W9-BOL-251

The Presidency of

JAMES EARL
CARTER, JR.

AMERICAN PRESIDENCY SERIES

Donald R. McCoy, Clifford S. Griffin, Homer E. Socolofsky
General Editors

George Washington, Forrest McDonald
John Adams, Ralph Adams Brown
Thomas Jefferson, Forrest McDonald
James Madison, Robert Allen Rutland
John Quincy Adams, Mary W. M. Hargreaves
Martin Van Buren, Major L. Wilson
William Henry Harrison & John Tyler, Norma Lois Peterson
James K. Polk, Paul H. Bergeron
Zachary Taylor & Millard Fillmore, Elbert B. Smith
Franklin Pierce, Larry Gara
James Buchanan, Elbert B. Smith
Andrew Johnson, Albert Castel
Rutherford B. Hayes, Ari Hoogenboom
James A. Garfield & Chester A. Arthur, Justus D. Doenecke
Grover Cleveland, Richard E. Welch, Jr.
Benjamin Harrison, Homer B. Socolofsky & Allan B. Spetter
William McKinley, Lewis L. Gould
Theodore Roosevelt, Lewis L. Gould
William Howard Taft, Paolo E. Coletta
Woodrow Wilson, Kendrick A. Clements
Warren G. Harding, Eugene P. Trani & David L. Wilson
Herbert C. Hoover, Martin L. Fausold
Harry S. Truman, Donald R. McCoy
Dwight D. Eisenhower, Chester J. Pach, Jr., & Elmo Richardson
John F. Kennedy, James N. Giglio
Lyndon B. Johnson, Vaughn Davis Bornet
James Earl Carter, Jr., Burton I. Kaufman

The Presidency of

JAMES EARL
CARTER, JR.

Burton I. Kaufman

UNIVERSITY PRESS OF KANSAS

For

Albert Slavin

© 1993 by the University Press of Kansas
All rights reserved

Published by the University Press of Kansas (Lawrence, Kansas 66049),
which was organized by the Kansas Board of Regents
and is operated and funded by Emporia State University, Fort Hays State
University, Kansas State University, Pittsburg State
University, the University of Kansas, and Wichita State University

Library of Congress Cataloging-in-Publication Data

Kaufman, Burton Ira.
The presidency of James Earl Carter, Jr. / Burton Ira Kaufman.
p.   cm. — (American presidency series)
Includes bibliographical references and index.
ISBN 0–7006–0572–X (alk. paper)
ISBN 0–7006–0573–8 (pbk. : alk. paper)
1. United States—Politics and government—1977–1981.
2. Carter, Jimmy, 1924–
I. Title.   II. Series.
E872.K38   1993
973.936—dc20   92–18134

British Library Cataloguing in Publication Data is available.

Printed in the United States of America

10 9 8 7 6 5 4 3 2 1

The paper used in this publication meets the minimum requirements
of the American National Standard for Permanence of Paper
for Printed Library Materials Z39.48–1984.

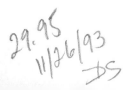

CONTENTS

FOREWORD

The aim of the American Presidency Series is to present historians and the general reading public with interesting, scholarly assessments of the various presidential administrations. These interpretive surveys are intended to cover the broad ground between biographies, specialized monographs, and journalistic accounts. As such, each wil be a comprehensive work which will draw upon original sources and pertinent secondary literature, yet leave room for the author's own analysis and interpretation.

Volumes in the series will present the data essential to understanding the administration under consideration. Particularly, each book will treat the then current problems facing the United States and its people and how the president and his associates felt about, thought about, and worked to cope with these problems. Attention will be given to how the office developed and operated during the president's tenure. Equally important will be consideration of the vital relationships between the president, his staff, the executive officers, Congress, foreign representatives, the judiciary, state officials, the public, political parties, the press, and influential private citizens. The series will also be concerned with how this unique American institution—the presidency—was viewed by the presidents, and with what results.

All this will be set, insofar as possible, in the context not only of contemporary politics but also of economics, international relations, law, morals, public administration, religion, and thought. Such a broad approach is necessary to understanding, for a presidential administration is more than the elected and appointed officers composing it, since its work so often reflects the major problems, anxieties, and glories of the nation. In short, the authors in this series will strive to recount and evaluate the record of each administration and to identify its distinctiveness and relationships to the past, its own time, and the future.

The General Editors

ACKNOWLEDGMENTS

I wish to thank first David Alsobrook, Martin Elzy, and the rest of the staff of the Jimmy Carter Library for the assistance they gave me over a period of six years. They were always ready to answer questions and to locate materials for me, and they made the research room at the Carter Library a pleasant place to do research. I also want to thank my former graduate student David Snead, a fledgling historian, who was given the unenviable task of helping to cut a manuscript that was far larger than this final product and did the job extremely well. In addition, I am grateful to my colleagues in the Department of History at Virginia Tech for commenting on a paper I gave at a departmental seminar when I first began to formulate my thoughts on the Carter presidency. I am particularly grateful for the help of Bill Ochsenwald, who read and commented on my chapter on the Camp David accords and the Iranian Revolution, and Tom Adriance, who encouraged me to reformulate my introduction.

I deeply appreciate also the help of the editors of the American Presidency Series, particularly Donald McCoy, for their assistance, encouragement, and support. Both Fred Woodward and Michael Briggs of the University Press of Kansas have been models of patience and kindness. My wife, Diane, and my daughter, Heather, have continued, with love, to put up with my absences and moodiness while I was writing this book. I am especially indebted to my son, Scott, who, for reasons unknown to me, has also decided to be a historian and spent several summers assisting me at the Carter Library. He is probably as familiar with the Carter presidency as I am.

I dedicate this book to my uncle Albert Slavin, Lillian L. and Harry A. Cowan Professor Emeritus, Northeastern University, whose life and career I have tried to make a model for my own.

1

★ ★ ★ ★ ★

INTRODUCTION

In his book *In the Absence of Power*, the journalist Haynes Johnson referred to the Jimmy Carter presidency as a "tragedy,"[1] and most other commentators writing during and soon after the Carter presidency have also regarded it as at least a failure if not quite a tragedy.[2] More recently, however, scholars have begun to look more kindly on the former president and his conduct of affairs while he was in the Oval Office. In *The Trusteeship Presidency*, for example, Charles O. Jones made the point that Carter saw his role as president to be that of a trustee of the public welfare, even when that meant he had to make unpopular and politically damaging decisions. Similarly, Erwin C. Hargrove argued in *Jimmy Carter As President* that the most striking criticism of Carter is that he did not calculate the political consequences of his actions. Richard V. Pierard and Robert D. Linder maintained in *Civil Religion and the Presidency* that Carter's difficulties as president stemmed from the fact that he "told the American people what they did not want to hear—that they would have to renounce their profligate lifestyles," and Aaron Wildavsky concluded that although "Carter did not do brilliantly [as president] he did a lot better than he was credited with doing."[3]

More generally, the people engaged in reassessing the Carter presidency have maintained that anyone entering the White House in 1977 would have faced a herculean task. The Vietnam War, the Watergate affair, a breakdown of the historically strong party system, cracks in the congressional system of seniority, and the appearance of hundreds of political action committees (PACs) had compromised the power of the presidency and raised questions as to just how governable the nation really was. Despite the difficulties Carter faced, moreover, his defenders have pointed to a number of

1

significant achievements during his administration: the Panama Canal treaties of 1978, civil service reform, energy legislation, a measure setting aside large areas of the Alaskan wilderness, and, of course, the Camp David agreement of 1978.[4]

Finally, there is the argument that the Carter presidency would receive a more favorable assessment if there were better ways to evaluate modern presidential administrations. Given the political, institutional, and social constraints imposed on the modern presidency, these analysts have contended that existing standards are inappropriate because they emphasize an administration's legislative accomplishments instead of evaluating a president on the basis of policy goals and personal style. According to this view, Carter was not interested so much in what was politically possible or expedient as in what was politically right. He saw a nation faced with major problems that needed to be recognized and dealt with irrespective of partisan considerations. It was on this basis that he organized his administration and functioned as president. And it is on this basis that his administration should be evaluated. "Carter worked with a concept of what was 'right' for the American people," Charles O. Jones wrote, "a concept that excluded both the 'fabled special interests' and also bargaining to accommodate those interests." Mark Rozell reached similar conclusions in his study of Carter and the press: "Focusing on what [Carter] did *not* do tells us little about how the Carter presidency did seek to lead."[5]

Paralleling the more positive reassessment of the Carter administration has been a more positive public image of the president as a result of his activities since leaving office. His efforts on behalf of international peace and social justice, including his outspoken support for human rights and political democracy in Central America and elsewhere; the support and leadership he has given to Habitat for Humanity, the nonprofit organization that builds homes for the homeless; and the work of the Carter Presidential Center in Atlanta, Georgia, which seeks to eradicate hunger and malnutrition in Africa and other poverty-stricken places, have led a number of commentators to suggest that if Carter was not the country's best president, he has been its best ex-president.

The reader will find that I am sympathetic with the thrust of the recent writing on Carter insofar as it concerns the problems he faced as president and his personal character. It is almost a cliché to talk about the enormous burdens and responsibilities of the chief executive, and certainly most modern presidents have faced difficult issues when they took office. But the problems Carter had to face when he entered the White House were arguably more complex and intractable than the problems encountered by most of his predecessors. Carter also deserves considerable credit for the quiet manner in which he furthered the earlier efforts of President Gerald Ford to heal some of the wounds caused by the Vietnam War and the Watergate affair. And there can be no doubt that, as Jones and others have suggested, Carter viewed himself as trustee of the public good and often acted irrespective of the political consequences of his actions. Personally, the president was extremely intelligent and well-informed. By most accounts he was one of the nation's brightest chief executives, and unlike his predecessors, Lyndon Johnson and Richard Nixon, he was neither mean-spirited nor conspiratorial. Both privately and publicly President Carter was considerate, compassionate, gracious, and self-possessed.

I am persuaded, however, that the earlier critics of his administration were justified in giving the president mediocre marks—and largely for the reasons they cited. First, I am not convinced that the nation was as ungovernable as some of Carter's defenders contend. Second, I find that the people who have called for a fresh look at the Carter presidency have too easily passed over the elemental fact that, for better or worse, there is a political process in any system of representative government which no leader can simply ignore on the basis of being above the fray, especially one who, like Carter, lacks a political mandate from the voters. Indeed, as Mark A. Peterson has suggested, the very fact that Carter viewed himself as the representative of the whole populace and the national interest was all the more reason for him "to operate in a tandem-institutions world," that is, to work closely with Congress.[6] Third, it is troubling that those people who comment favorably on Carter's concept of a "public trustee" ignore a real danger inherent in that concept—namely, that the trustee has a wisdom about the national welfare superior to the collective wisdom of the nation's elected representatives on Capitol Hill—and disregard the need for a person in the Oval Office to be attentive to the pluralistic nature of American society. Fourth, I find that while Carter viewed himself as a trustee of the public good, he never adequately articulated an overarching purpose and direction for his administration.

Finally, and perhaps most important, I conclude that Carter failed to establish the base of public support and political legitimacy he needed in order to be successful in his role as a trustee president. Instead, the events of his four years in office projected an image to the American people of a hapless administration in disarray and of a presidency that was increasingly divided, lacking in leadership, ineffective in dealing with Congress, incapable of defending America's honor abroad, and uncertain about its purpose, priorities, and sense of direction. In my view, this contemporary image of the Carter presidency was, unfortunately, all too accurate and helped assure a mediocre, if not a failed, presidency.

2

★ ★ ★ ★ ★

WHAT MAKES JIMMY RUN?

Jimmy Carter is a southerner, an engineer, an agribusinessman, and a politician. He is not a nuclear physicist, a populist, or even a dirt farmer as he and his followers have sometimes claimed. He is a Southern Baptist and an evangelical, but not a fundamentalist. He is deeply religious but not theological. He can be—and most of the time is—courteous, compassionate, and gracious, but he can also be—and frequently has been—calculating and opportunistic. He is a person of deep moral conviction and principle; at the same time, during his career, he has often been devious and politically pragmatic. He is highly intelligent, introspective, and thoughtful, but he is not ideological, philosophical, or conceptual. His successful quest for the White House was made possible by the news media, but he was not an especially effective media candidate. He is, in other words, an individual whose personality and career are replete with contradictions and inconsistencies. For that reason, the people who voted for him in 1976 probably did so more as an act of faith and as a measure of hope than as a statement of their abiding commitment to him or to the programs he espoused.

The future president was born James Earl Carter, Jr., on 1 October 1924, in Plains, Georgia, a community of about five hundred in the southwestern part of the state. His father, Earl, was a successful local businessman who owned a considerable amount of real estate and operated a warehouse and brokerage in peanuts. His mother, Lillian Gordon, was a registered nurse. Jimmy also had two sisters—Gloria, born in 1926, and Ruth, born in 1929—and a much younger brother, Billy, born in 1937, when Jimmy was already a teenager.

Finishing high school in 1941, Carter spent the next two years boning up on his science background at Georgia Southwestern College and then the Georgia Institute of Technology before being admitted to the U.S. Naval Academy, which had been his goal since he was six years old. Rushing through accelerated wartime courses, he worked hard, excelled in his studies, and received high grades, finishing sixtieth out of a class of 822. Aside from his good academic record, there was little else noteworthy about his term at the academy. After graduating from Annapolis in 1946, Jimmy married Rosalynn Smith, who was also from Plains. Although they had known each other from childhood, they did not begin to date until after Jimmy returned home on leave from Annapolis. Like Jimmy, Rosalynn had set high standards for herself, graduating from high school as class valedictorian, and she shared his desire to see more of the world beyond Plains.

Carter spent the next seven years in the navy. In 1951 he was assigned to what he regarded as "the finest Navy billet available to any officer of [his] rank—the development of the first atomic submarine." Before he received the assignment, he had to be screened by the person most responsible for the navy's atomic submarine program, Capt. (later admiral) Hyman Rickover, a brilliant but demanding naval officer. As the lengthy interview was ending, Rickover asked the junior officer whether he had done his best at Annapolis. After reflection, Carter said that he had not, to which Rickover countered, "Why not?"[1]

The interview had a profound and lasting impact on Carter. "Why Not the Best?" would be the theme of his drive for the presidency and the title of his campaign autobiography. A perfectionist, Carter saw Rickover's question as a challenge that demanded an ongoing process of self-examination. Rickover always remained bigger than life for Carter, a figure who would haunt him long after he left the navy. Even as governor of Georgia, more than a dozen years later, he would break out in a cold sweat whenever he was told that Admiral Rickover was on the telephone waiting to speak to him.

Rickover accepted the young officer into his program and put him to work on the *Seawolf*, one of the prototypes of the nuclear submarine. Moving to Schenectady, New York, where the submarine's reactor was being built, Carter took classes at Union College in reactor technology and nuclear physics; although these were accelerated, one-semester, noncredit courses, they provided the basis for his later claim that he had been trained as a nuclear physicist. Carter's future now seemed settled. He was a seasoned submariner and lieutenant senior grade, working on the latest submarine technology under the direction of an exacting and sometimes even abrasive superior for whom he had the greatest respect and admiration. He had been selected to be chief engineer of the *Seawolf* when it put to sea. He was also the father of three children—John William (nicknamed "Jack") born in 1947, James Earl Carter III (nicknamed "Chip") born in April 1950, and Donald Jeffrey born in August 1952. Both Rosalynn and he loved the navy life—the work, the new experiences, the camaraderie that existed among the officers. He would, therefore, pursue his career in the navy.

Then word came from Plains that Jimmy's father was dying, and his life abruptly changed. Since his departure from Annapolis, he and Earl had drifted apart, as they had less and less in common. Jimmy was saddened by the lack of rapport with his father, for he had grown up with a robust sense of family and home, and he sometimes felt he had deserted his roots to follow his own ambitions. After his father's death, Carter went through a type of midlife crisis. "I began to think about the relative significance of his life and mine," Carter remarked. "He was an integral part of the community, and had a wide range of varied but interrelated interests and responsibilities. He was his own boss, and his life was stabilized by the slow evolutionary change in the local societal structure." The more he compared his life with his father's, the more he was convinced his father's way had been the more satisfying one. In 1953, he, Rosalynn, and their three boys came home to Plains to stay.[2]

During his seven years in the service, Carter had proved that he was a good officer—intelligent, resourceful, able to carry out difficult assignments with a minimum of direction. As part of Rickover's team, he had also dealt frequently and effectively with government officials. Yet there was no indication that he was on the fast track to high command. He had not seen service in the Korean War, and his fellow officers had not singled him out as a leader of men. Indeed, he tended to be more aloof than most officers, usually rushing home to his family as soon as he was off duty. Perhaps that is why Carter had so few regrets about leaving the navy once he decided to resign. "I had only one life to live," he recalled, "and I wanted to live it as a civilian, with a potentially fuller opportunity for varied public service."[3]

Jimmy's first years back in Plains were difficult as he and Rosalynn tried to readjust to rural living and rebuild his father's faltering warehouse peanut business during one of Georgia's worst droughts. But things soon improved, for the drought of 1954 was followed by the rains of 1955 and a bumper peanut crop. Jimmy became skilled at raising peanuts, and after a few years, his business was prospering. Active in community affairs and serving as a deacon of the Plains Baptist Church, he had become by 1960 one of Plains's most respected business and civic leaders.

Although Carter had shown little interest in politics to this point, he came from a politically active family. Earl Carter had served on the county school board and had been elected to the state legislature the year before he died. Jimmy had gotten his first taste of politics when he worked on behalf of an unsuccessful referendum to consolidate the county schools. As his business flourished, he had more time for outside interests. When some of his friends encouraged him to run for office, Carter needed little persuasion. The ambition that had made him so determined and competitive was still a driving force of his personality. In this sense, public office was another of Carter's quests for greater achievement, but it is undeniable that he also had a real commitment to civic duty.

As his first bid for public office, Carter chose to run for a seat in the Georgia Senate in 1962. His initiation into elective politics was characterized by exceptional energy and enthusiasm, as all his campaign efforts would be. As in future races, he made personal character—his compared with that of his opponents—the central campaign issue. It was "an amateurish and whirl-wind" effort, Carter later remarked. Although he had lost the primary by 139 votes, the election had involved a tampered ballot box; forcing a new election, Carter won by a comfortable margin.[4]

Carter served two terms in the state senate, from 1963 to 1966. He was an industrious and hard-working legislator, and he established a record as a moderate progressive who supported "good government" measures and educational reform, lashed out at lobbyists for special interests, and stressed the importance of caring for the poor, the underprivileged, and the underrepresented in government. By 1965, Carter was named in a Georgia newspaper poll as one of the state's most influential legislators. Spurred by this to seek higher office, the next year he announced he was running for governor.

Virtually unknown outside his own district, Carter conducted a grueling gubernatorial campaign, even by Georgia standards. At first not taken seriously by most political pundits, his candidacy appeared increasingly more viable as he traveled through the state meeting an estimated 300,000 Georgians. On the eve of the election, he fully expected that he would be in a runoff against either former Governor Ellis Arnall or Lester Maddox, a restaurant owner who had gained national notoriety for defying integration by standing in the doorway of his establishment holding an ax handle. The next morning, however, Carter learned that he had finished a close third. Rather than being satisfied that he had gone from being practically unknown in the race to almost winning a runoff spot, he was devastated and fell into a deep depression, which was lifted only by the solace he found as a born-again Christian.

Although religion had always been an important part of his daily life, Carter had not been devout. At age eleven he had announced that he had accepted Jesus Christ as his personal savior, but religion was not at the core of his very existence. Now Carter went through a second experience of conversion, and his renewed Christian faith only intensified his commitment to public service. Although he never thought that his faith provided unerring answers to contemporary problems, he was more convinced than ever that his purpose was to serve God's will, and he interpreted this to mean serving humanity. He also accepted theologian Reinhold Niebuhr's aphorism that "the sad duty of politics is to establish justice in a sinful world." As a result, his secular sense of public duty became firmly wedded to a gospel of service based on his strong religious convictions.

At peace with himself and convinced that he had good work to do, Carter decided to run for governor again in 1970 and to win whatever the cost. The result was a campaign that even his own advisers would later regret. To defeat former Governor Carl Sanders, his chief opponent in the Democratic primary, Carter appealed to segregationist and white supremacist elements in the state. He spoke out against busing, visiting a segregated private academy, and said he would welcome a meeting with Alabama's openly racist governor, George Wallace. He also attacked Sanders for his wealth, for his alleged conflicts of interest, and for his association with liberal Democrats such as Hubert Humphrey. In the primary runoff, Carter easily beat Sanders and then went on to an overwhelming victory in the general election in November.

Unquestionably, the campaign had not been one of Carter's finest moments. He had acted with a ruthlessness and disregard of principle that was difficult to excuse even on grounds of the ends justifying the means. Yet the governor-elect also owed his election to hard work. For almost four years, he had crisscrossed the state, delivering more than eighteen hundred speeches to almost any group that invited him. He pored over old Georgia budgets in order to master state finances and developed an extensive mailing list of anyone he met who might support his candidacy. Although Carter's fourth child and first daughter, Amy, was still a toddler (she was born in 1967), Rosalynn joined him on the campaign trail, and he expanded his group of advisers and consultants to include Jody Powell, a graduate student at Emory University who became his chauffeur and personal confidant, and Stuart Eizenstat, a young Atlanta attorney and recent Harvard Law School graduate who became his issues coordinator. Already on board were Hamilton Jordan, who as a student at the University of Georgia in 1966 had worked in Carter's gubernatorial campaign and quickly became one of his shrewdest political advisers, and Charles Kirbo, an Atlanta lawyer and Carter's closest friend. These four formed the nucleus of the so-called Peanut Brigade, which would play such a prominent role in the Carter White House.

Considering his campaign pitch, almost no one could anticipate that as governor Carter would promote racial moderation and become known as a reform leader, yet that is precisely what happened. In his inaugural address in January, Carter surprised his listeners by promising to steer Georgia into a new era of racial equality and economic and social justice, and in fact he did achieve an impressive list of reforms. During his tenure, the number of black state employees increased from 4,850 to 6,684 as a result of his efforts. Carter established a special commission to improve services for the mentally and emotionally handicapped and authorized 111 new community mental health centers. He worked successfully for environmental protection, for tax, welfare, and judicial reform, and for consumer protection—all programs that would receive similarly high priority during the Carter presidency. He also instituted the practice of "zero-base budgeting," a system requiring an annual review of budgetary priorities as a means of promoting and measuring efficiency.

However, Carter's main goal as governor was to reorganize state government to improve its operation and cost effectiveness. A reorganization measure easily passed the state assembly but ran into considerable opposition in the senate. Carter responded by throwing the full weight of his office behind the legislation, making it a test of his own authority as governor. The results were inconclusive. Although the senate passed the bill, it authorized only the preparation of a reorganization plan, not its implementation. In the months that followed, Carter appointed teams of experts and prominent citizens to design a set of proposals that he could then submit to the legislature for its approval. Meeting regularly with these groups, the governor impressed them with his mastery of detail and his management skills. To win public support for reorganization, he initiated a massive media campaign orchestrated by Gerald Rafshoon, an Atlanta advertising executive who became another member of the Peanut Brigade.

At times, Carter was his own worst enemy, committing many of the same strategic and tactical mistakes he would make as president. For example, he unnecessarily antagonized powerful state officials by attempting to turn the battle over reorganization into a morality play, in which he was the guardian of the public welfare and his opponents were tools of special interest groups. He compounded his mistake by resisting efforts at compromise and coalition building when the reorganization proposal was finally submitted to the Georgia General Assembly. Yet Carter did succeed in getting most of his program passed by the legislature. Although many aspects of the plan were more cosmetic than corrective—that is, it eliminated agencies that did not meet or consolidated agencies without cutting back their expenditures—the outcome overall was a more effective, efficient, and responsive state government than had existed before.

By the end of his second year in office, Carter had earned a solid record of achievement. He appeared to typify a new group of southern governors known for their moderate racial views and progressive response to economic and social change in the South. Indeed, as early as May 1971, *Time* magazine featured Carter on its front cover as the representative of this new political leadership in the South. "Soft-voiced, assured, looking eerily like John Kennedy from certain angles," *Time* reported, "Carter is a man as contradictory as Georgia itself, but determined to resolve some of its paradoxes."[5] Indeed, Carter *was* a man of opposites. In him, consummate personal ambition was linked to a compelling sense of public purpose; though spiritually content and eminently successful in nearly everything he did, Carter was not complacent but driven. His cousin Hugh Carter, who served as majority leader of the state senate while Jimmy was governor, later framed the question, "What made Jimmy run?" He concluded that Jimmy ran because he perceived himself as a "lay missionary" who saw only harmony between his own ambition and his larger spiritual and political purposes.[6]

So it was that in 1972, after only two years as Georgia's governor, Carter turned his attention to the nation's top political prize—the White House. The Georgian decided to run for president following Richard Nixon's overwhelming defeat of Senator George McGovern in November. Even though he was virtually unknown outside of Georgia, he was encouraged to seek the Democratic nomination by Hamilton Jordan and Dr. Peter Bourne, a psychiatrist who headed Georgia's drug-abuse program. They recognized what more seasoned politicians had missed: the significance of the change in the nominating process, and the shift in the nation's political temper.

Jordan and Bourne realized that McGovern had won his party's nomination because the party's guidelines for selecting delegates had been revised to provide for a more democratic selection process and for proportional representation of minorities and women at national conventions. To assure compliance with these standards, a record number of states were filling their slates through direct primaries. Only fifteen states had held primaries in 1952; in 1972 there were twenty-one, and by 1976, there would be at least thirty. This meant that the nomination would increasingly be determined at the ballot box, not by the party's hierarchy. If Carter could build political momentum by winning some of the early primaries, his advisers reasoned that he could win the nomination.

Jordan and Bourne also sensed a real advantage in the fact tht Carter was a political outsider and not part of the Washington establishment. By the early 1970s, a wave of cynicism had surged over much of the country, manifested in a widespread distrust of politics and politicians. The reasons for this feeling were complex, but it arose in part from a growing conviction that the politicians had failed to deal with the great issues that had confronted the nation over the past ten years—among them, war, poverty, increased inflation, and economic stagnation. McGovern had been able to capitalize on this anti-Washington sentiment, and Carter's advisers believed he could do the same.

Jordan explained all this to Carter in a lengthy, seventy-two-page memorandum he wrote in 1972 outlining a strategy for victory in 1976. "Perhaps the strongest feeling in this country today," he told Carter, "is the general distrust of government and politicians at all levels. The desire and thrust for strong moral leadership in the nation was not satisfied with the election of Richard Nixon."[7] Brilliantly conceived, Jordan's brief became the blueprint for Carter's campaign. In fact, the only major difference between Jordan's recommendations and the strategy adopted was Carter's decision to enter as many primaries as possible instead of running in a carefully chosen few as Jordan had advised. "Our strategy was simple," Carter later recalled; "make a total effort all over the country."[8]

Beginning in January with a talk before the National Press Club, Carter threw himself into the presidential race with all the intensity and diligence that had marked his previous campaigns. For the next two years, he traveled throughout the country, meeting people, shaking hands, appearing on television, and holding news conferences. In order to gain more foreign policy exposure (another of Jordan's suggestions), he also joined the Trilateral Commission, a private international organization founded by David Rockefeller of the Chase Manhattan Bank, whose purpose was to promote closer ties between the United States, Europe, and Japan.

Wherever he traveled, Carter remained intentionally vague on the issues—stating publicly, for example, that he could not support an anti-abortion constitutional amendment (already a heated campaign issue) but allowing that he might back a "national statute" limiting abortions. Similarly, in foreign affairs, he declared that the policy of detente with the Soviet Union had gone too far without explaining how much too far. Only on a few matters did he take a firm stand, favoring strict enforcement of the antitrust laws, enactment of gun control legislation, and welfare reform. He also stressed the need to reorganize the federal bureaucracy, following the state of Georgia's lead.

The emphasis, however, was on values. Government, Carter said, had to measure up to the honesty and integrity, the love and compassion, the idealism and heroism of the American people. He talked about his own character and career as a successful farmer and businessman, a dedicated family man, a military officer and veteran, a trained engineer and nuclear scientist, and an efficient and progressive state governor. In this way he was able to project himself differently—but effectively—to a variety of constituencies across a broad political spectrum.

Since Carter's message was the failure of government to be worthy of the character and principles of the American people, he could reap the fallout from the Watergate scandal and Richard Nixon's subsequent resignation in August 1974. But the most important early development benefiting the Carter candidacy was the decision by Massachusetts Senator Edward ("Ted") Kennedy in September 1974 to take himself out of the presidential race. Carter's advisers had acted on the assumption that Kennedy would run and had the best chance of getting the Democratic nomination. The senator's withdrawal thus opened the way for other aspirants, more liberal than Carter, to vie for the nomination. If the liberal vote divided among a number of candidates—most notably, senators Birch Bayh of Indiana and Henry Jackson of Washington, former Senator Fred Harris of Oklahoma, and Congressman Morris Udall of Arizona—Carter could co-opt the political center and compete for the political right and left of the party. He could also appear as a progressive alternative to George Wallace who, although now confined to a wheelchair, had announced his candidacy for president in November 1975 and remained a wild card in the campaign.

Just as Jordan had hypothesized, Carter won the Democratic nomination after key victories in the caucuses and early primaries. His first break-through came in January 1976 in Iowa, where he won 27.6 percent of the vote, more than twice that of his nearest rival, Birch Bayh. Although less than 10 percent of the registered Democrats had actually participated in the Iowa caucuses and the largest bloc of votes went not to Carter but to uncommitted delegates, the news media declared Carter the winner; this gave him the momentum he needed to win the next month in New Hampshire, which held the first election of the primary season. Soon Carter's face was appearing on the covers of *Time* and *Newsweek*, and he was being widely touted as the front-runner in the race for the Democratic nomination.

Even so, Carter's victory in the 9 March Florida primary was just as crucial as his successes in Iowa and New Hampshire. The contest was largely between Carter and Governor Wallace, since the other candidates, except Jackson, sat out the primary, believing the state was Wallace country. Between New Hampshire and Florida, Carter had suffered a major defeat in Massachusetts, where he had finished a poor fourth in the state's primary. If he lost in Florida, he would probably be through as a serious candidate. But if he beat Wallace in the South, his claim to be the moderate southern alternative to the Alabama governor would stay viable, and his strategy of running as a centrist candidate acceptable to the mainstream of the Democratic party would be justified.

Carter's plan worked brilliantly. He finished with 34.3 percent of the primary vote in Florida compared with Wallace's 30.6 percent and Henry Jackson's 23.9 percent. As *Time* reported, Carter "dominated the center on the issues, had the best organization and had the broadest appeal of all the candidates." He won large majorities among voters under age twenty-five, blue-collar workers, and Democrats identifying themselves as liberals. "I don't see anybody who can beat me," Carter said after the primary, "but I see a lot of hard political scraps ahead."[9] In the weeks that followed, Carter won easily over Wallace in Illinois and North Carolina, but he lost badly in the New York primary in April and beat Udall by less than 5,000 votes in Wisconsin. Because Jackson and Udall had not run in Illinois, Carter had yet to demonstrate that he could succeed against strong opposition in a northern industrial state. Pennsylvania, the site of the next major primary, became the proving ground.

Before campaigning in Pennsylvania, Carter made one of his few serious blunders of the primary season by telling reporters that he had "nothing against" an ethnic community "trying to maintain the ethnic purity of their neighborhoods." As he explained later, what he meant to say was that he was opposed to using the power of the federal government to "artificially" change the ethnic character of a neighborhood, but that he would not condone discrimination against any family wishing to move into the neighborhood. However, the phrase "ethnic purity" captured the attention of the press and made the headlines. Soon Carter was being loudly criticized by such black leaders as the Reverend Jesse Jackson of Chicago, who called Carter's views "a throwback to Hitlerian racism," and Mayor Richard Hatcher of Gary, Indiana, who referred to Carter as a "Frankenstein monster with a Southern drawl."[10]

For two days Carter refused to retract his statement, insisting that it had been taken out of context. Only after considerable coaxing from Rosalynn did he finally acknowledge his mistake, stating at a news conference in Philadelphia that he too had been bothered by the word "purity." This was enough to mollify most black leaders: Detroit Mayor Coleman Young said that Carter's apology was "satisfactory" and that the whole matter had been a "phony issue." Other black leaders concurred.[11]

One of the intriguing questions about the campaign is how a rural southern white candidate could enjoy such support from blacks. In Florida, Carter had received 70 percent of the black vote; in North Carolina, 90 percent. Even in his Massachusetts defeat, he had led the other candidates in the nearly all-black Boston neighborhood of Roxbury. Part of the explanation for Carter's appeal in such states as Florida and North Carolina was that blacks there would have backed almost anyone against Wallace. In addition, as governor of Georgia, he had opened the doors of state government to many more black employees and had made the important gesture of putting a portrait of Martin Luther King, Jr., in the rotunda of the state capitol. As a result, he had gained the strong support of such respected black leaders as Martin Luther King, Sr., and Atlanta Congressman Andrew Young. His deputy campaign coordinator, Ben Brown, one of the nineteen blacks on Carter's paid staff of two hundred, also had close connections with influential blacks throughout the country, who were able to mobilize black voters in behalf of Carter. Finally, evangelical blacks could relate to Carter's own religious background and to his call for a national renewal of spiritual values.

Accordingly, Carter was able to carry the black vote in Pennnsylvania by a substantial margin. He also managed to sway a large number of blue-collar workers despite the endorsement of Henry Jackson by Pennsylvania's powerful labor leaders. Together, these groups gave Carter the victory he needed in a northern industrial state. After the loss in Pennsylvania, Jackson announced he was withdrawing from the race; meanwhile, Hubert Humphrey, who had been considering entering the campaign, said in a press conference that he would not actively seek the nomination. New polls showed that voters considered Carter the strongest possible Democratic candidate and that he would defeat President Gerald Ford by as much as 10 percent.

Carter's decision to participate in every primary, combined with party rules that awarded delegates on a basis proportional to a candidate's vote, now worked to his advantage. Although he actually lost most of the remaining primaries, including major ones in California and New Jersey, to latecomers Senator Frank Church of Idaho and Governor Edmund Brown of

California, he managed to win at least one election every primary Tuesday. As a result, he was able to maintain his political pace and to pick up enough delegates, even in the states he lost, to assure his nomination when the Democrats held their convention in July.

Carter had performed a political miracle. In 1972, when he announced to his mother that he was going to run for president, Lillian had responded, "President of what?" In winning his party's nod, Carter had pursued George McGovern's route of four years past—running actively in as many primaries as possible, avoiding the formal Democratic party structure, and relying instead on thousands of volunteers throughout the primary campaigns. He had also finessed his opponents by appealing to all sectors of the party, liberals as well as conservatives, through his focus on unobjectionable values instead of specific issues and his exploitation of the nation's anti-Washington mood.

For a revolt against Washington was what the election was all about. American voters, most polls showed, felt that government was far too meddlesome and intrusive, that it was unmovable and overbureaucratized, and that it was out of touch with the American people and insensitive to their ability to manage their own affairs. Disgruntled Americans sought new ideas, fresh faces, and a style of leadership predicated on openness, truthfulness, and public responsiveness. Indeed, morality was the emerging keynote of the campaign—a desire to restore a sense of purpose, trust, fairness, and civic responsibility to American life. Carter understood the national mood perfectly, and he attacked Washington in a positive way, emphasizing not so much what was wrong in the nation's capital as the power of the American people to set things right and appealing not to their cynicism but to their idealism.

By the time of the Democratic National Convention in July, Carter's nomination was a foregone conclusion. He won on the first ballot when Ohio's 132 votes put him over the top. As his running mate, he selected Senator Walter Mondale of Minnesota, a liberal and a Washington insider who could balance the ticket and heal any rifts left over from the campaign. Opposing them were President Gerald Ford, who won the Republican nomination in August after a close battle with former California Governor Ronald Reagan, and his vice-presidential nominee, Senator Robert Dole of Kansas.

The election seemed to be Carter's to win. In contrast to the Democrats, the Republicans remained badly split between moderates who had backed Ford and conservatives who had supported Reagan. The polls indicated, moreover, that while Americans appreciated Ford's honesty and personal character and though he had restored integrity to the office of the president, they still had serious doubts about his competence as president. Even Ford's own campaign plan acknowledged that "the President has not shown the capability of causing a sharp increase in his approval rating for a sustained period of time."[12]

Realizing that voters generally had a positive image of Carter but found him obscure on the issues, Ford's advisers decided to hammer away at his vagueness. The Democratic candidate himself defined "trust of the people in government" as the campaign's major issue, and Ford responded by accusing Carter of "fuzziness." Republican strategy soon began paying dividends. In August, Carter had a 15-percent lead over Ford, but by the beginning of September it was clear the gap was closing fast. Carter's uninspiring rhetoric helped to fuel the Republican critique. Yale historian C. Van Woodward marveled at "Carter's remarkable propensity . . . for fusing contradictions and reconciling opposites," remarking that "the result was an unusual assortment of unified ambiguities and ambiguous unities." Political commentators Rowland Evans and Robert Novak suggested that the Democratic candidate was "allergic to all efforts at eloquence."[13] Polls conducted by the Ford campaign showed that the Republican candidate was gaining ground in southern states, including Texas, Louisiana, Mississippi, Virginia, and North Carolina. Another poll revealed that although Carter still had a six- to eight-point lead over Ford in California, his support was "soft."

The last two weeks of September and the first week of October were a disaster for Carter. First he was heckled by angry anti-abortionists over his opposition to an anti-abortion constitutional amendment. Then he displeased pro-abortion forces by modifying his position, telling a group of Catholic bishops that while he would not support an anti-abortion amendment, neither would he oppose one. His statement merely added credence to another of Ford's claims—that Carter "flip-flopped" on the issues.

Carter's meeting with the bishops had been intended to dispel Catholic concerns about his born-again Christianity. During his campaign, the Democratic candidate had neither hidden his deep religious faith nor harped on it. Nevertheless, it had become an issue. All of the polls indicated that, because of his religion, Carter would do well among the nation's 30 million white evangelical Protestants but that his support was weak among traditionally Democratic Catholics, who feared fundamentalist intolerance. Compounding the religious rift was the displeasure of ethnic Catholics in urban areas at Carter's efforts to reach out to blacks. As a result, many Catholics indicated that they would stay home on election day or vote Republican.

Of more immediate importance to the Carter campaign than Catholic disaffection, however, was public reaction to an interview the Democratic candidate gave to *Playboy*, in which he used risqué language and said that he had "committed adultery in [his] heart many times." The story exposed him to ridicule and raised questions about his judgment in granting an interview to *Playboy* in the first place and then using such terms as "screw" and "shacks up." Prospects dimmed further for Carter after his poor showing in his first televised debate with Ford, which was held in Philadelphia on 23 September. Although neither candidate was particularly impressive, Ford appeared composed and in charge of the evening—less discursive, more articulate, better able to project himself to the television audience, and more on the offensive than Carter, frequently accusing Carter of being evasive in his responses or a big spender. A *New York Times*/CBS poll four days later showed that by a margin of 37 percent to 24 percent, the people surveyed named Ford the winner of the debate; the remaining 39 percent expressed no opinion or thought the debate was a draw.

By the end of September, the impulse toward victory had clearly shifted from Carter to Ford. Dick Cheney, one of the president's campaign strategists, informed Ford on 30 September that the latest polls showed him "closing the gap in the South." A member of the White House staff, Doug Bailey, commented that the "President's major opportunity to win the election" was the second debate, set for 6 October in San Francisco."[14] The first encounter had concentrated on the domestic economy, but the second was to handle foreign policy and defense issues. Ford staffers expected the second debate to be the trump card of the president's campaign. Ford would characterize his foreign policy as one of peace through strength. Because of the military might of the United States and its allies, his administration had been able to lower the level of tensions with the Soviet Union. In fact, as a result of his policies, the danger of war in Central Europe had been greatly reduced, Berlin was no longer a source of constant friction, and limitations had been placed on the size of the Soviet nuclear arsenal. All of this would make the president appear the more statesmanlike of the two candidates.[15]

The plan backfired. Predictably, Carter was much more aggressive in the second debate, accusing Ford of showing "an absence of leadership and an absence of a grasp of what this country is and what it ought to be." Ford countered by charging that his Democratic opponent would cut the defense budget by $15 billion (actually, Carter had proposed a $5-billion to $7-billion cut). But then Ford made what proved to be the great gaffe of the campaign. In response to a question about Eastern Europe, he said that there was "no Soviet domination of Eastern Europe, and there never will be under a Ford administration."

The query about Eastern Europe was not unexpected. Anticipating that it would be raised at some point in the debate, the president's staff had carefully prepared a response for him. "The peoples of Europe," he was told to say, "have a right to freedom and national independence, and the United States has not, and will not abandon them." However, in longhand, Ford had added the following note to the briefing materials he had received: "No Soviet sphere of influence in Eastern Europe. Agreement borders cannot be changed by force." Apparently, Ford had simply misread or misinterpreted the information provided by his staff.[16]

Ford's mistake disrupted the momentum of his campaign and brought an abrupt halt to his improved showing in the polls. A survey conducted immediately after the debate by his pollster found a majority of voters still planning to vote for Ford over Carter (54–36 percent). But as reporters pressed Ford to clarify his remarks, which were now blazoned in the headlines, the seriousness of his blunder became apparent. When his pollster conducted another poll the next night, he found Carter *leading* Ford by almost the same percentage (54–37 percent) that he had trailed the president a day earlier. Democrats (although not Carter) had argued that Ford was not smart enough to be president, and his gaffe about Eastern Europe seemed to prove that. Moreover, his remarks cost him heavily among ethnic Catholics, many of whom still had families in Eastern Europe.[17]

Ford's comment also galvanized Carter's own candidacy. The Democratic candidate stayed permanently on the offensive, even accusing the president of being "brainwashed" on Eastern Europe. In his third and final debate with Ford, on 22 October at Williamsburg, Virginia, he seemed more quick-witted and sharper than the president, who appeared distraught and agitated. Although Ford made no great error as he had in the second debate, almost all observers agreed that Carter had outperformed him.

Even so, the race was not over yet. Ford had defused his blunder over Eastern Europe somewhat by acknowledging his mistake. What he had meant to say, he remarked, was that he would not concur in Soviet domination of the region. In addition, the fuzziness label still worked with great effectiveness. During a whistle-stop train ride through Illinois, Ford said of Carter, "He wavers, he wanders, he wiggles, and he waffles and he shouldn't be President of the United States." The president hammered away at this theme with some success for the remainder of the election, assisted by the specter of the infamous *Playboy* interview.

As the campaign drew to a close, the polls indicated a virtual dead heat between the two candidates. On the morning of the election, the Harris poll placed Carter ahead by one percentage point, the Gallup poll had him trailing by the same amount. The candidates' own surveys showed that neither of them had generated much excitement or aroused intense loyalty among the voters. The "vast number of voters," commented Jerald ter Horst, a Ford campaign staffer, "have looked at the two men and see no practical difference." Indeed, if there was a consensus in the country, it was that these candidates were not the best that the parties had to offer the voters.[18]

As the polls predicted, the election proved to be one of the closest in the nation's history. Carter won with about 41 million popular votes (50.1 percent) to Ford's 39 million (48 percent). In electoral votes, Carter received 297 to Ford's 240. However tiny his margin of victory, the once-obscure former governor of Georgia had beaten all the odds by running against Washington. The question now was whether he could make a smooth transition from political outsider to presidential helmsman.

3

★ ★ ★ ★ ★

TRANSITION AND HONEYMOON

At first glance, it appeared that Jimmy Carter had won the presidency by restoring the old political coalition established by Franklin Roosevelt forty years earlier but crumbling since the 1950s. Like Roosevelt, Carter carried the South as well as the big industrial cities of the North and upper Midwest. For the first time in almost twenty-five years, Democrats captured every southern and border state except Virginia. Organized labor, which had deserted the Democratic party in the presidential election of 1972, went strongly Democratic in 1976 and handed Carter about 62 percent of its vote. Blacks also turned out in record numbers to support the Democratic candidate, casting five out of every six of their ballots for him. Without the union and black vote, Carter would have lost the election.

In several respects, however, Carter's coalition bore little resemblance to Roosevelt's. In the 1930s, for example, it was a white South that had supported FDR, since most southern blacks were disfranchised then. But in 1976 it was the black South that made the difference for Carter. The majority of white southerners voted for Ford, although not as many as had supported Republicans in 1968 and 1972. Similarly, *both* union and nonunion labor had voted for Roosevelt; in 1976, nonunion workers voted for Ford over Carter by 52 percent to 48 percent. Finally, Roosevelt had enjoyed stronger support from Catholic voters than Carter did.

Indeed, in an election in which Carter defeated Ford by a margin of less than 2 percent, the president-elect owed a good part of his victory to Republican crossovers. For example, he had solid backing from professional and business groups, particularly among their younger voters, whose members typically cast their ballots for Republicans. Even more important, he cut into normally Republican terrain in rural Protestant areas. While Ford garnered a higher percentage of the Catholic vote than had historically been given to Republican candidates, he could not match Carter's gains among rural Protestants. This was especially true in the South, where pride in a native son blended with shared religious beliefs to reduce the majorities Republicans had been winning among white voters in earlier presidential elections. Together with the black vote, a return of white southerners to the Democratic party assured Carter of a larger share of the vote (54 percent) than any Democratic candidate had received since 1948—and twice George McGovern's share four years earlier.

Carter's inroads were not limited to the South. His ethical convictions and religious passion had great national appeal, especially among fellow evangelical Protestants. Although many Americans, especially religious minorities, found his publicly stated commitment to Christian principles worrisome, many others were attracted to his call for a spiritual reawakening after a decade in which the integrity and morality of the nation's political leaders had come under fire.

The nature of Carter's victory had important implications for his presidency. In the first place, Carter lacked a political mandate from the American people. Not only had the election been close, but a record number of voters, apparently unimpressed with either of the two major candidates, did not cast their ballots. Only in the deep South was voter turnout larger than in 1972. And different constituencies expected different things from the president-elect. Professional people tended to be economic conservatives while blacks were more likely to put economic growth—especially jobs—and civil rights ahead of other concerns. Similarly, younger voters were generally more interested in such issues as the environment and quality of life than older voters, who turned their attention to matters involving health and social security. Organized labor, which had conducted a massive get-out-the-vote campaign, had its own agenda for the new president, which included a broad program of social welfare legislation and measures to stimulate the economy. Given Carter's narrow victory and his ambiguous platform, each of these constituencies could—and did—take credit for his election. They also anticipated his unequivocal support for their particular interests, even when they conflicted with one another or with Carter's own legislative proposals.

There were several indications already that the new president would have trouble persuading Congress to approve his programs. Although Democrats maintained their two-to-one majority in the House and their three-to-two majority in the Senate, most of the House members had assumed office since 1972, and nearly one-fifth of the senators were newly elected. Because Carter had campaigned as much against the Washington establishment as against the Republican party, few members of the new Congress felt politically obligated to him. As for party loyalty, lawmakers gained and held office more by building personal organizations than by being staunch Democrats or Republicans. Moreover, institutional changes had taken effect on Capitol Hill in recent years that limited the authority of hitherto powerful committee chairmen while augmenting that of more junior subcommittee heads. Taken together, these developments meant that Carter faced an increasingly independent and even intractable Congress and a decline in the cohesiveness of the legislative process.

The flip side of more assertive Congress, moreover, was an increasingly encumbered presidency. As early as 1960, Harvard University Professor Richard Neustadt had written that presidential power to reverse policy direction was limited by political and bureaucratic barriers and scarce resources. In response to the Vietnam War, the Watergate scandal, and charges of an "imperial presidency," Congress enacted legislation in the 1970s that further circumscribed the authority of the Oval Office. For example, the War Powers Act of 1973, approved over President Richard Nixon's veto, curtailed the president's power to engage in military action abroad without congressional consent; that same year, Congress banned funds for combat activities in Indochina. In addition, Congress responded in 1974 to Nixon's attempts to impound appropriated funds by passing legislation forcing him to release the funds. This was part of a larger overhaul of the entire budgetary procedure—including the establishment of new House and Senate budget committees and a Congressional Budget Office—intended to give Congress greater control over government spending.

Congress's determination to redress what it considered an imbalance between the executive and legislative branches of government posed a formidable challenge for the incoming president. Indeed, to some observers, there was a fundamental question as to just how governable the United States was at the time Carter entered the White House. In 1974, the National Academy of Public Administration and the Committee for Economic Development co-sponsored a three-day conference, attended by some of the nation's leading authorities on the presidency, to discuss the problems associated with governing the nation. Their final report contained over 140 recommendations for improving the institutional relationships between the Oval Office, Congress, the press, the federal bureaucracy, state and local governments, the major political parties, and the public. "A President confronts a splintered and shell-shocked nation," commented Ernest S. Griffith of the Library of Congress in summarizing the conference's suggestions.[1]

The next year, political scientist Thomas E. Cronin published a highly praised volume on the state of the presidency, in which he asserted that the American public expected more from a president in terms of making the nation a better place to live than he could deliver. The presidency was an "underdefined institution" constitutionally and historically, and the American people seemed to want a strong and effective chief executive who was also open and democratic. Yet these worthy objectives were not always compatible. The public also longed for leadership but was skeptical of the nation's leaders. Indeed, Cronin pointed to a fundamental paradox of the presidency. "A president will always have too much power for the realization of that cherished ideal—government by the people—yet never enough to solve all the problems we expect him to solve." In addition, he is "asked to represent the unrepresented and the under-represented, yet he [is] expected to be responsive to the electoral majority."[2]

Another complication for Carter as the incoming president was the widely held perception of him as inexperienced. Even his own advisers acknowledged his image problem, in part the result of a campaign that had been more about style than substance, so that most Americans still did not know where he stood on the issues. According to all the polls, the public's greatest concern was the state of the economy. Despite a drop in the inflation rate from about 12 percent in 1974 to around 6 percent by the end of 1976, the economy remained sluggish. The nation's output of goods and services (the gross national product or GNP) had risen at an annual rate of only 3 percent during the last three months of 1976, the lowest since the spring of 1975. Unemployment also stood at a high 7.8 percent of the work force; to lower that figure, economists estimated that the GNP would have to grow at an annual rate of at least 4 percent.

Disturbing demographic trends also confronted Carter as he prepared to take office. In 1976, the United States was a nation of about 215 million people, with 158 million living in urban areas of 50,000 or more. The fastest growing segment of the population was the elderly. Since 1970 the number of children under age ten had declined by 5.5 million, while the size of the population sixty-five and over had grown by 3 million, or 14.8 percent; more than 10 percent of the population were now in this age group. These statistics meant rapidly rising costs for social security and health care. The number of people living below the poverty level also continued to grow, from 11.2 percent in 1974 to 12.5 percent in 1976, and a staggering 50 percent of all black female heads of households fell into this category. Overall, the nation's social safety net was distended by tremendous strains.

The United States was also a nation on the move—mostly to the sunbelt. The population of the thirteen states of the West and the sixteen states of the South grew by about 9 percent over the last five years, compared with a 2-percent growth for the rest of the nation. Similarly, most urban centers of the North and East either declined in numbers or increased only marginally, while the fifteen fastest growing metropolitan areas were in Florida, Texas, Arizona, and Colorado. These population shifts contributed to a deepening blight in the nation's oldest and largest cities and an ongoing erosion of the traditional power base of the Democratic party. Paralleling the urban trauma was the havoc inflicted on the American environment. Natural habitats for wildlife continued to shrink as a result of such activities as drainage projects and subdivisions of western lands for mining and logging. Three million acres of farmland and 4 billion tons of topsoil were being lost each year as a result of urbanization, flooding, and wind and water erosion.

Finally, the political nation was moving toward what Harvard University Professor Samuel H. Beer later referred to as a "new and destructive pluralism"—that is, a society of organized groups that are bound together by common goals, represented by professional lobbyists, and relying on public authority to support or actively promote their private interests. As Beer described this development, the centralizing tendencies of a burgeoning federal bureaucracy were being offset by the fragmentation inherent in specialized knowledge, economic and political differences, and growing tolerance of social and cultural diversity. Within the multitude of groups arising out of this process, it was difficult to build lasting coalitions based on shared views of public policy. Leaders of these groups looked to Washington for leadership and direction and were aggrieved when Washington felt short. But they were concerned more with problem solving than with matters of public philosophy and national purpose.[3]

Yet the institutional and demographic developments Carter faced were not entirely dismal. The American people were better educated, held down more white-collar jobs, and took home higher salaries than ever before. Between 1970 and 1976, the number of high school students increased from 14.4 million to 15.8 million, or 8.9 percent, and the number of college students rose from 7.1 million to 9.7 million, or 26.8 percent. During this same period, the number of white-collar workers increased by about 3 percent each year, while the number of blue-collar workers decreased by about the same amount. In addition, median family income nearly doubled between 1970 and 1976 (although, because of inflation, this represented a gain in real purchasing power of only about 3 percent).

Despite the Vietnam War, Watergate, and other evidence of corruption in high government places, surveys also showed that Americans retained their faith in the nation's basic institutions and were anxious to "feel good about things" once more. Although the presidency was beleaguered and some of the president's authority diminished, he still wielded enormous power in terms of setting the nation's agenda and priorities and marking its direction. "The promise of the American presidency may have been oversold, overstated, and stretched beyond reality," Cronin observed in 1975, "but denying the importance and the need for presidential leadership would be to overstate the case, as well as misleading." Finally, the American people tended to see the president-elect as a potentially stronger and more decisive leader than President Ford had been. Carter would bring a new way of doing business to the government; he would be a practical "anti-politician" truly concerned about doing something for the "average person."[4]

Even on Capitol Hill, there were circumstances that augured well for the incoming Democratic president. Over the past fifty years, conservative southern Democrats and northern Republicans in the House had combined to defeat legislation sponsored by more liberal Democratic presidents. But since 1958 southern Democrats had been losing their seats to Republicans, while outside the South mostly liberal Democrats had replaced Republicans. Meanwhile, the Democratic caucus, which had spearheaded the change limiting the power of committee chairmen, actually increased the authority of the top Democratic leadership. This was especially true for the Speaker, who was now in charge of committee assignments and had the exclusive right to appoint the powerful House Rules Committee, which controlled the flow of legislation onto the House Floor. As presidential scholar Nelson Polsby noted, "Congressional reform devolved not only downward . . . but also upward," and the outcome was "an increased potential for favorable results for any President willing to work with the congressional leadership in establishing legislative priorities and strategies."[5]

The president-elect's pollster, Pat Caddell, explained many of these demographic and structural developments to Carter in a fifty-five-page postmortem on the election. He also warned Carter of some of the political obstacles that awaited him, including opposition on Capitol Hill to his programs from such Democrats as Edward Kennedy, George McGovern, and Morris Udall—all of whom Caddell described as "traditional Democrats . . . in many ways . . . as antiquated and anachronistic a group as are conservative Republicans." Although he advised Carter to seek good relations with these liberals, he also recommended that the Democratic National Committee (DNC) be "'Carterized' and made a political wing of the White House" and that the president use the DNC "to reward supporters [and] co-opt adversaries." As for the economic issues confronting the new administration, he told Carter not to handle them by "resort[ing] to old Democratic dogmas," which, he said, no longer appealed to younger and more prosperous voters. Instead, he urged the new president to "devise a context that [was] neither traditionally liberal nor traditionally conservative" but rather that cut "across traditional ideology." Indeed, he was concerned almost as much with questions of ideology and the administration's long-term plans for the country as he was with more pressing economic and political matters.

Yet Caddell's lengthy report was flawed in several important respects. First, while he believed that, in order to succeed, the new president would have to provide an "articulated vision" of where the country was going, he failed to offer Carter any sense of what that vision should be or what ideological perspective should guide his leadership. He also ignored such fundamental considerations as the interests and priorities of the congressional leadership, and although he encouraged Carter to focus his attention on legislative issues that would have "the greatest impact on the public," he never articulated these issues for the president or placed them in the context of long-range goals. Nevertheless, Carter digested the report carefully, described it as "excellent," and ordered that it be read by his other political advisers. In fact, the legislative and political course that the new president pursued after he took office was the one Caddell had laid out for him.[6]

Soon after his primary victory in Pennsylvania, Carter had followed the recommendation of Jack Watson, a young attorney who had worked for him while he was governor, and established a policy planning organization to prepare for his transition from candidate to president should he win in November. Over the summer and fall, a group headed by Watson produced a series of briefing books and option papers on the issues most likely to confront an incoming Carter administration; they were transmitted to Carter at the end of October—a week before the election. The most important of these was a paper on the budget, in which the transition team asserted that it was possible to fulfill campaign promises of holding government spending down and balancing the budget by fiscal 1981. In fact, the writers projected a budget surplus in 1981 of $52 billion.

Like the Caddell postmortem, however, the budget memorandum was deficient in several respects. First, it made light of the fact that achieving a $50-billion–$60-billion budget surplus by 1981, even under optimum economic conditions, would require a policy of fiscal restraints that was certain to cause confrontation with liberal Democrats on Capitol Hill. Second, it assumed a 5.5 percent to 6 percent annual growth in the GNP and a decline in the inflation rate from 6 percent to 5 percent by 1981. Even Charles Schultze, Carter's chairman-designate of the Council of Economic Advisers (CEA), conceded that these goals were "optimistic."[7]

Besides drafting policy papers for a Carter presidency, the Watson group concerned itself with staffing the new administration, and its involvement in this process provided early insight into a recurring problem of the Carter presidency: weak or conflicting delegation of authority. Although the Watson team reviewed thousands of resumés on potential Carter appointees, the president-elect never gave it exclusive responsibility for staffing. As a result, much of its work was duplicated in a separate operation at the Democratic National Committee. Making matters worse, Hamilton Jordan wanted to be in charge of White House personnel. When Watson submitted a transition budget giving him only one staff member, Jordan exploded, accusing Watson of trying to undercut him. The president-elect was finally forced to intervene. On 15 November, he announced that Jordan would assume primary responsibility for presidential appointments, in effect stripping Watson of much of his power.

Selection of cabinet and other high administration officials also proceeded slowly, in part because Carter insisted on lengthy review procedures, including consideration of at least one minority and one woman for each cabinet-level post. For more than three weeks, the president-elect remained virtually sequestered in his home in Plains, examining dossiers and checking references for each key position within the new administration. Not until December, exactly one month after his election, did he announce his first appointments, naming his close friend, Atlanta banker Bert Lance, as director of the Office of Management and Budget (OMB) and choosing former defense official Cyrus Vance as his secretary of state. A week later, he selected the chief executive of the Bendix Corporation, Michael Blumenthal, as his Treasury secretary and decided on Washington Congressman Brock Adams as his secretary of transportation. Other appointments soon followed: former Budget Director Charles Schultze as chairman of the CEA, Columbia University Professor Zbigniew Brzezinski as national security adviser, President Harold Brown of the California Institute of Technology as secretary of defense, Georgia Congressman Andrew Young as ambassador to the United Nations, and Idaho Governor Cecil Andrus as secretary of the interior. But not until the beginning of January, when Carter named Theodore Sorensen, former aide to President John F. Kennedy, as director of the Central Intelligence Agency (CIA) and former defense secretary James Schlesinger as his presidential assistant for energy, were all the top positions in the Carter administration finally filled. Of the newly elected presidents since 1952, Carter was the slowest in choosing his cabinet.

In assembling his administration, the president-elect made a concerted effort to appoint blacks and women to high government positions, as he had promised he would do during the campaign. It proved a harder task than he expected, since several prominent blacks, including mayors Thomas Bradley of Los Angeles and Coleman Young of Detroit, declined offers to join the Carter team. But he was eventually able to persuade Duke University Vice-President Juanita Kreps to serve as commerce secretary and a former dean of Howard Law School, Patricia Harris, to become secretary of housing and urban development (HUD). Both women were black.

Carter was less successful in opening the door to Washington outsiders for key administration slots. Among his cabinet appointments, only Ray Marshall, a University of Texas economist whom the president-elect named as his secretary of labor, could be regarded as a genuine newcomer to Washington. Most of the other "unknowns" were fellow Georgians, already being referred to by some as the "Georgia Mafia." In addition to Lance, the new faces included Hamilton Jordan as his chief staff aide and indeed his most trusted adviser; Jody Powell as his press secretary; Stuart Eizenstat as head of the Domestic Policy Staff (DPS) reponsible for providing him with options on major domestic policy issues; Jack Watson as his cabinet secretary; and Atlanta judge Griffin Bell as his attorney general.

Aside from these Georgians and a few others, the top positions in the Carter administration, including the three most important posts—state, defense, and Treasury—went to individuals with considerable Washington experience. Vance was a former secretary of the army and deputy secretary of defense under presidents Kennedy and Lyndon Johnson and a successful Washington lawyer; he epitomized the Washington establishment. Brown had also served under Kennedy and Johnson, first as director of research at the Pentagon and then as secretary of the air force. Blumenthal had served from 1961 to 1967 as deputy assistant secretary of state for economic affairs and as chairman of the United States delegation to the Kennedy round of tariff negotiations at Geneva.

In picking his cabinet, the president isolated himself from the diversity of viewpoint that might have better informed his own leadership and furnished the White House with a broader perspective. As it was, he chose Vance, Brown, Blumenthal, and the rest of his cabinet-level officials not because they were original thinkers, grand strategists, or innovative planners, but because he respected their managerial talents, believed they would make skilled negotiators, felt they could be relied on for sound advice, and thought they would follow instructions from the Oval Office.

Carter organized the White House staff intending that his cabinet secretaries have direct access to him. In particular, there was to be no chief of staff able to control and regulate the vital arteries of communication between the Oval Office and the rest of the administration—as had H. R. Haldeman during the Nixon administration and, to a lesser extent, Richard Cheney and Donald Rumsfeld during the Ford administration. But without a chief of staff, who would be ultimately responsible for running the White House? delegating authority? protecting the president's time and energy? watching over the flow of paper to and from the Oval Office? Decisions on these and similar structural questions had still not been made when Carter took the oath of office on 20 January.

The incoming president had also spent too much time on detail and not enough on providing overall leadership; no previous president-elect had been so directly involved for so long in choosing his administration. While surrounding himself with valued subordinates in good management style, Carter had neglected executive policy planning; nor, as a manager, had he implemented efficient procedures or delegated authority along clearly established organizational lines.

For a politician who had been remarkably successful in defying the odds by winning the White House, Carter also displayed lapses in political judgment. His appointment of Griffin Bell as attorney general stirred up a hornet's nest because of Bell's decisions in earlier desegregation cases and his membership in two segregated social clubs. The transition team at the Department of Justice had warned the president-elect of the outcry that would follow Bell's nomination and had recommended that he choose someone who was more "respected by responsible minority leaders." But Carter refused even to meet with civil rights leaders to discuss the appointment.[8]

Ten weeks after the election, Carter remained a veiled figure. During the campaign, he had often been referred to as a Populist—a voice of the people outside the mainstream of American politics, who promised to rid Washington of its entrenched leadership and to seek justice for the common people by eradicating concentrations of political and economic power. In reality, the new president was closer to the Progressives than the Populists, attempting to make government more competent and administratively more rational. Like the Progressives of the early twentieth century, he stood for responsible and efficient government, spoke out against vested interest groups, and talked about the importance of subordinating self-interest to a broader national interest. Similarly, he assumed that those who opposed his programs acted from selfish motives rather than from their own perception of the public good. Thus he was loath to compromise on what he regarded as matters of principle. Envisioning himself as a trustee of the public welfare, he also perceived one of his major tasks as president to be that of arousing the public conscience. But he was not a social reformer seeking fundamental changes. As a result, when the new administration undertook a vast array of initiatives in its first few months in office, it did so without any well-articulated sense of direction or long-term objective.

From the time Carter assumed office on 20 January, he was warned by his own White House staff to proceed slowly and set priorities in developing his legislative program. But the president ignored these admonitions. "Everybody has warned me not to take on too many projects so early in the administration, but it's almost impossible for me to delay something that I see needs to be done," he noted in his diary a week after taking office.[9]

As a result, Carter presented the 95th Congress with a legislative docket whose passage would have taxed the political skills of any president, much less one as unfamiliar with Washington's *modus operandi* as Carter. Among the proposals he submitted to the new Congress during his first six months in office were cuts in water projects, a measure to establish an agency for consumer affairs, executive reorganization authority, programs of urban and welfare reform, an ethics in government bill, changes in social security, hospital cost containment legislation, a bill to create a Department of Energy, and a comprehensive energy program.

Of the items Carter sent to Capitol Hill, however, none was more important than a package designed to stimulate the sluggish economy by giving all citizens a $50 tax rebate, cutting corporate taxes by $900 million, and allocating modest increases in public works and other job-creating programs. The president's plan underscored a shift in his economic philosophy. During the campaign, Carter had defined the most serious economic problem facing the nation as the high rate of unemployment. Yet as president-elect, he emphasized the need to avoid a reacceleration of the rate of inflation.

The administration's program reflected Carter's own admitted fiscal conservatism. On other issues, such as civil rights, the environment, and "helping people overcome handicaps to lead fruitful lives," he claimed to be "quite liberal," but this proved to be an untenable dichotomy. Carter's stance raised real questions about achieving "liberal" ends through "conservative" means—for example, could he "help people overcome handicaps" without large federal expenditures? Politically, it challenged powerful elements within Carter's own party, who denied that liberal ends could be reached by conservative means without distorting those ends—for example, if his proposals defined "handicaps" so as to exclude people lacking basic job skills.[10]

The response to Carter's economic package exposed the dissonance within Democratic ranks, and reaction ranged from mixed to negative, with the sharpest attacks coming from groups that had mobilized behind Carter during the campaign. The U.S. Conference of Mayors said his proposals did not do enough to help the cities. Seeking a much larger package, including a $30-billion public works program for 1977 alone, the AFL-CIO called the plan "a retreat from the goals we understand President-elect Carter to have set during last year's election campaign." Although Carter worked hard on Capitol Hill to sell his ideas, lawmakers were highly critical of the administration for relying too heavily on a tax refund to stimulate the economy instead of bringing down the rate of unemployment by creating more public-sector jobs. Yielding to the criticism that a rebate given to high-income taxpayers had no real economic benefit, the administration agreed to limit it to people with incomes of less than $30,000. However, the basic suspicion persisted that such tax measures would not be enough to energize the economy.[11]

By March 1977, organized labor was in open rebellion against the administration, not only because it disliked Carter's economic stimulus package but also because it had not received White House backing on a number of other issues, such as an increase in the minimum wage from $2.30 to $3.00 an hour. Labor leaders were also disappointed that the president gave only lukewarm support to a common situs picketing bill, which would have allowed a union striking against a single subcontractor to shut down an entire construction site. According to Lane Kirkland, secretary-treasurer of the AFL-CIO, Carter had simply failed to keep his campaign promises to "working people."[12]

Contrary to Kirkland's contention, Carter was neither unmindful of nor unsympathetic to labor's interests. But his primary concern was with the unorganized, bottom rung of the labor market rather than with more highly paid union members. Not only did he agree to a more modest, twenty-cent increase in the minimum wage, he took a strong stand against a proposed "split" that would have set a lower minimum for employees not covered by federal minimum wage laws before 1966 (primarily service and farm workers and workers in the retail and wholesale trades). "The differential hurts the most vulnerable workers," he told Eizenstat; supported by most of his economic advisers, it was still unacceptable to him.[13]

Carter also had difficulties in his relations with Capitol Hill. In December, the president-elect had come to Washington to confer with President Ford and leaders of the new Congress. In a private conversation with Carter, House Speaker Thomas ("Tip") O'Neill lectured him on the need to separate the rhetoric of the campaign from the reality of the legislative process. But according to O'Neill, "Carter didn't seem to understand." On the contrary, he told the Massachusetts congressman that, as governor of Georgia, he had taken his message to the people when the state legislature had blocked him; if, as president, he faced a similar situation with Congress, he would not hesitate to employ the same methods. He later repeated that statement to a group of lawmakers, telling them, "I can talk to your constituents easier than you can."[14]

The new president also provoked many lawmakers when, immediately after he took office, he honored a campaign promise to pardon Vietnam War draft evaders. Republican Senator Barry Goldwater of Arizona was enraged and described Carter's action as "the most disgraceful thing that a President has ever done." His nomination of Theodore Sorensen to head the CIA also caused considerable consternation. Because Sorensen had registered for the draft as a conscientious objector and had admitted to removing classified information without authorization while working at the Kennedy White House, even liberal Democrats opposed his appointment. Foreseeing certain defeat in the Senate, the president withdrew the nomination—but only after the whole episode had turned very nasty, warning of things to come.[15]

Nowhere was the early conflict between the White House and Capitol Hill more evident than in the flap over Carter's announcement at the end of February 1977 that he was targeting a number of dam and water projects (his so-called hit list) for possible elimination in the fiscal year 1978 budget. Again, his action arose from a campaign pledge—this time, to end waste and pork-barrel projects in the federal government. Unfortunately for Carter, pork-barrel politics had been sacrosanct on Capitol Hill for many decades. Lawmakers also viewed the hit list as further evidence of presidential indifference to Congress. Even the president acknowledged that his new administration had sometimes "inadvertently" given Congress cause for complaint by not conferring with the congressional leadership.[16]

By April, Congress and the president were at loggerheads over the water projects. Although Carter modified his hit list by dropping some items and adding others and promised to meet with lawmakers "to establish a dialogue and close cooperation in this issue," he was determined to excise the remaining projects. "Prepare dam project statement listing those which will be eliminated or cutback," he instructed Eizenstat. "In every case, itemize objections in strongest terms." Congress responded by soundly defeating (252 to 143) an administration-sponsored admendment to cut $100 million of funding for water projects from the budget.[17]

Relations between the president and lawmakers on Capitol Hill became even more strained after Carter announced unexpectedly on 14 April that he was rescinding his administration's proposal for a $50 tax rebate. The president had intended the measure as a one-time expedient to energize the economy, but since the economic picture continued to improve after he took office, there seemed less need for it. Nevertheless, the decision to drop the tax rebate angered congressional leaders who had agreed to back the White House despite their own reservations. "It was a little less than fair to those of us who supported it against our better judgment and worked hard to get it passed," complained Chairman Al Ullman of the House Ways and Means Committee.[18]

By early spring, therefore, Carter had already alienated many groups that had been instrumental in his election and whose support he needed if his legislative programs were to succeed. Yet the president remained extremely popular with the American public. Before he took office, his advisers had told him that, as president, he should project himself in the same way he did as a candidate—as a political outsider committed to restoring to government the values that had been the basis of America's greatness as a nation. Vice-President-elect Walter Mondale also recommended that he present himself as a leader "who is close to the people, who cares about their problems and is determined to give them a government that is courteous, compassionate, and helpful."[19]

Following this advice almost to the letter, Carter authorized an extensive public relations campaign after taking office that would portray him as a "citizen-president" and champion of traditional American values. Breaking with the pomp and circumstance surrounding the presidency, he disposed of most of the White House's fleet of limousines, ended the practice of having "Hail to the Chief" played whenever the president made a public appearance, placed his nine-year-old daughter, Amy, in the public schools, carried his own suitbag whenever he traveled, and ordered members of his administration to spend more time with their families. After holding a televised "town meeting" in Clinton, Massachusetts, on 16 March, he spent the night at the home of a local family before traveling the next day to Charleston, West Virginia, for a grass-roots discussion on energy problems. All of this had great appeal for a nation whose people, according to commentator Hugh Sidey, were "looking for smaller dimensions [and] for more simplicity in their lives." Carter's popularity was reflected in the polls: A Gallup survey taken at the end of April gave Carter a 71-percent approval rating, while a Harris poll gauged the rating four points higher, at 75 percent.[20]

The president wielded his popularity to win congressional authorization to reorganize sectors of the federal bureaucracy. What made this victory so impressive was that it was achieved over the strong opposition of lawmakers who objected to the legislation's carte blanche, since Carter could revamp the executive branch without seeking Congress's preliminary approval. Even so, the first three months of the Carter administration were characterized more by brisk activity than by actual accomplishments. Work was under way at the White House on a new urban and regional policy based on what Carter had referred to during his campaign as "federalism," or shared decision making between Washington and local government and public-private partnerships in urban development programs. The administration was also preparing major messages on the environment and consumer affairs. In addition, the president endorsed the establishment of a Consumer Protection Agency (CPA) and named Esther Peterson, a leading proponent of consumer rights recommended to him by consumer-advocate Ralph Nader, as his special assistant for consumer affairs.

Aside from the economy, the most pressing legislative matter for the president was the nation's worsening energy crisis. Since the 1973 Yom Kippur War, the price of foreign oil had more than doubled, from about $6 to over $12 a barrel. At the same time, U.S. dependence on foreign oil had risen from about 35 percent to over 50 percent of its total supply. Virtually every public official, including the president, agreed that unless something was done to curb this energy appetite, the nation's future would be mortgaged to the oil producers of the Middle East.

The brutal winter of 1976/77 underscored how critical the situation had become. Because of a shortage of natural gas, schools and factories throughout the nation were forced to close. According to White House estimates, by the end of January, as many as 400,000 workers had been laid off for a day or more since November as a result of fuel deficiencies. A number of states even declared energy emergencies. The administration responded to this crisis quickly and decisively. The Interstate Commerce Commission ordered railroads to give priority to oil tank cars and permitted trucks licensed to do business in only one state to cross state lines in order to deliver fuel. The Federal Energy Administration directed refineries to curtail production of jet fuel in favor of heating oil. President Carter dramatized his own concern for the plight of the people hardest hit by the freeze by making a quick trip to ice-bound Pittsburgh and then declaring eleven states disaster areas.

In February, the White House also asked for emergency authority to deregulate the price of gas piped across state lines. Because interstate gas was regulated at $1.44 per 1,000 cubic feet while unregulated gas (that is, gas sold within the producing states) sold at $1.90 or more, pipeline companies preferred to sell their gas intrastate. As a result, gas-producing states had plentiful supplies, while the other states faced a fuel emergency. If interstate gas was sold at the market price instead of the regulated price, then gas would flow to wherever it was most needed. Congress responded with inordinate speed to Carter's request. On 2 February, just six days after he had asked for the legislation, lawmakers passed the Emergency Natural Gas Act, giving the president the authority he wanted.

For Carter and his advisers, the natural gas shortage only highlighted the full-scale energy crisis threatening the country. Until the United States had a comprehensive energy program that would cut energy consumption, develop new sources of energy at home, and wean the nation away from its reliance on foreign oil, new and more serious shortages lay ahead, with catastrophic consequences for the American economy. In an address to the nation delivered the same day he signed the Emergency Natural Gas Act into law, Carter spelled out the alternatives facing the nation, adding that he would present Congress with an energy program by 20 April. A few days later, he sent to Capitol Hill a proposal to establish a cabinet-level Department of Energy.

Meanwhile, the president struggled with the problem of how to get the American people to conserve energy. In his view, there had to be a significant increase in energy costs to discourage waste and to encourage further development of national energy resources, yet the increase could not be so steep as to throw the nation into recession or even depression. Nor should the oil and gas producers be allowed to make such enormous profits that the American people would reject the program outright. Although the administration attached considerable importance to generating public support for such an energy plan, the actual drafting was done in great secrecy by Carter's energy adviser, James Schlesinger, and a small group of his assistants. The complex strategy they developed contained 113 separate provisions, the most important of which placed a tax on all domestic oil production and a standby gasoline tax each year gasoline consumption exceeded stated targets. The program also imposed a "gas guzzler" tax on automobiles with low fuel efficiency, penalized heavy industrial users of oil and natural gas, and instituted tax credits and other incentives to encourage conservation. On 18 April, the president spoke to the nation on energy, referring to his energy program as the "moral equivalent of war." Although some pundits later pointed out that the acronym for "moral equivalent of war" was "meow," the public response to his program was overwhelmingly favorable. "For the first time, a strong activist President had seized the initiative on energy," *Newsweek* later commented.[21]

Unfortunately, the energy program had been put together with such a total disregard for any review process that it bristled with technical flaws and raised a number of unanswered questions, such as the effect of the gas guzzler tax on the automobile industry, the inflationary impact of the standby gasoline tax, or the conversion costs of switching from oil and natural gas to coal as mandated by the legislation. Even Treasury Secretary Blumenthal and CEA Chairman Schultze complained about having no opportunity to scrutinize the program. Consequently, when the White House finally briefed House and Senate leaders on the plan, administration officials often contradicted one another on specific matters. But the president chose to blame his difficulties on the lobbying power of vested interest groups rather than on problems internal to his administration.

After three months in office, the White House remained in an organizational tangle, with such fundamental questions as the delegation of authority and the administrative structure of the staff still largely unresolved. Complicating matters was the president's commitment to a form of government in which cabinet officers were given an unusual amount of autonomy, including making subcabinet appointments without first clearing them through normal White House and Congressional channels. Much of the friction with Capitol Hill came about as a result of this practice. Carter also failed to delineate clearly the authority of agencies whose purview overlapped, such as OMB, CEA, and the Treasury Department. As a result, competing interests often tried to win his support by offering advice they thought he wanted to hear rather than recommendations worked out after careful deliberation. "*A great premium is placed on anticipating what you want instead of providing you with frank and hard analysis,*" Hamilton Jordan thus told the president in March.[22]

The president buried himself in an endless flow of paper, distancing himself from his own staff and curtailing his time for thought and reflection. When he first took office, he had anticipated a fifty-five-hour work week, of which about fifteen hours would be spent reading and responding to the material in his "in box." By April, his work week had grown to about eighty hours, of which more than thirty hours were given over to paperwork. As a result, by the time he delivered his energy message, his staff had become overwhelmed by the amount of paper circulating through the Oval Office. "Look, we are trying to do too much," Jody Powell finally told Carter in April, but to little avail.[23]

Undoubtedly, obtaining approval for a comprehensive energy policy would have been grueling for any person in the Oval Office. Opponents of the energy program had begun lobbying against it even before the president addressed the joint session of Congress. Critics denounced the package as being too complex, going too far, not going far enough, and not presenting an accurate picture of the energy industry. Carter might have undercut the opposition to his program by bringing congressional leaders—those who were more in touch with the political pulse on Capitol Hill than the president—into the preparation process and by seeking allies within the energy industry itself. But viewing himself as a trustee of the nation's welfare, who had to conduct his administration above the political fray and according to his perception of the national interest, he refused to engage in the type of power-brokering that had been utilized by successful presidents since at least Woodrow Wilson.

There are certain parallels between Wilson and Carter that permit of a highly instructive comparison. Both leaders were progressive southerners and devout Christians who believed in the gospel of service and considered political office a form of ministry. In contrast to Carter, however, Wilson had a clear sense of purpose. He also had a better grasp than Carter of the attainable and a better understanding of the negotiable and the expendable. Unalterably committed to certain basic values, he could be cunning and devious in achieving his aims, but he understood that flexibility and compromise on specific issues did not entail repudiation of fundamental principles. As a result, he managed to get through Congress a program of economic and social legislation that ranks his administration among the most productive in the nation's history.

Unlike Wilson, Carter's progressive mentality seemed to blind him to the realities of American politics and public life. The special interests he assailed were a reflection of the pluralistic nature of American politics, in which there was not a single constituency but an array of them, with often conflicting but legitimate interests. To rally the American people behind his programs, he needed to be a creative and flexible leader with a well-defined sense of purpose that commanded broad respect. This latter requirement especially would pose a stumbling block throughout his four years in office.

4

★ ★ ★ ★ ★

MORALITY AND
FOREIGN POLICY

Although President Carter undertook a full agenda of domestic initiatives in his early months in office, he also devoted considerable attention to matters of foreign policy. Indeed, there were some striking similarities between his handling of foreign policy and his management of domestic affairs. In both cases, he was determined to play a dominant role, proposed a number of bold new measures, angered constituencies that had helped to elect him, and tried to do too much too quickly.

From the time Carter took office, he intended to take charge of his own foreign policy. Secretary of State Cyrus Vance would be the diplomat transacting the nation's business abroad, but the president alone would establish priorities, set direction, and make the final decisions. Foreign policy would originate in the Oval Office, not the Department of State. In fact, Carter believed he had to overcome what Hamilton Jordan called "an elitism and arrogance at the State Department that is reflected in our foreign policy." Although he had great personal respect for Vance and considered him an able diplomat, Carter selected him—as he did most of his cabinet—primarily because he thought he would be a tough and competent manager who would make a good team player.[1]

With Carter as the decision maker and Vance as the diplomat, Zbigniew Brzezinski would serve as the idea man of the administration. In choosing the Columbia University professor and former director of the Trilateral Commission as his national security adviser, the president-elect clearly wanted someone who thought in broad geopolitical terms and could provide him with a comprehensive overview of international developments. He regarded Brzezinski as a "first rate thinker"—impulsive and sometimes wrongheaded but possessing the ability to grasp and clarify the fundamental interrelationships of global politics. Distrusting the bureaucracy of the State Department, Carter believed the National Security Council (NSC) would furnish a more favorable setting for developing and analyzing strategic concepts. In conducting foreign policy, therefore, Carter would be able to balance the bureaucratized but rationalized professionalism of the State Department with the intellectual ferment of the NSC.[2]

Carter also predicated his foreign policy on open diplomacy and the linkage between morality and power. During his presidential campaign, he attacked Secretary of State Henry Kissinger for his closed and secret diplomacy. "Our Secretary of State simply does not trust the judgment of the American people," he told the Chicago Council on Foreign Relations in March 1976. Carter also contended that the United States as a world power had an inherent moral responsibility to match its conduct of foreign policy to the basic principles of human rights as set forth in the Helsinki accords of 1975.[3]

The new president had not always felt this way. At the Democratic Issues Conference in 1975, he had criticized the Jackson-Vanik amendment on free emigration from the Soviet Union—a rallying point for human rights activists—as unwarranted interference in Soviet internal affairs. Increasingly, however, he had become disturbed by what he regarded as an excessive degree of realpolitik and even amorality in the Ford administration's handling of foreign affairs. His campaign strategists also saw human rights as a "no-lose issue," which might even win Carter votes from foreign policy hardliners because of its implicit attack on the Soviet Union. Beginning with a speech to the B'nai B'rith in early September 1976, therefore, Carter had made human rights a resounding campaign theme, assailing the Ford administration for its alleged neglect and promising, when in office, to make the United States once more "a beacon light for human rights throughout the world."[4]

In addition to open diplomacy and human rights, Carter was also strongly committed to creating a community of nations in which the United States would work closely with its allies. Echoing the position of the Trilateral Commission, he declared that the "time has come" for the United States "to seek a partnership between North America, Western Europe, and Japan." Attacking Kissinger for ignoring the Western European powers in his effort to improve relations with Moscow, he also argued that "[to] the maximum extent possible," Washington's relations with the communist powers "should reflect the combined view of the democracies."[5]

Carter, of course, was not opposed to bettering relations with the Soviet Union and the rest of the communist world. In fact, he was convinced that global interdependence should replace global confrontation, and, in terms reminiscent of Woodrow Wilson, he spoke of a new world order based on mutual cooperation, stability, justice, and peace. None of these ideals could become reality without a continuation of the policy of détente begun under Nixon and Ford and an end to the arms race. For that reason, Carter strongly supported the 1972 SALT I agreement between the two superpowers, which placed ceilings on different types of intercontinental ballistic missiles (ICBMs). Carter maintained, however, that détente should not be pursued at the expense of human rights, nor should foreign policy be exclusively focused any longer on the Cold War rivalry between Washington and Moscow. Further, the United States should drive a harder bargain with Moscow than it had under Ford. "We talk about détente," he said in his second debate with President Ford. "The Soviet Union knows what they want in détente, and they've been getting it. We have not known what we've wanted, and we've been outtraded in almost every instance."[6]

Another area of concern for the new administration was arms control, especially since it was an issue Carter had raised repeatedly throughout the campaign. Although he approved of the SALT I agreement, due to expire in 1977, he lambasted the Ford administration for not reaching a new and more extensive accord. Even after being elected president, he continued to express his dismay at the size of the nuclear arsenals owned by the United States and the Soviet Union. "I went over the complete inventory of U.S. nuclear warheads, which is really a sobering experience," he recorded in his diary on 28 December.[7]

By the time Carter moved into the White House in January 1977, therefore, the general outlines of his foreign policy were fairly well established, yet problems soon arose over implementation. Some of the difficulties stemmed from the same organizational woes that hampered the administration's domestic agenda. It was not always clear, for example, who spoke for the president before Congress. Carter also complained that he was receiving too many undigested briefings on foreign policy issues. "Get together and from now on give me *one coordinated* briefing book—collected from the myriad sources," he instructed Brzezinski and his staff.[8]

A far more serious development was the administration's approach toward Soviet-American relations. There can be no question that Carter hoped to carry on the policy of détente, since he said as much in a letter to Soviet leader Leonid Brezhnev six days after moving into the White House. But his advisers mistakenly believed that he could speak out against Soviet infringements of human rights without jeopardizing relations between Moscow and Washington. "Surely the Soviets are sophisticated enough to understand that the domestic flexibility we need to make progress in other areas is enhanced by your position on human rights," Jody Powell told the president in February 1977. Carter agreed, reminding news correspondents that he did not single out the Soviet Union as the only place where human rights were being violated.[9]

It soon became clear that the president and his press secretary were being extremely naive, and the first clash between Washington and Moscow over human rights occurred only a week after Carter took office. In a public statement, the Department of State accused Czechoslovakia of violating the 1975 Helsinki agreements by harassing a group of Czechoslovakian intellectuals who were demanding domestic reforms. Two days later, it issued another statement calling the Soviet dissident Andrei Sakharov "an outspoken champion of human rights" and warning the Soviets that any effort to "intimidate" him would "conflict with accepted international standards of human rights." Carter even sent a personal note to Sakharov, pledging his support worldwide for human rights.[10]

The Soviets were infuriated. In their view, the Carter administration had broken an unwritten agreement between the two superpowers not to comment on each other's internal affairs. The State Department broadsides also represented the first time that Washington had publicly condemned an East European country for not abiding by the Helsinki agreements. Meanwhile, Moscow had already decided to step up its efforts to block contact between dissident leaders in the East and their sympathizers in the West. As Soviet Ambassador to the United States Anatoli Dobrynin met with Vance to protest Carter's letter to Sakharov, the Soviets intensified their repression of political dissidents, making a point of arresting such leading critics as Alexander Ginsburg and Yuri Orlov. Rumors circulated in Washington that they would be deported to the West along with Sakharov.

Ignoring the growing strain in Soviet-American relations, the White House mounted a diplomatic offensive to win a new arms reduction agreement with Moscow. With the SALT I treaty set to expire in October, the Soviets were also anxious to resume arms limitation talks, which had been stalled since 1974 when Ford and Brezhnev agreed at Vladivostok to impose a ceiling of 2,400 strategic missile launchers on both the United States and the Soviet Union. Carter remained dissatisfied with the accord since it did not reduce existing stockpiles but only created parity at a level beyond which neither nation sought to build. He was also worried about a new generation of Soviet ICBMs with enormous warheads and greatly improved accuracy. The president made clear to Moscow his desire for a comprehensive agreement, which would include a significant reduction in the nuclear arsenals of both sides. As a fallback position, he was willing to settle for a pact based on the Vladivostok accord but with a ceiling about 10 percent lower.

In his opening remarks in Moscow, Secretary of State Vance laid out the administration's proposals, and Soviet leaders responded bitterly. Almost all the major cutbacks would be in weapons categories in which the Soviets held an edge, and there would be few restrictions on submarine or air-launched weapons, the classes in which the United States had the clear advantage. In addition, both sides would have to cease making improvements in warhead accuracy, again leaving the United States far ahead. What angered the Soviets almost as much as the specifics, however, was the fact they were offered publicly. Taken together with Carter's avowed support for Soviet dissidents, Soviet leaders were convinced that the American call for a major reduction in nuclear weapons was part of a duplicitous campaign to embarrass them. They were determined not to be sucked into what they regarded as Washington's ploy. At a meeting with Vance, Brezhnev rejected the American proposals without even offering any counterproposals. He then ended the meeting and cancelled the rest of the negotiating sessions scheduled during Vance's visit.

In its first few weeks in office, therefore, the Carter administration had made a muddle of U.S.–Soviet relations. The president and his advisers had tried to impose their values and perspectives on Moscow, and their efforts had backfired. Carter had assumed that the Soviets were just as anxious as he was for arms reductions, but he had miscalculated the effects of his outspoken criticism of the Kremlin and his well-publicized arms proposals on the secretive, paranoid Soviet government. In fairness to the president, he was under severe constraints in negotiating with the Soviets. There had already been a battle over his nomination of Paul Warnke as the nation's chief arms negotiator, which had revealed the depth of the opposition to any agreement seeming disadvantageous to the United States. A close friend of Vance's, Warnke was widely regarded in Washington as a "dove" on arms control, and his critics feared he would make too many concessions to the Soviets. Although the president managed to get Warnke confirmed, the closeness of the vote (fifty-eight to forty) indicated the difficulty he would have in getting the two-thirds majority needed in the Senate for ratification of a new SALT agreement.

Regardless, there was ample warning that the Soviets would never accept the arms deal the president was offering them and that his public sympathy for Soviet dissidents was undermining his chances for successful negotiations with the Kremlin. In a speech in March, Brezhnev lashed out at Carter's human rights campaign, warning that such "interference in the internal affairs of the Soviet Union [along with a] slanderous campaign in the United States about the myth" of the Soviet military threat stood in "direct opposition to further improvement of Soviet-American relations." The American ambassador to the Soviet Union, Malcolm Toon, was summoned to the Foreign Ministry, where he had to listen to a tirade directed against the United States. Even Carter himself later acknowledged that he misjudged the Kremlin's reaction to his human rights campaign.[11]

Despite the failure of the first Moscow meeting, both sides were still willing to return to the bargaining table. The Soviet Union wanted a formal conclusion to the Vladivostok agreement of 1974, while the United States was under increasing pressure domestically and from its allies to recover some of the ground lost as a result of the March fiasco. In May, the arms limitation talks resumed in Geneva, and after three days of negotiations, the two sides reached agreement on the broad outlines of a new SALT II accord that would run through 1985. Reluctantly, Vance accepted the ceiling of 2,400 strategic launchers as the starting point for SALT II. In return, Soviet Foreign Minister Andrei Gromyko indicated Soviet readiness to consider paring down each side's strategic arsenals by as much as 10 percent. He also agreed to a protocol restraining the development and deployment of American cruise missiles (relatively inexpensive pilotless drones that could fly at altitudes low enough to escape radar detection) and Soviet backfire bombers (aircraft that Washington maintained could be modified to strike the United States). Both weapons threatened the delicate strategic balance between the two superpowers.

Nevertheless, Washington and Moscow remained far apart on the size of any arms reduction and on numerous other specifics. In particular, the administration wanted to limit the number of missiles able to carry more than one warhead (multiple independently targetable reentry vehicles, or MIRVs) on all classes of ICBMs, not just the ones with the heaviest thrust (or throw power) as it had earlier proposed. The Soviets believed that this would unduly benefit the United States, since it had already put multiple warheads on its sea-launched missiles (SLBMs) while they had not, so Moscow rejected the proposal.

Carter's human rights campaign also remained a festering sore point in Soviet-American relations. Even though the president moderated his censure of Soviet violations, he did not desist entirely. In a commencement address at Annapolis, he criticized Moscow's refusal to tolerate free speech and to grant all Soviet citizens the right to emigrate. To the Kremlin, it appeared that Carter was meddling again. When the president wrote Brezhnev in June offering to meet with him at a mutually acceptable time and place, the Soviet leader told Ambassador Toon that a summit meeting was possible only after a SALT agreement had been reached. Brezhnev also took the occasion to deliver an angry, table-thumping attack on Carter's Soviet policy. He then prohibited Toon from giving a Fourth of July address to the Soviet people because Toon made reference to the administration's efforts on behalf of human rights.

By midsummer 1977, relations between the two superpowers had dipped to such a low that Carter felt it was imperative to adopt a more conciliatory posture toward Moscow. In a speech before the Southern Legislative Conference, he emphasized the need for cooperation between the United States and the Soviet Union in order to bring about a "gentler, freer, more bountiful world." He also noted that the "whole history of Soviet-American relations teaches us that we will be misled if we base our long range policies on the mood of the moment." Nevertheless, Soviet-American dealings remained icy.

Closer to home, Carter was running into trouble because of his attempt to conclude a treaty between the United States and Panama that would transfer the Panama Canal and the Panama Canal Zone (an area five miles wide on both sides of the Panama Canal) to Panama. The negotiations, which had been going on sporadically since 1964, had not been a point of contention in the Democratic primaries, although they were in the Republican contests. While Republican candidate Ronald Reagan slashed away at Gerald Ford for agreeing to the gradual transfer of the canal and canal zone to Panama, Democratic hopefuls paid little attention to the issue. In November 1975, on one of the few occasions Carter mentioned the canal, he came out in favor of maintaining American sovereignty.

Reagan had remarked during the primaries that the United States had built and paid for the canal and so "we should tell [the Panamanian government of General Omar] Torrijos and Company that we are going to keep it." This struck a responsive chord among the American people, and negotiating a treaty with Panama became an important issue during the general election. Carter avoided the question as much as possible, but when queried, he reiterated his stand against relinquishing American hegemony. "I would never give up complete control or practical control of the Panama Canal Zone," he commented during the presidential debates.[12]

After the election, however, Carter changed his mind, convinced now that turning over the canal to Panama was morally right, that it would enhance the United States' image throughout Latin America, and that gaining Senate ratification of a canal agreement would demonstrate to the American public his willingness and ability to tackle difficult assignments. The president had also been warned by the State Department that if a settlement was not reached with the Torrijos government, violence might erupt in Panama threatening the very security of the canal.

A new round of negotiations with Panama began on 14 February, but they were almost immediately broken off because of the United States' insistence on retaining the right to use military force if necessary to keep the canal open. The Panamanians balked at what they regarded as an infringement of their sovereignty. The talks were not resumed again until May when the Panamanians agreed to a U.S. proposal for two treaties. The first would transfer control of the canal to Panama after 1999; the second would give the United States an indefinite right to defend the neutrality of the canal but only against external threats. On this basis, the two sides reached final agreement in August.

By this time, however, the Panama Canal had become a cause célèbre on Capitol Hill. The White House was flooded with letters from lawmakers, some supporting the administration's decision to negotiate with Panama, most angrily denouncing it. Although Republicans led the charge, many Democrats joined them in accusing Carter of surrendering one of the nation's great treasures. Opinion polls differed substantially over the degree of public opposition to the agreement, but it was clearly significant and well-organized.

Meanwhile, Carter had become ensnarled in the enormously complex and seemingly endless Mideast crisis. During the campaign and after the election, he had been warned by his advisers not to get involved in the Mideast quagmire. But as he later wrote, his concern about Israeli security, the rights of Palestinians, the possibility of Soviet influence in the region, and the West's dependence on Arab oil led him to ignore their counsel.

Carter's campaign statements on the region had been unexceptional. Very early in his candidacy, he had urged Israel to withdraw from most of the territories it had seized during the Six Days' War of 1967, and he had later endorsed the establishment of a Palestinian state on the West Bank of the Jordan River. But in an obvious effort to court the Jewish vote, he increasingly emphasized the importance of strengthening ties with Israel and came out in support of Israel's demands for "defensible borders," a term generally understood to mean continued occupation of the areas taken in 1967. He also stated that he would not recognize the Palestinian Liberation Organization (PLO) "or other government entities representing the Palestinians" until he was convinced that they acknowledged Israel's right to exist.[13]

Once in office, Carter claimed he would "rather commit suicide than hurt Israel." Nevertheless, he decided to wield American influence to resolve the Arab-Israeli conflict even if it meant placing himself at odds with Israeli leaders and the American Jewish community. Rejecting the "step-by-step" approach pursued by former secretary Kissinger, the president preferred a comprehensive settlement to be achieved by reconvening the 1973 Geneva Conference. That strategy was risky. First, there were logistical problems; it was doubtful that such a complex gathering could even be arranged by year's end. In the meantime, moderate Arabs might not be able to withstand pressure from more radical groups to renew military action against Israel. Second, Egypt would want to send its own delegation to Geneva in order to negotiate bilaterally with Israel, while its Arab archrival Syria would hold out for a single Arab delegation in order to keep Egypt from reaching a separate agreement with the Israelis. But the most intractable problem concerned the status of the PLO at a Geneva conference. Would the PLO try to send its own delegation to Geneva, or would it accept membership in a pan-Arab delegation? More to the point, would Israel permit PLO representation under any circumstances? To explore these issues and prepare the groundwork for a Geneva conference, President Carter sent Vance in February 1977 to the Mideast.

Although no progress was made toward an actual settlement, Vance and Carter were encouraged by the reception the secretary of state received, especially from Egyptian President Anwar Sadat. According to Vance, Sadat "showed more flexibility on the question of peace" than any of the other Arab leaders he met. But even President Hafaz-al-Assad of Syria, whom Vance described as "the hardest" of the Arab leaders, appeared willing to make some compromises, indicating, for example, that he might be prepared to accept something less than full autonomy for the Palestinians. As for Israel, Prime Minister Yitzhak Rabin said his country might compromise on borders (although it would never return to the pre-1967 lines). He even suggested that Israel might tolerate the presence of Palestinians at a Geneva conference if they came as part of the Jordanian delegation. Most important, every one of the leaders Vance met endorsed the goal of holding a meeting at Geneva before the end of 1977.[14]

The optimism of February, however, soon faded. In March, Rabin came to Washington, the first of the Mideast heads of state to call on Carter. Over the next three months, other Mideast leaders, including Egypt's Anwar Sadat, Crown Prince Fahd of Saudi Arabia, and King Hussein of Jordan visited the White House. In May, Carter also flew from London, where he had been attending an economic summit with other Western leaders, to Geneva where he met with Syria's President Assad.

For the most part, these talks were unproductive. Contrary to what he had indicated earlier, Rabin now told the president that he would oppose a Geneva conference if the PLO or other Palestinian representatives were present. He also stated that he would not agree to total withdrawal from the West Bank or Golan Heights or permit the establishment of an independent Palestinian state on the West Bank. Discussions with other Mideast leaders were not much more fruitful. Although Carter was clearly charmed by Sadat's good-natured friendliness and had great admiration for the Egyptian leader, not even their talks produced any significant breakthroughs.

Meanwhile, relations with Israel began to sour. Israeli leaders reacted angrily to remarks Carter had made on several occasions in favor of some form of Palestinian homeland or political entity, and they were afraid the president was trying to impose his own peace settlement on the Mideast. Also, with a May election approaching, they were worried that Carter's meeting with Assad would play into the hands of the hard-line Likud party headed by Menachem Begin. As they feared, on 23 May Israelis gave the Likud party a stunning victory in the national elections.

The president's comments about a Palestinian homeland and his courting of the Arab powers also offended many American Jewish leaders, who had voted for Carter in November but had done so reluctantly, wary of his avowed evangelical Christianity. In an effort to solidify their favor, the president had Brzezinski and Vice-President Walter Mondale meet with them soon after he took office to underscore his continued support for Israel. More important, he strongly backed a measure prohibiting American firms doing business in the Middle East from participating in an Arab trade embargo against Israel. Although most American Jewish leaders appear to have genuinely appreciated the president's efforts on behalf of the antiboycott legislation, two other decisions Carter made soon after cancelled out whatever goodwill he had just earned. First, he blocked the sale by Israel to Ecuador of twenty-four Kfir fighter-bombers whose engines were of American manufacture; then he announced that he was reviewing a campaign promise by Ford to supply Israel with concussion bombs. These moves were actually part of Carter's stated policy of limiting arms sales to Third World countries, but Jewish leaders perceived them as slaps against Israel. Fuel was added to the fire in March when Carter mistakenly shook hands with a representative of the PLO while standing in a reception line after delivering a speech at the United Nations.

Jewish leaders also complained to Carter about the proposed sale to Saudi Arabia of Hawk and Maverick missiles, which Congressman Benjamin Rosenthal of New York said would undermine Israel's capacity to defend itself. The president tried to mollify these critics, telling Rosenthal that the United States' commitment to Israel's security was "unequivocal." But as Hamilton Jordan later commented, there was *"widespread concern* in the American Jewish community over the President's positions on Israel."[15]

On 19 July, Prime Minister Begin arrived in Washington for meetings with the president. Carter had been shocked to learn that Begin would be Israel's new leader. A hard-liner whom *Time* labeled a "superhawk," Begin referred to the West Bank and Gaza Strip as "liberated territories, part of the land of Israel," and even called the West Bank by its biblical names of Judea and Samaria. In the president's view, Begin's election hardly boded well for the peace process.[16] However, he was pleasantly surprised after talking with the Israeli leader for two days. Contrary to what he had anticipated, Begin proved to be an intelligent, courteous, and even charming figure, who listened attentively both to the president's reassurances that he would not impose a peace plan on Israel and to his objections about the building of Israeli settlements in the occupied territories. In response, the prime minister stated his own desire for a Geneva conference. He also stressed that all issues were negotiable at Geneva and that the deliberations should be based on United Nations Resolutions 242 and 338 calling for the withdrawal of Israeli troops from the occupied territories in return for Arab recognition of the state of Israel.

The Carter-Begin talks did much to dispel the president's worst fears about Begin's inflexibility. Momentarily, they also helped to mend fences between the president and American Jewish leaders. Based on his conversations with the Israeli prime minister, Carter even told reporters that he saw "the convening of a Geneva conference as being very likely." Yet major differences still existed between Begin and the American president. The Israeli leader interpreted UN Resolutions 242 and 338 to mean withdrawal of Israeli forces from "some" occupied territories; Carter construed the resolutions to mean from "all" territories. Under no circumstances, moreover, would Begin give up the West Bank, parley with the PLO, begin talks in Geneva with a combined Arab-Palestinian delegation, agree to a Palestinian homeland, or stop the construction of Israeli settlements in the occupied territories.

Soon after returning to Israel, in fact, the prime minister announced plans for a large number of new settlements on the West Bank. Coming as it did on the eve of Vance's Mideast mission to coax the Arab states to the negotiating table, the administration responded by angrily condemning Israel's action. A sharp exchange then followed between Washington and Jerusalem over the settlements issue. These events rekindled earlier concerns among American Jews about the administration's Mideast policy and pushed relations between them and the White House to the breaking point.

Politically and diplomatically, therefore, Carter's Mideast policy was a disaster. No progress had been made toward resolving the Mideast crisis, yet the president had alienated the Jewish community and lawmakers on Capitol Hill who were sympathetic to Israel. As the president himself later observed, "My own political supporters were coming to see me, groups were meeting with Cy Vance, and stirrings within Congress were becoming more pronounced."[17]

Another battle on Capitol Hill formed around the president's pledge to withdraw U.S. troops from South Korea. Carter's determination on this matter was another legacy of his campaign. Although he favored a buildup of American ground forces in Europe, where Soviet troops outnumbered NATO forces, he saw no useful military purpose for American troops in Korea, which, he believed, could be better defended with U.S. air and logistical support. He also considered the politically repressive government of Park Chung Hee to be morally repugnant. For both these reasons, he promised to begin removing American ground forces from Korea soon after taking office.

On 26 January, the president announced at a press conference that he intended to carry through with his campaign pledge. The news was not well received by powerful circles in Japan and the United States. The Japanese feared instability in the Korean peninsula and were worried about the implications of the withdrawal in terms of the United States' security commitments to Japan. They were also miffed that they had not been consulted before Carter made his decision. In the United States, the president's announcement drew strong opposition from foreign policy hard-liners and senior military officials who believed the pullout might encourage North Korea to launch a second invasion of South Korea. In May, Gen. John K. Singlaub, the third-ranking army officer in Korea, told the *Washington Post* that, in his view, the removal of 32,000 ground troops from South Korea would lead to war.

Replicating President Harry Truman's firing of Gen. Douglas MacArthur in 1951 for questioning official policy, Carter immediately relieved Singlaub of his command and ordered him home. Critics of the redeployment seized on Singlaub's dismissal as a way of pressuring Carter into reversing his decision. On Capitol Hill, influential Democratic senators, such as John Glenn of Ohio, Sam Nunn of Georgia, Henry Jackson of Washington, Daniel Inouye of Hawaii, Hubert Humphrey of Minnesota, and Gary Hart of Colorado, joined Republicans in opposing the president. Opinion ran against the plan even within the White House: Of Carter's senior advisers, only Brzezinski approved of the president's resolve. Although Carter refused to budge from his public commitment to take the troops out of Korea, it was clear by the end of the summer that he had dug himself into a hole over this issue. Opposition to troop removal was so great that he wisely deferred implementation, but he had every reason to expect a donnybrook on Capitol Hill should he later go ahead with the withdrawal. As Secretary of State Vance noted, "Congress continued to hammer home warnings of a political explosion if the withdrawals actually proceeded."[18]

Loud reverberations from Capitol Hill could also be heard at the White House over Carter's decision to scrap the development of a new class of B-1 bombers. For more than a decade, a fight had raged in Washington over whether to build this new bomber as a replacement for the United States' aging fleet of 330 B-52s, many of which were more than twenty years old. Pentagon planners and others argued that the B-1, which could fly faster (up to 1,320 miles per hour) and lower than the B-52s, was needed to penetrate Soviet air defenses. Opponents of the B-1 argued that the plane was not only outlandishly expensive but a dinosaur in the age of rocketry.

Over a period of five months, Carter met with Defense Secretary Brown, the Joint Chiefs of Staff, and other defense experts to assess the military value of the B-1 bomber. Most Washington observers anticipated that he would approve production of at least some, perhaps as many as 120, of the B-1s the air force was requesting. Secretary Brown was known to have supported the plane when he was air force secretary under Lyndon Johnson. Also, Carter included the construction of five B-1 bombers in the Defense Department authorization bill for 1978. Certainly the president gave no indication before June that he intended to cut the entire program.

But that is just what he decided to do. Impressed particularly by his conversations with Brown—who had been persuaded against the B-1 bomber by his own studies of its cost effectiveness—Carter stunned reporters at a news conference on the last day of June by announcing that he was discontinuing production of new weapons systems. The president's move was a courageous one, and he was fully aware of the political flak it would generate from the many people having an economic stake in the huge project and from defense hard-liners and political opponents of the administration. Never before had a president killed so large a program so close to production. Speaker O'Neill congratulated the president for being so bold, remarking that Carter was "the only President who doesn't have to rely on the Pentagon to make his military decisions."[19]

Yet Carter might have served his administration better had he done something to soften the impact of his announcement on congressional and public attitudes—such as seeking some Soviet concessions in return for eliminating the B-1 bomber or simply delaying any action until the conclusion of the SALT II talks. As it was, the president indulged in the worst possible timing by cutting the B-1 program two days after the House voted down a measure to cancel production of the bomber. Proponents of the B-1 accused him of purposely trying to embarrass the Congress, and they also charged him with failing again to provide for national security.

Although Carter was criticized at home for not being firm enough on national defense, he was attacked in Europe for being too inflexible in his conduct of foreign affairs. European leaders found his approach to the human rights issue to be preachy, and they maintained that few nations in the world had spotless records. In addition, many believed that Carter was unnecessarily provoking Moscow. West German Chancellor Helmut Schmidt, who had openly supported Ford during the election, was especially critical of Carter's foreign policy. In particular, he was irate because the administration, committed to nuclear nonproliferation, was attempting to undercut a $4.7-billion sale by West Germany to Brazil of a complete nuclear fuel facility, on the grounds that Brazil could use part of the facility to develop its own nuclear weapons capability. Schmidt was also upset that the Pentagon appeared ready to renege on an agreement to buy German Leopard II battletanks because of their alleged inferiority to American tanks. Finally, he resented the administration's pressure on him to stimulate the German economy as part of a coordinated effort with the United States and Japan to prevent a global recession.

At the beginning of May, Carter traveled to London where he participated in a summit meeting with Schmidt and the other leaders of Western Europe, Canada, and Japan. Much of the summit was spent considering ways to deal with the worldwide economic problems of high inflation and unemployment and the rising global trend toward protectionism. By all accounts, Carter was a smashing success. He had prepared carefully for the meeting, and he impressed the other leaders at the summit with his grasp of economic issues, his willingness to listen, his easygoing friendliness, his lack of pretension, and his deliberate manner. He also seemed to get along famously with Schmidt.

Despite this amity, the president continued to bicker with the German chancellor and other European leaders over his policy toward Moscow and his human rights advocacy. French President Valéry Giscard d'Estaing, who was angry with Carter for not revoking the New York Port Authority's ban on the Concorde supersonic airliner, gave a magazine interview in which he accused the president of having "compromised the process of detente" by being clumsy in his dealings with Brezhnev. On 13 July Schmidt came to

Washington carrying with him a message from the leaders of all the Common Market countries urging Carter to moderate his campaign on behalf of human rights.

As fall approached, there was a growing perception, even among Democrats, that the administration's foreign policy was seriously flawed. According to *Time*, "Quite a few members of the mainly Democratic foreign policy establishment are beginning to wonder whether [the president] is really up to the job." As if to confirm this view, former Undersecretary of State George Ball observed that the human rights campaign "to some extent . . . had become a stuck needle, getting in the way of things which might be more important in the long run."[20] Carter's foreign policy, then, was being questioned both at home and abroad, among Democrats as well as Republicans and liberals as well as conservatives. Meanwhile, the president had succeeded in alienating his own constituencies while providing ample ammunition for the opposition to use against him. But all this paled in comparison with the problems he faced on the domestic front, especially a developing scandal involving his close friend and OMB Director, Bert Lance.

5

★ ★ ★ ★ ★

THE DOG DAYS OF
SUMMER AND FALL

By the fall of 1977, Carter's public approval rating had begun a precipitous decline from which it never recovered. A Harris poll taken in March had given the president a resounding 75 percent rating on his ability to "inspire confidence"; by late September, that figure had dropped to 50 percent. Moreover, an NBC poll taken a few weeks later showed that only 46 percent of the people surveyed approved of his performance as president.

Part of the reason for Carter's dramatic drop in the polls was simply that high ratings are normally given to presidents early in their administrations. Indeed, the new president's approval rating after three months in office, while impressive, was not unprecedented. At the same point in their administrations, John F. Kennedy had a favorable grade of 83 percent, Dwight Eisenhower, of 74 percent, and Lyndon Johnson, of 73 percent. However, their support was not as soft as Carter's. As chief executive, Carter satisfied the American people but did not motivate them; he sought to awaken the national conscience but was unable to inspire public confidence; he won supporters but did not gain committed followers.

Early spring had gone well enough for Carter. After much difficulty and delay, the White House was able to negotiate a deal with the House and Senate on the president's hit list of water projects. Like most compromises, this one did not represent a clear victory for either side. Because the agreement still included several of the most expensive and least environmentally sound ventures, Stu Eizenstat advised the president against signing it. Even Carter remarked later that he rued the day he had agreed to compromise on "those worthless dam projects." Nevertheless, as a result of his persistence, only half the projects he targeted for elimination were funded, and appropriations were cut by more than half (from $147 million to $63 million).[1]

Meanwhile, the president could take considerable satisfaction from the fact that the economy appeared to be moving ahead strongly. Despite the severe winter, the rate of economic growth in the first quarter of 1977 was 5.2 percent, and preliminary calculations for the second quarter placed it at 6.4 percent. "This estimate seems more likely to be revised up than down as more data becomes available," CEA Chairman Schultze told the president at the end of June. The rates of inflation and unemployment were also down as food prices moderated and more people found jobs.[2]

On Capitol Hill, most of Carter's economic stimulus package was winding its way through committee without the tax rebate, which the president had decided to scrap. On 5 May, Congress passed a $20.1-billion measure to increase employment through various job programs. In June, it approved a one-year extension of the Comprehensive Employment and Training Act under which most federal job and training programs operated. The next month it passed yet another bill establishing a number of job projects for disadvantaged youth. In addition, lawmakers simplified the tax laws, as the president had requested, and approved a plan for countercyclical aid to help state and local governments avoid cutbacks during economic slowdowns.

Carter could, therefore, point to a substantial list of accomplishments during his second trimester as president, but his achievements were again clouded by major economic and political uncertainties. In the first place, not all the economic news the White House received was good. Foreign trade deficits were growing, and the Commerce Department forecast that business investment for the latter half of 1977 would be sluggish. If that happened, Schultze admitted that his projections of economic growth for 1977 and 1978 would be too high. Similarly, the Congressional Budget Office reported that while it was possible for the president to meet his goals of reasonably full employment (near 5 percent) and a balanced budget by 1981, it was unlikely without further measures to stimulate the economy. Eizenstat informed Carter that, in all likelihood, the administration would have to choose between full employment or a balanced budget.

There was never much doubt about which of these two alternatives Carter would favor. The president was committed to reducing inflation and balancing the budget, even if that meant a restrictive fiscal policy and higher levels of unemployment than he preferred. This became evident in Carter's proposal for overhauling the nation's labyrinthine system of public welfare. Shortly after his victory, the president-elect had asked Joseph Califano, whom he was considering for secretary of health, education, and welfare (HEW), how fast a welfare reform plan could be developed. Caught off guard and not expecting to be taken literally, Califano responded that it could be ready by 1 May. Much to his alarm, Carter took him at his word, informing his newly appointed cabinet in December that May would be the month for welfare reform. Over the next few weeks, Califano told Carter repeatedly that he needed more time, but the president-elect flatly turned him down.

Misunderstandings over what reform entailed became even more apparent after Carter took office. Califano assumed that welfare reform would involve more money, yet the president meant to keep spending at existing levels. Analysts at HEW and the Labor Department, who were supposed to be working together in developing the legislation, also differed over the best approach to take. HEW officials emphasized the importance of improving the efficiency of existing maintenance programs for welfare recipients and the working poor. Spokesmen from the Labor Department stressed the need to provide more jobs for recipients who could work. Even representatives of welfare recipients were divided as to what modifications were most needed.

By late March, HEW had come up with a series of options for reforming the system, ranging from modest administrative changes to a guaranteed annual income for most people on welfare. Califano decided to brief Carter on these options, since the president had not involved himself in the planning process. "I wanted to give him a picture of the existing system and of the problems involved in shaping a reform proposal," the secretary recalled. He also hoped to move back the 1 May deadline and to get an idea of the type of welfare system Carter expected, including the level of funding to which he was prepared to commit.[3]

His meeting with the president on 25 March did not go well. Carter instructed Califano to redesign the whole proposal at current levels of funding. Both Califano and Labor Secretary Ray Marshall, who advocated a program of guaranteed public service jobs for the unemployed poor, were keenly disappointed. Marshall even considered not giving the president any zero-cost alternatives, believing they would be unrealistic. Califano sent Carter a ten-point memorandum of reform principles in which he called once more for "funding increments above zero-cost to increase equity and make the package more politically attractive."[4]

Over the next month, officials from the departments of HEW and labor developed three zero-cost reform plans, which reflected their inability to reconcile their differences. One plan featured Marshall's jobs program; a second, favored by HEW, proposed to replace the existing system of nine separate programs with a so-called negative income tax, or direct cash payments to the poor based strictly on need; and a third, supported by the AFL-CIO, included a jobs program and cash assistance for people who could not work. When Califano met with Carter again on 11 April, he argued that, without additional funding, many welfare recipients would be worse off no matter which option the president selected. The president became irate. "Are you telling me that there is no way to improve the present welfare system except by spending billions of dollars?" Carter asked. "In that case, to hell with it!

We're wasting our time." After the president cooled down, however, he told the HEW secretary to come to terms with Marshall and to present him with an outline that he could broadcast on 1 May.[5]

Over the next three weeks, the conflict between the Labor Department and HEW, which had been relatively subdued, became more pronounced as each agency sought to protect its institutional interests. At the same time, representatives of the poor continued to air their own grievances, charging that both the HEW's plan for a negative income tax and labor's proposed jobs program were inadequate. When Califano and Marshall met with the president on 30 April, just one day before his promised announcement on welfare reform, they still had not been able to reach a consensus. Determined to meet his May commitment, Carter resigned himself to a general statement of principles on which welfare reform would be based rather than the presentation of a legislative package, which was now put off until August.

The public bickering and interagency squabbling that characterized this episode left Carter totally frustrated. His mood had become so dark that, toward the end of April, Hamilton Jordan advised him to get away from Washington and relax at Camp David. "If you work all weekend on welfare reform, you will begin the week tired," Jordan told the president. Yet many of the difficulties could be traced back to Carter himself. His unrealistic deadlines were intended to force action, but they gave officials at HEW and the Department of Labor little time to wade through the complexities involved in changing the welfare system—much less to develop a carefully structured program on which there was widespread agreement.[6]

The president had also failed to make the hard choices or to provide the guidelines demanded by the type of major overhaul of the welfare system that he wanted. Left unresolved were such fundamental issues as who should be required to work or excused from work, what should be the minimum level of subsistence for individuals and families, to what extent the government should be expected to provide jobs for the unemployed, and whether the poor should be aided primarily through the negative income tax favored by HEW, the jobs program preferred by the Labor Department, or some combination of the two. Indeed, there was no consideration of whether it is even possible to have a welfare system that is both fair and simple at the same time.

In the final analysis, though, it was Carter's fiscal conservatism, as evidenced by his determination to hold welfare spending to existing levels, that made it virtually impossible for his administration to reach agreement by his 1 May deadline. Because the president wanted only a redistribution of extant resources without indicating who should be helped or hurt under a reallotment, both the departments of HEW and Labor were unable to reconcile their differences without adversely affecting the constituencies they served, something they were loath to do.

In August, the president finally sent to Congress his proposals for welfare reform. Illustrating his emphasis on the work ethic, Carter's program provided jobs for welfare recipients who could work and a "decent income" for those who could not, such as the disabled and single parents with children. Initial reaction to the plan was overwhelmingly favorable, but as lawmakers and others examined it more carefully, they began to object strongly to some of its provisions. Senator Russell Long and other congressional conservatives expressed alarm at the large number of people who would be added to the "welfare rolls." The AFL-CIO claimed that the huge jobs programs paying minimum wage would weaken local labor markets. Welfare advocates decried the scheme's complexity.

Lawmakers also began to raise questions as to the proposal's real costs. Although the president wanted welfare reform held to current budgetary limits, he agreed over the summer to $2.8 billion in additional spending as a way of supplying more fiscal relief to the states. But in order to balance the books, the administration had to include in its cost estimates compensatory savings and new revenue sources. Many of the projected offsets, such as savings in extended unemployment insurance and a wellhead tax on oil, were problematic.

By this time, the president had also suffered a major reversal on his farm program, and many of his other legislative proposals, including energy and tax reform, were also in trouble. A massive grain sale to the Soviet Union in 1972 had wiped out most of the nation's surplus grain accumulated during the 1950s and 1960s. At the same time, droughts, poor harvests, and rising populations in other countries had caused farm prices to soar as demand boomed worldwide for America's plentiful agricultural production. As a result, in 1973 Congress replaced the existing program of high fixed price supports—which, by encouraging overproduction, had created most of the nation's farm surpluses—with a more flexible system of target and loan prices for farm commodities. Because these prices were considerably below market prices, few expected the government to be back in the business of storing excess grain.

The situation had changed by Carter's inauguration in 1977. A worldwide agricultural recovery, including an unexpected bumper crop in the Soviet Union in 1976, led to tumbling farm prices. By the end of 1976, the price of wheat, which had sold for as much as $5.32 a bushel in February 1974, was selling for only $2.85. A 1975 emergency farm bill, which would have raised target and loan prices, was vetoed by President Ford on the grounds that it was too expensive and would undermine the existing market-oriented farm policy. This cost Ford heavily among farmers a year later when he ran against Carter. As the new administration assumed office, therefore, farmers' organizations and lawmakers from farm states looked to the new president for relief, warning about an agricultural crisis unless help was forthcoming.

They were sorely disappointed. Although Carter had made the farm crisis a campaign issue, accusing Nixon and Ford of causing farm income to drop and promising new legislation to assure support prices at least equal to the cost of production, he discovered after he took office that his promise conflicted with his higher commitment to a balanced budget by 1981. As a result, his farm program, which Secretary of Agriculture Bob Bergland sent to Congress at the end of March, contained support prices even lower than existing prices.

Not surprisingly, therefore, the plan soon came under heavy fire. In the House Agricultural Committee, Chairman Thomas Foley told Bergland that even with an all-out effort, he could muster no more than five of the committee's forty-six votes in favor of the administration's proposal. With his usual candor, Jordan admonished Carter for presenting Congress with such a politically untenable program. "Instead of being considered seriously by the Congress and having an impact on the final outcome of the legislation," he said, "the Administration's position on [price supports] will be discarded and the likelihood is that Congress will come up with a more expensive program than would have been originally acceptable to the various interests if we had come in with a *politically credible proposal.*"[7]

Yielding to the widespread dissatisfaction within and outside his administration, Carter agreed on 18 April to accept higher target prices for wheat, corn, cotton, and rice. Although he warned that he would veto any measure with still-higher supports, the Senate ignored his threat, approving its own, more expensive farm bill by a margin of sixty-nine to eighteen, more than the two-thirds vote needed to override a presidential veto. At first, Carter responded angrily and at a news conference on 26 May, he renewed his veto pledge. But by July, when the House took up the farm bill, there was little question that lawmakers would overwhelmingly approve price supports higher than what the administration wanted.

Aware that the opposition had enough votes to cancel his veto, the president adopted a more conciliatory line and merely urged Senate and House conferees to accept the least costly provisions in the two bills. In the final legislation, which both houses approved in September, the target price of wheat was set at either $3.00 or $3.05 a bushel depending on the size of the wheat crop. Although the president objected to the expense of the program, he signed the measure into law at the end of September.

In retrospect, there were several reasons why Carter lost the contest over price supports. First, falling agricultural prices and a near-record grain harvest in the summer of 1977, after a record harvest a year earlier, evoked nationwide sympathy for the plight of farmers. Second, wheat growers and lawmakers from wheat-producing states conducted an enormously successful lobbying effort on behalf of higher target prices; farmers from the Midwest came to Washington by the hundreds to press their case. Further, the farm bill itself was a multifaceted piece of legislation, which allowed ample opportunity for bargaining. Since it also authorized funding for food stamps, lawmakers from the grain-producing states were able to horse-trade with their urban counterparts to win approval for higher prices.

The president, however, also helped to undermine his own farm program by failing to give Agriculture Secretary Bergland or anyone else the authority needed to coordinate farm policy. As a result, the administration continued to bicker internally over the size of the price supports it should recommend. Bergland found himself pitted against CEA Chairman Schultze and OMB Director Lance, both of whom favored lower price supports than he did. When Carter's own people were unable to thrash out their differences, it left the president hard-pressed to sell his farm program to Congress. It did not escape the notice of a number of House and Senate members that Bergland's support for the program was lackluster.

Elsewhere on the president's agenda, the combined efforts of Speaker O'Neill and the White House's own lobbying produced a crucial legislative victory in August when most of Carter's energy program was accepted by the House. Regarding passage of the energy package as a test of whether a Democratic president and Congress could work together, O'Neill short-circuited the regular legislative process by having the program quickly funneled to a forty-member ad hoc Committee on Energy, which he established. The Speaker also made sure that the majority of the committee's members supported Carter's energy proposals. In this way, he sought to prevent the five volumes of legislation from being carved up and then mutilated by the nine House committees and subcommittees, which normally would have been responsible for sending the legislation onto the House floor. "This bill was going to pit one region of the country against another," O'Neill later explained. "I *had* to get that bill through—and quickly, so that Congress could move ahead on other fronts."[8]

Meanwhile, the White House succeeded in turning back an effort to decontrol the price of natural gas, which was not part of Carter's program but was broached by House members from energy-producing states. It had less success with its proposed standby tax on gasoline, since House members believed it was not politically feasible; the measure never resurfaced after it was rejected by the Ways and Means Committee. Except for that provision and the House's refusal to give tax rebates to buyers of small cars, which it thought would amount to a subsidy for foreign imports, Carter's program was approved on 5 August by a vote of 244 to 177.

House passage of the energy plan represented a major coup for Carter, made even sweeter by the fact that he had just signed the legislation establishing the new Department of Energy. But as both advocates and critics of the president's program realized, the real battle over energy still lay ahead in the Senate, where procedural rules made it easier than in the House for a small group to block legislation or to amend it to death and where much of the leadership was in the hands of lawmakers from energy-producing states. Because the plan was built around increased taxes to discourage the use of energy, its fate would be largely determined by the Senate Finance Committee and its powerful chairman, Russell Long of Louisiana. Although Long remained closemouthed about his own position on Carter's proposal, it was clear, even to the White House, that the energy industry would get a much more sympathetic hearing before his committee than it had received in the House.

Carter's program for tax reform was also in trouble. The president had made a firm commitment during the campaign to clean up the tax system, which he described as "nothing less than a disgrace." As a candidate and as president-elect, he promoted three fundamental objectives for tax reform: 1) It must be comprehensive; 2) the result must be a fairer, more progressive tax system; and 3) it must achieve simplification. He called for taxing capital gains at the same rate as ordinary income, eliminating tax shelters, limiting business expense deductions (such as first-class travel and "two martini" lunches), tightening the rules on other tax deductions (such as large charitable gifts), and shifting more of the tax burden from low- and middle-income families to wealthy people and corporations.

One of the changes in the tax code that Carter hoped to accomplish— simplifying and increasing the standard deduction for individual and joint returns—was included in the tax portion of his economic stimulus package, but the president considered this only the first step. As early as February, he had instructed Treasury Secretary Blumenthal to devise an inclusive tax reform and simplification package, to be presented to Congress in the fall. In May, Blumenthal gave Carter a preliminary outline of his proposals, which contained many of the features the president wanted—such as discarding preferential treatment for capital gains and placing some restrictions on tax-deductible business expenses. However, the Treasury secretary allowed deductions on many other business expenses and eliminated "double taxation" on corporate income paid out as dividends (by taxing only income and not dividends, both of which were subject to taxes under existing law). In addition, the current schedule of tax rates, which ranged from 14 percent to 70 percent, was changed to one that varied from 13 percent to 50 percent.

At the White House, Stuart Eizenstat reacted angrily to Blumenthal's suggestions. He and the Treasury secretary were not on the best of terms. As Treasury secretary, Blumenthal chaired the steering committee of the Economic Policy Group (EPG), which had broad authority over virtually every economic issue facing the administration. Eizenstat had never been happy with the oversight power delegated to Blumenthal because it intruded into his own domain as the president's assistant for domestic affairs and head of the White House's Domestic Policy Staff. But Eizenstat objected to the Treasury secretary's tax recommendations mainly because he thought they favored the rich and were not based on a complete review of all special tax provisions. "*If you want a really comprehensive review of the tax system with all major issues and options presented to you for decision,*" he told Carter in May, "*you will have to instruct Treasury to that effect.*" Carter's chief speechwriter, Jim Fallows, also warned the president of the political damage the proposals might cause. "I am not an expert in taxes," he remarked, "but I believe we should start now to measure this plan against the expectations we have built up."[9]

Following the advice he received from Eizenstat, Fallows, and other White House aides, Carter assumed a more active role in putting together his administration's tax package. He instructed Blumenthal to simplify his plan and make it more progressive. Blumenthal agreed to reduce the tax on the lowest income bracket from 14 percent to 12 percent, rather than to 13 percent as he had originally recommended. He also proposed to limit deductible personal interest payments to $10,000 and to tighten business deductions for entertainment. Eizenstat estimated that under the latest version of the reform program, all income classes below $30,000 would bear a smaller share of the total tax burden and those above $30,000 would shoulder a larger share. But he and CEA Chairman Schultze continued to object to the tax breaks given to business.

With the administration itself divided over tax reform and Congress already handling a full legislative docket, the president decided, on the advice of the congressional leadership, to delay sending his tax proposals to Congress until the very end of the session. Thus, after a promising start in early summer, by autumn most of Carter's legislative agenda had stalled or was in serious trouble. The president had made an energy bill, welfare reform, and tax reform three of his highest priorities, and all faced an uncertain future.

There were also signs of pending economic woes as the robust economy of the first half of 1977 became increasingly sluggish. The growth rate for the first six months of 1977 had been about 6.8 percent, and CEA Chairman Schultze had predicted this would continue for the entire year. Yet third-quarter growth slowed substantially to around 4 percent. While Schultze still thought the economy would improve in the fourth quarter, he was not as optimistic as he had been. "It appears to us that, in the absence of additional measures to stimulate growth," he told Carter in October, "the rate of expansion will fall well short of our 5 percent target for next year." Inflation, which was still running at around 6 percent, also remained a nagging concern. Contrary to his earlier estimates, Schultze was now forecasting that inflation would continue to hound all the major nations, including the United States.[10]

No problem, however, caused Carter greater grief or did more harm to his presidency in its first year than the scandal resulting from the banking and business practices of his OMB director and close friend Bert Lance. The

"Lance affair" (as it came to be called) struck at the very foundation of a vulnerable administration. Although Lance was eventually forced to resign his post, Carter's unfailing support of his friend, well beyond the bounds of political prudence, raised questions not only about his political judgment but also about his publicly stated commitment to the highest ethical standards in government.

The episode began innocently enough. After his election, Carter directed all of his appointees to reveal their financial holdings and to divest themselves of any that might lead to a conflict of interest. In accordance with this policy, the president-elect asked Lance to dispose of his considerable assets in the National Bank of Georgia (NBG), which he had headed along with the much-smaller First National Bank of Calhoun. Lance agreed to place his NBG stock, valued at $3.3 million, in a blind trust, with instructions to the trustee to divest it of all NBG stock by the end of 1977.

However, the value of his NBG holdings began to drop after it was learned that the bank planned to charge off various bad loans, which would affect its ability to continue its dividend payments. By July Lance's NBG holdings were worth only $1.7 million; his annual income had also declined. Faced with worsening economic prospects, the OMB director went to Carter for help. After conferring with Charles Kirbo, the president sent a letter to Democratic Senator Abraham Ribicoff of Connecticut, chairman of the Senate's Governmental Affairs Committee, which had confirmed Lance, asking for an unlimited extension of the 31 December deadline.

In addition to his promise to sell his bank stock by the end of the year, Lance had also pledged during his confirmation hearings to disqualify himself from participating in any matter involving banking regulation so long as he held NBG stock. Yet reports, which were later confirmed, circulated in Washington that he had met in his OMB office with NBG officials and had written to Senate Banking Chairman William Proxmire of Wisconsin against an anti-redlining proposal that would require banks to give priority to the credit needs of their communities in making loans. Even more serious, columnist William Safire accused the OMB director of peddling his political influence to obtain a $3.4-million loan with deferred interest from the First National Bank of Chicago; the *Washington Post* claimed the loan was made in return for a $200,000 deposit of NBG funds in a non-interest-bearing account. The U.S. Comptroller's Office began an investigation of these charges, Senator Ribicoff summoned Lance before his committee for an explanation, and Senator Proxmire, the only senator to oppose Lance's confirmation, undertook his own probe.

Lance's appearance before the Ribicoff committee failed to produce the fireworks many Washington observers had anticipated. Denying Safire's charge of a "sweetheart loan," Lance said he was paying a respectable .75 percent above the prime interest rate on the loan. He also maintained that the

NBG's account with the First National Bank of Chicago was long-standing and that he had not acted illegally or unethically either before or after being appointed OMB director. That seemed to satisfy the committee, which granted him the extension he sought.

On 18 August, Comptroller John Heimann released his agency's eagerly awaited report on Lance's banking practices. In a massive 394-page document, Heimann determined that Lance had done nothing illegal. As far as the White House was concerned, that amounted to the OMB director's vindication. At a news conference, the president personally announced the report's central conclusion; turning to Lance, who was standing next to him, he remarked, "Bert, I'm proud of you." Later, Hamilton Jordan commented that while the controversy over Lance would not end "tomorrow or next week . . . it won't go on much longer." As for Lance, he made it clear that he intended to stay in office.[11]

The president had badly misinterpreted the comptroller's report, however, and the normally prescient Jordan had likewise missed its political implications. Although Carter believed the report gave Lance a clean bill of health, it actually revealed that the former banker had skirted the edge of probity and ethical behavior—for example, his custom as chairman of the Calhoun bank of permitting sizable overdrafts on the personal accounts of its officers and their relatives. More generally, the report accused Lance of "unsafe and unsound banking practices."[12]

Instead of vanishing, the Lance affair mushroomed over the next two weeks, as new charges were leveled against the OMB director. One involved his private use of the NBG's two airplanes, including unreported free trips by Carter while he was campaigning for president. It was also alleged that an investigation had been under way into the Calhoun bank's handling of overdrafts on accounts maintained by Lance's campaign organization when he ran for governor in 1974, but that the probe had been squashed by the U.S. Attorney's Office in Atlanta the day before Carter announced Lance's appointment as OMB director. The Internal Revenue Service (IRS) undertook its own investigation to determine the validity of these claims. The *New York Times* charged that Lance was not making the same financial disclosures that the White House required of other high administration officials and that he still had business associations that were conflicts of interest.

By the beginning of September, the White House was in a near state of siege over the Lance affair. On 3 September, senators Ribicoff and Charles Percy of Illinois, the ranking Republican on the Governmental Affairs Committee, sent the president a memorandum outlining a number of matters concerning Lance that had not been covered in the comptroller's report. "Information has been brought to our attention," they told Carter, "which would appear to substantiate allegations that the Justice Department acted improperly in failing to fully investigate potential criminal violations of Federal banking law growing out of the Lance for Governor campaign and Mr. Lance's personal affairs during that time."[13] Pressure mounted for a special prosecutor to be named to examine Lance's tangled affairs and for the OMB director to resign. On 6 September, the White House received a second report from Heimann, which showed "a pattern" of borrowing by Lance from other correspondent banks "similar to that established in the other report." Heimann also informed the White House that his office was referring the issue of the private use of the NBG airplane to the Justice Department and IRS for investigation. "The referral to Justice," Carter's counsel, Robert Lipshutz, informed him, "will undoubtedly increase pressure for the appointment of a Special Prosecutor." Both *Business Week* and the *Los Angeles Times* called for Lance to step down, and the *Wall Street Journal* declared that Lance could no longer be effective as budget director.[14]

Carter's visceral reaction to the outcry for Lance's resignation was to stand by his friend. As late as 15 September, he defended Lance before a group of news directors, saying that the OMB chief was neither dishonest, incompetent, nor unethical. But the pressure on him to ask for Lance's resignation continued to rise. Hamilton Jordan even flew down to Lance's vacation home on Sea Island, Georgia, during the Labor Day weekend to tell him that the controversy was becoming a huge liability for the president. On Capitol Hill, a large and growing number of lawmakers urged Carter to dismiss his friend. Unable to stem the call for Lance's head, the president began reluctantly to back away from his support of the OMB director, acknowledging, for example, that Lance's use of overdrafts was "obviously a mistake." He did ask that no final judgment on Lance be made until after he went before Ribicoff's Governmental Affairs Committee. "Bert would be permanently disgraced if he left office without having some chance to defend himself," the president later commented.[15]

Lance's appearance before the Senate committee on Friday, 17 September, was his last hurrah. In a two-hour opening statement and then in subsequent testimony carried on national television, the OMB director defended himself well, even putting his accusers on trial. "The basic American principle of justice and fair play has been pointedly ignored by certain members of this committee," he charged. "The rights that I thought that I possessed have, one by one, gone down the drain." By the time the committee adjourned for the weekend, many observers predicted that Lance might yet be able to keep his job.[16]

On Saturday, however, Carter met with Jordan, Vice-President Mondale, Press Secretary Powell, and Charles Kirbo, who had flown up from Atlanta. As the president recorded in his diary, they agreed that Lance had "won a great victory and now should step down." Returning to Washington from Camp David that afternoon, the president called Lance, asking to see him the next morning. He also telephoned Majority Leader Robert Byrd to get his reaction to Lance's performance. Although Byrd believed that Lance had been "a good, affable, strong witness," he warned that the Lance affair was not going to vanish and that it was doing serious damage to Carter on Capitol Hill. The presidency was more important than any single individual, he said.[17]

After a sleepless night, Carter met Lance in the morning. He congratulated his friend on his appearance before the Governmental Affairs Committee, saying that his critics had suffered a setback. But he added that the opposition was regrouping, and he strongly suggested that Lance consider resigning. Before deciding, Lance wanted to discuss the situation with his wife, LaBelle, and his attorney, Clark Clifford. After a game of tennis that afternoon, Lance indicated that he planned to resign. "I didn't argue with him," the president recorded in his diary. But on the following day, 21 September, which the president described as "one of the worst days I've ever spent," Lance informed Carter that his wife was convinced he should stay in office and that he did not know what he should do. The president replied he had made the right decision on the tennis courts, and that afternoon Lance agreed to step down—although LaBelle adamantly opposed his decision and told Carter that he had betrayed his best friend. A few hours later, the president announced the resignation to a news conference that had actually been scheduled for earlier in the day.[18]

After the announcement the White House was flooded with telephone calls, telegrams, and letters, most of which, according to Carter, condemned the press and the Congress for their relentless attacks on Lance. Ironically, one of the letters the president received was from H. R. Haldeman, who had been forced out of his position as former President Richard Nixon's chief of staff and later sent to prison. "Although it may seem odd in view of the source," Haldeman wrote Carter, "I want to express my concern and sorrow over the outcome of the Lance affair."[19]

In his letter, Haldeman also stated his hope that this "sort of problem" would now "be behind" him and that he could devote his "full energies and abilities to the really important matters facing" him. But the scars of the Lance affair could not be erased so readily. Although most people polled by Pat Caddell in the aftermath of Lance's resignation approved of the way the president had handled the episode, there seems little question that his support of Lance did irreparable harm to his administration. Even the president later conceded this point. Not only did the controversy distract the administration from more pressing domestic and foreign policy matters and help poison relations with Congress, it undermined public trust in Carter, which he had worked so hard to foster and which was so essential to his success as president.

Yet the problems confronting Carter extended beyond Bert Lance. As one reporter correctly observed, that muddle was "only the tip of the iceberg." While the president had enjoyed some success in both his domestic programs and his conduct of foreign policy, most of his legislative agenda had not been passed and some of the United States' closest allies were openly expressing reservations about his ability as a world leader. Perhaps even more important, public cynicism about government remained as hardened as ever. "The optimism we saw in December," Pat Caddell told the president in September, "has faded and voters see the past, present, and future as quite similar. They are becoming resigned to the idea that problems like inflation, poverty, and war will be ever with us."[20] By the fall of 1977, then, it appeared to an increasing number of Americans that the outsider from Georgia had not been able to elevate the level at which the affairs of government were conducted and that his administration was already giving signs of crumbling from within.

6

★ ★ ★ ★ ★

CAN CARTER COPE?

Although there was a mounting perception among American voters that the still-young Carter administration was in disarray, polls at the end of 1977 indicated that the voters were not yet ready to pass final judgment on the president. When asked for whom they would vote if they could choose again between Carter and Ford, the people surveyed still chose Carter over Ford by 44 percent to 41 percent, with 15 percent not sure. These figures compared favorably with Carter's 2 percent margin of victory in 1976 and suggested that voters would elect him by about the same plurality a year later.

But these surveys also revealed a growing sense among the American people that the president had not lived up to his campaign promises and that he seemed unable to get things done. In particular, respondents doubted whether he could cope with inflation and high unemployment, the issues that most concerned them. Only 18 percent of the interviewees in one poll had "a lot" of confidence in the president's ability to deal with the economy, while 23 percent had "practically no" confidence. Voters also complained that the president was trying to do too much at once, that he was trying to do too much by himself, that he had compromised on too many issues, that his staff was insular, inexperienced, uncoordinated, and error-prone, and that he had yet to master the art of congressional relations. While most of these criticisms were not new, they were being stated with increasing frequency, leading more and more Americans to ask, "Can Carter cope?"

Carter's defense of Bert Lance had done him considerable political damage. At the very least, he had displayed an obstinacy and blind spot regarding his friend that seemed to belie his reputation for cool judgment and high moral standards. But Lance was not the only member of his administration to embarrass Carter or present him with major complications. Also undercutting the president politically was Andrew Young, the United States' first black ambassador to the United Nations. By advocating support for newly emerging nations, openly attacking the apartheid policies of Rhodesia and South Africa, and working on behalf of majority rule in Rhodesia and Namibia, Young was instrumental in gaining African confidence in the United States. But at the same time, he created enormous controversy by his uninhibited candor and sometimes reckless remarks—such as his suggestion in a *Playboy* interview that a race war in South Africa would cause whites in the United States "to panic" and attack American blacks, or his comment in the same interview that Soviet dissidents were only a "literary elite who had tasted a little freedom and wanted more." The latter statement in particular caused a public furor. American Jewish leaders and others called the White House demanding that Young apologize for his comments. Although the ambassador tempered his remarks over the next several months, his bluntness continued to rankle many Americans, and there were rumblings that he should be forced to resign.[1]

Conversely, many liberal Democrats complained that Vice-President Walter Mondale was not playing the vital role in Carter's administration that had been promised by the president. In reality, this charge was grossly exaggerated. Although Mondale's political liberalism sometimes clashed with Carter's economic conservatism, the vice-president quickly became one of the president's closest advisers. Not only was he kept fully informed on all domestic issues by Eizenstat and his staff, he was one of only four people—along with the president, secretary of state, and national security adviser—to have a daily intelligence briefing. Nevertheless, the doubts expressed in the news media about Mondale's influence within the administration, when coupled with the largely negative reporting on Young, raised new accusations that the White House was controlled by the "Georgia Mafia" and further weakened Carter's already tenuous political standing with Congress.

Just how vulnerable the president had become on Capitol Hill was evident when House Speaker Tip O'Neill decided to cancel a pending vote on legislation sponsored by the White House and supported by a coalition of consumer groups to establish a federal office for consumer affairs. Even though the administration lobbied hard for this bill, congressional opposition to the measure remained so strong that O'Neill pulled it off the House calendar the day before it was scheduled for a floor vote.

The president suffered an even more far-reaching defeat when the Senate gutted his energy program and then locked horns with the House in conference committee. In the House, the president's energy legislation was contained in one omnibus measure, but in the Senate it was divided among six separate bills. Four were relatively noncontroversial, including one requiring new electric utility and major industrial plants to burn coal or other fuels instead of oil and natural gas and another providing $1.02 billion for a broad range of conservation measures. Except for a ban on "gas guzzling" cars, which the Senate approved in place of the tax passed by the House, this quartet sailed through the Upper Chamber.

That was not the case with the president's proposals to bring intrastate gas under federal regulation for the first time, thereby rationalizing gas distribution and pricing, and to key the price of new natural gas to the heating equivalency of oil—that is, the same output of heating for the same cost, or about $1.75 per 1,000 cubic feet. Although this represented an increase of almost $.30 over the current ceiling price of $1.46, lobbyists for the oil and gas industry wanted total deregulation of new gas within five years. By a narrow 50–46 vote, the Senate ratified legislation placing a price cap on new gas of $2.46 for two years, after which the price would be fully deregulated.

The Senate also rejected Carter's proposal to raise the price of domestically produced oil to the world price by 1980 through a crude oil equalization (COE) or wellhead tax. Opposition to the plan was led by Chairman Russell Long of the Finance Committee. Since his home state, Louisiana, had an economy dependent on oil and gas, Long had complained from the moment Carter announced his energy program that it did not provide adequate incentives for increasing oil and gas production. While he was willing to consider a wellhead tax whose revenues would be returned to the oil industry, he was not prepared to accept a plan which involved a rebate to taxpayers. On 21 October, his committee reported out a bill whose only revenue raiser was an extension of the existing four-cents-per-gallon tax on gasoline. After six days of debate, the full Senate approved the measure.

The president had badly misread the Senate and its differences with the House. At a news conference on 13 October—after the Senate had already voted to deregulate natural gas and the Senate Finance Committee had mangled the tax portions of his program—Carter conceded that "in retrospect it would have helped had [he] had more meetings with the members of the Senate." Even then he expected that Senator Long would come up with an acceptable energy package on which both houses of Congress could compromise. But the divisions between the House and the Senate over deregulation of natural gas and the imposition of a wellhead tax were so fundamental that they were unable to resolve their disagreements in conference committee. Instead, final action on the energy legislation had to be postponed until the next session of Congress.

Once Congress reconvened in January, the White House was determined to win swift passage of its energy program. Delayed action, Eizenstat told the president, would be "disastrous" since it would divert attention on Capitol Hill from the other economic issues the administration had targeted for 1978. Yet the White House also recognized that it would have to make concessions to oil and gas producers in order to reach final agreement. Meeting with reporters in January, Carter declared that passage of his energy legislation would again "be the first order of business . . . the first priority." Because he was willing to strike a bargain, he also predicted that a bill "acceptable to me and to the country . . . will come very early in this session."[2]

There was no quick resolution of the issues that separated the House and Senate, however, and the energy package languished in conference committee. Russell Long made it clear that he and the other Senate conferees would not discuss the tax provisions of the president's program without a compromise on natural gas. As a basis for negotiation, the administration made an offer just before Christmas that kept some controls on natural gas until 1985 but increased producer revenue by $17 billion by raising the ceiling price for newly discovered gas. Later, it even proposed shortening the interim until complete deregulation and increasing even more the revenue industry would receive. But that failed to resolve the legislative impasse.

As hopes for accommodation dimmed, the White House decided to intervene in the negotiations. On 12 April, Carter called the conferees to the White House. After meeting for thirteen hours, a small group of the House and Senate lawmakers announced that they had reached a shaky compromise that imposed price controls on both interstate and intrastate natural gas, thus creating a unified national market; in return, federal controls on new natural gas would end by 1985. But House members protested the secrecy of the talks, and within a week, the agreement fell apart. Other efforts at compromise also became unglued at the last moment. On 9 May, House Speaker O'Neill threatened for the first time to split up the five-part energy package the House had passed—a move that almost certainly would have killed the unpopular wellhead tax, which the president had described as the centerpiece of his energy program.

During the Senate debate, Stu Eizenstat and James Schlesinger had told the president that, in terms of domestic legislation, his administration's performance would be measured in large part by the outcome of his national energy plan; the president had agreed. With the fate of the package in peril, the administration was in line for a poor evaluation. But criticism of the Carter White House extended beyond any single piece of legislation to the instability within the administration itself. This was illustrated by the next testing ground for the White House—a Supreme Court case involving alleged reverse discrimination against a white applicant, Allan Bakke, who was denied admission into the University of California Medical School at Davis.

In the decade since the peak of the civil rights movement in the mid-1960s, affirmative action laws had been passed to create avenues of opportunity for minorities (and women) in education and employment. Special programs had been established to ensure minority hiring and job promotion, even over employees with seniority. Colleges and universities encouraged minority applications and set aside slots for minority students. These developments produced a backlash among some whites who claimed that as a result of affirmative action programs, they had fallen victim to "reverse discrimination." In 1973, Bakke, a Marine veteran who had twice been denied admission to the Medical School at Davis, filed suit alleging that the university had discriminated against him by accepting minority students with college grades and aptitude-test scores lower than his own, under an affirmative action program that had reserved sixteen places for disadvantaged students. After the California Supreme Court upheld his complaint, the regents of the University of California appealed the decision to the U.S. Supreme Court, which agreed to hear the case. Immediately, *Bakke* v. *Regents of the University of California* became the most important civil rights case since the 1954 *Brown* v. *Board of Education*, not only pitting proponents against opponents of affirmative action but dividing advocates between those who supported and those who denounced racial quotas.

Almost any position the White House adopted with respect to the case was bound to alienate one of the administration's traditional constituencies. American Jewish leaders, for example, generally favored affirmative action programs if they were based on goals rather than quotas. Most of organized labor opposed affirmative action entirely, viewing it as a frontal assault on its prized seniority system. The black community supported affirmative action programs, including ones utilizing racial quotas.

The *Bakke* case, therefore, presented Carter with a no-win situation. Almost as soon as the Supreme Court agreed to hear the case, Paren J. Mitchell of the Congressional Black Caucus wrote Attorney General Griffin Bell and President Carter to urge that the Justice Department file an amicus curiae brief on behalf of the University of California regents. In contrast, the Anti-Defamation League of the B'nai B'rith and other Jewish organizations urged Carter not to intervene. Moreover, Carter himself was ambivalent about affirmative action. As a matter of principle, the president opposed all quotas, whatever their purpose. "I hate to endorse the proposition of quotas for minority groups, for women or for anyone else," he remarked in response to a reporter's question on the *Bakke* case. At the same time, he recognized that previous patterns of racial discrimination might have to be addressed in a way that could be injurious to particular individuals.

In August, Attorney General Bell gave Carter a draft of the Justice Department's brief on the *Bakke* case, which challenged the Davis plan because it established separate admissions procedures for whites and minorities. At the same time, Bell tried to reassure Carter by telling him and special counsel Robert Lipshutz that the Justice Department intended to "stand for affirmative action" even though it supported Bakke. As Lipshutz, Eizenstat, and other members of the administration read the document, however, they found its defense of affirmative action equivocal and murky. Although the brief ultimately concluded that some forms of affirmative action were appropriate, it also argued that all racial classifications were "suspect," including "even ostensibly benign classifications." Indeed, it stated that race was "presumptively pernicious as a basis on which to bestow or withhold benefits."[3]

Eizenstat and Lipshutz tore the document apart, warning the president that the brief did "not clearly express this Administration's firm commitment to affirmative action." Instead of asking the Supreme Court to declare the Davis Medical School's affirmative action program unconstitutional, the brief should firmly endorse affirmative action programs and clearly differentiate between racial goals and quotas. The pair also strongly recommended that the Justice Department seek to have the case remanded to the lower courts in order to determine whether the sixteen places reserved for disadvantaged students in the Davis program represented a goal or a rigid quota.[4]

The president thought that remanding the case might be "ill advised," although he did not explain why. But he agreed that the brief should be rewritten to include an unequivocal statement of support for affirmative action. Accordingly, he sent it back to the Justice Department for redrafting. When one of the lawyers involved in the revision told HEW Secretary Califano that it was impossible to write a brief defending a special admissions policy, Califano exploded. "Like hell it's impossible," he responded. Similarly, Vice-President Mondale reminded the attorney general that the *Bakke* case represented an extremely important policy decision and that the president wanted any administration pronouncement to be consistent with his position of standing for affirmative action but against quotas. The chairman of the Equal Employment Opportunity Commission, Eleanor Holmes Norton, and Secretary Califano also prepared legal arguments in opposition to *Bakke*, which they submitted to Bell.[5]

In accordance with the president's instructions, the new brief, which the Justice Department filed with the Supreme Court on 19 September, contained a strong endorsement of affirmative action. "In our view," the document concluded, "only one question should be finally resolved in the present posture of this case: whether a state university admissions program may take race into account to remedy the effects of social discrimination."[6]

The Supreme Court did not decide the *Bakke* case until the following June. In a five to four decision, it sanctioned affirmative action programs but found that the Davis Medical School had employed an unconstitutional quota system in denying Bakke a place. It therefore ordered that Bakke be admitted with the school's next class. By this time, the case had ceased to be a political problem for the White House. Blacks and other civil rights activists were generally pleased with the position the administration had taken on *Bakke*. Indeed, black leaders pointed to the Justice Department's brief as one of the administration's major contributions to the cause of civil rights.

On the negative side, *Bakke* had revealed divisions within the administration. Both Attorney General Bell and HEW Secretary Califano, who held substantially different views on affirmative action, later complained about the hurdles they encountered—Bell attributing it to liberal elements within the administration, Califano to the Georgia clique supposedly running the White House. In a sense, both men were right. Certainly the two persons who most influenced the president in the *Bakke* case were Eizenstat and Lipshutz, two moderately conservative Georgians, but they were balanced by Mondale, a liberal outsider. According to Bell, in fact, Mondale was his greatest irritant in civil rights cases (a statement that directly contradicted the claims about the vice-president's diminished status within the administration).

Throughout most of the discussion on *Bakke*, the president had remained surprisingly disengaged. Califano saw him as determined "to walk the tightrope between affirmative action and reverse discrimination," while Bell believed he was attempting "to gloss over [the] fundamental differences" in political philosophy between Carter and Mondale. According to the attorney general, this detachment "helped produce the unclear, all-things-to-all-people voice that the public heard so often from the administration."[7] In fact, because much of the internal bickering over *Bakke* was leaked to the press, it contributed to the perception of an administration incapable of commanding the loyalty of its own people. Even Jordan criticized the White House's conduct of the case. "I would like to share with you my serious concern about the manner in which we are handling . . . the Bakke case," he wrote the president. "If you knew and were aware of the approach that is being taken on your behalf, I don't think you would be either happy or satisfied." Indeed, Supreme Court Chief Justice Warren Burger and Associate Justice Harry Blackmun told Solicitor General Wade H. McCree, Jr., that the entire Court was offended and displeased by the news leaks that had taken place.[8]

Bakke had been a sensational case that had elicited vocal opinion from all sides on the affirmative action issue. Far more mundane were the daily reports of a sinking economy, yet it was this issue that solidified the administration's increasingly unfavorable image among the American people. Like the White House itself, the economy seemed more and more chaotic and lacking direction. The administration also sent out conflicting signals, which created confusion and uncertainty within business and financial circles.

After a year in office, there was still no single person to whom the president routinely deferred for economic advice or who spoke for him on economic issues. Eizenstat and Charles Schultze came closest to serving Carter in these capacities, but neither of them set policy. Eizenstat was not a trained economist, and Schultze was not part of Carter's inner circle. Although Treasury Secretary Blumenthal headed the administration's Economic Policy Group, he had already clashed with the White House over tax reform and had been largely ignored in the development of the administration's welfare and energy programs. Nor did the new director of the OMB, James

McIntyre—or, for that matter, anyone else—enjoy as much influence with the president as McIntyre's predecessor, Bert Lance, had.

As a result, when one of these officials took a public position, business leaders were never certain whether they were speaking for themselves or for the president. This was particularly unsettling because Eizenstat and Schultze tended to be more moderate on spending issues than Blumenthal and McIntyre. The business community remained uneasy over what the news media described as "stagflation," or an economy suffering simultaneously from low growth and high inflation. Although capital spending at the beginning of November was about 8 percent above that for 1976, the economy was still slack and the unemployment rate continued to hover around 7 percent. To stimulate the economy, some analysts recommended a substantial increase in federal spending, but others believed the 6-percent inflation rate had to be addressed first.

Finally, businesses were concerned about the economic impact of pending legislation for refinancing the ailing social security system and reforming the nation's tax structure, both of which were high priority items for the administration. Soon after taking office, HEW Secretary Califano had discovered that social security was drowning in a sea of red ink. Driven by inflation, benefits were increasing, but revenues were diminishing. Moreover, the population was aging, and the resultant additional strains on the system were projected to continue well into the next century. To keep the system solvent, Califano estimated that $83 billion more would be needed over the next five years, which he proposed to obtain through modest increases in social security taxes, supplemented in times of high unemployment by general revenue funds. Satisfied to follow HEW's lead on social security, Carter presented this plan to Congress on 9 May.

In the Senate the proposal was attacked as a raid on the federal treasury, but in the House lawmakers voted overwhelmingly for a large increase in both tax rates and the wage ceiling on which social security taxes were paid. With these changes, the maximum tax would rise from $965 in 1977 to $2,854 in 1986, a threefold increase in ten years. Even though the legislation flew in the face of the president's campaign promise not to raise payroll taxes, he decided to support the bill, hoping the Senate would trim it before sending it to the Oval Office for his signature. Failing that, he would try to compensate for the hike with cuts in the income tax as part of his tax reform proposal. Regardless of the reasoning behind it, the administration's support for a measure that promised to be the largest ever peacetime tax increase fueled business pessimism about the economy.

So did speculation about Carter's plans for tax reform. Because the administration had been divided over what changes to recommend in the existing system and was not even certain Congress would pass any reform bill, the White House had decided in October not to send its recommendations to

Capitol Hill until near the end of the session. In the interim, the president's economic advisers, including Blumenthal, Mondale, Schultze, McIntyre, and Eizenstat, reached a consensus on a tax package, which significantly slimmed down the one proposed by the Treasury secretary in September but included greater incentives for capital formation and more tax breaks for lower income groups. But until the specifics of the program were finally worked out and then made public, the business community did not know whether the White House would emphasize economic incentives for business, as Blumenthal wanted, or assault tax write-offs and business profits, as some business leaders feared.

Together with the administration's energy package, therefore, the proposal to increase social security taxes and the possibility of higher taxes as a result of tax reform suggested to the business community an alarming scenario of higher taxes, higher interest rates, runaway inflation, huge budget deficits, and subsequent recession. The lack of business confidence in the economy was reflected in the stock market, as the Dow-Jones average dropped to just over 800 by early November, its lowest level in two years and 195 points under what it had been on New Year's Eve. Apprehension about the economy also extended to the general public. According to a Harris poll taken about the same time the stock market was skidding toward its two-year low, only 26 percent of the public approved of the president's conduct of the economy, down from 46 percent in May. Of the people polled, moreover, 54 percent believed the country was in a recession, a view not held by most economists.

The surveys also revealed the extent to which Carter had antagonized many of the key voting groups that had helped get him elected in 1976. Blacks expressed dismay that he had not paid more attention to their problems. Labor remained miffed at his failure to endorse a larger increase in the minimum wage. Farmers did not forget that he had proposed lower price supports than those finally approved by Congress. These groups looked to Carter's budget for fiscal 1979 to discover the course he would follow in his second year as president. Since he had inherited Ford's budget for fiscal 1978, this proposal would be the first spending plan that carried Carter's imprint alone. Describing the budget as "tight and lean" but "compassionate" enough to meet the nation's social needs, the president announced in his budget message that this would be the year of the economy. "Our main task at home," he said, "is the nation's economy." The economic recovery of 1977 must continue in 1978 in order "to provide new jobs and better income, which our people need."

Anyone hoping for expanded government assistance or more innovative programs in the year of the economy was greatly disappointed. To offset increased social security taxes and to build on the economic expansion of the previous year, the president proposed a $25-billion tax cut. But the theme that resounded in his budget request was the scarcity of government's resources and its limited ability to correct society's woes. "Government cannot eliminate poverty or provide a bountiful economy or reduce inflation or save our cities or cure illiteracy or provide energy," he stated in presenting his budget to Congress. His priorities for fiscal 1979 would be to lower unemployment, fight inflation, and control federal spending.[9]

Hurt the most by the president's wielding of the budget ax were new funding proposals to aid urban areas. As far back as June 1976, two weeks before he won the Democratic nomination, Carter had told the U.S. Conference of Mayors that if he was elected president, they would "have a friend, an ally, and a partner in the White House." In January, one day before he was inaugurated, he sent eight cabinet-level members of his new administration to meet with a group of mayors gathered in Washington to assure them that he was going to give precedence to urban problems.

Over the next nine months, the president signed into law several of the mayors' recommendations, including an increase in the number of public service jobs and a $12.5-billion urban aid bill targeted at the nation's most distressed cities. He also established an Urban Regional Policy Group (URPG), headed by HUD Secretary Patricia Harris, whose mandate was to develop a national urban policy. To demonstrate his personal concern about the plight of the cities, he traveled at the beginning of October to the South Bronx, and with dozens of reporters in tow, he viewed the wreckage of that ravaged area. Obviously moved by what he saw, Carter returned to Washington and instructed the URPG to prepare a plan of action for the South Bronx that would "serve as a prototype for other blighted urban areas."[10]

Despite Carter's commitment to a national urban policy, however, he never intended any major additional spending for the cities. Rather, he was interested in improving the targeting, coordination, and efficiency of existing programs—supplying some (but not much) supplemental funding for economic development, encouraging more local and neighborhood planning, eliminating redlining in home purchases, and increasing private sector involvement in urban development projects.

The administration, therefore, rejected the URPG's 150-page draft report, which called for adding $8 billion to $12 billion to the $50 billion in aid that cities and towns already received. Instead, Eizenstat recommended to the president a much more restrained and less costly role for Washington. Unlike the Harris task force, which still believed that well-conceived federal programs could bring about urban revitalization, Eizenstat argued that Washington could be most useful serving as a catalyst, promoting "public-private partnerships at the local level," and facilitating "greater involvement by neighborhood and citizen's groups."[11] Carter agreed with his chief domestic adviser. "Don't tell me we'll spend more money all around and then we'll call it an urban policy," he said at a meeting with the URPG in December.

74

"Give me something worth funding if you want more money." The next day he instructed OMB Director James McIntyre not to include any urban initiatives in the 1979 budget.[12]

Aside from its price tag, the president had good reason to reject the URPG's report and to order the task force back to the drawing board. Many of its recommendations were conceptually flawed. Its much-touted proposal for an urban development bank, for example, assumed that the low cost of credit, which the bank would presumably make available to investors, would spur economic development in distressed areas. But the URPG did not analyze carefully the other critical factors affecting investment, such as operating costs, availability of land and a skilled labor force, government regulation, and crime rates.

In deciding not to include any additional funding in his budget for the cities, the president also displayed considerable political courage, for, as he anticipated, his action angered urban interests, whose support was so essential to his presidency. A spokesman for the U.S. Conference of Mayors stated that if the president failed to provide more aid to the cities, his administration would "be viewed as a traitor to urban America." Rather than being intimidated by such warnings, Carter made it clear that his urban policy would stress the role of state and local governments and of neighborhood and voluntary groups, not an infusion of federal dollars.[13]

The president lost a chance, however, to turn the "urban policy" issue to his own advantage. An essential part of his strategy for capturing the presidency, especially in the prenomination phase, had been to present himself as an alternative to conventional Democrats, as someone who was not an advocate of past programs or an apologist for past failures. He told the American people that more was not necessarily better and that there were limits to what the federal government could do, and voters responded by electing him. The issue of aid to the cities offered an excellent opportunity to build on these themes and to benefit from the swelling suspicion of big government that existed even within his own party. In this way, he might have gained some compensating political leverage for the losses he suffered among traditional Democrats as a result of his willingness to challenge standard liberal, and Democratic, dogma about the interventionist responsibilities of the federal government.

Yet Carter never seized the moment, largely because of his economic conservatism. Instead of making the case for a "new liberalism" based on a healthy skepticism about Washington and the need for better rather than more government, for citizen participation, and for grass-roots activism—all of which the polls said had great appeal among the nation's urban residents—he resorted to time-worn conservative arguments about fiscal economy and budgetary frugality. In the process, he neglected to articulate strongly enough his own view that what was required for the nation's cities was not new money but new approaches. What was impressed upon the minds of the public was not a president prepared to challenge convention, lead the nation in fresh directions, and help the cities in innovative ways, but a fiscal conservative at the head of a divided administration.

In fact, there was so little that was novel in any of his economic proposals that journalists commented on how his economic agenda could have been put together just as easily by former President Ford. In calling for tax reform and a $25-billion tax cut, for example, the president stated plainly that he still intended to rely primarily on the private sector to spur economic growth. The purpose of the cut in his view was not so much to stimulate the economy as to prevent it from going into a tailspin as a result of increased social security taxes.

Even so, Carter had not been able to win the confidence of the business community. In February, the Dow-Jones reached a thirty-four-month low of 753 as business and financial leaders continued to bet against the long-term prospects for economic growth under Carter. Inflation, which was still running at around 6 percent, remained an insistent problem. Interest rates had also jumped sharply over the previous twelve months, with the prime rate on business loans climbing from 6.25 percent to 8 percent during this time. Developments such as these led many businessmen to anticipate slow economic improvement at best and recession at worst.

Another area of concern to the business and financial communities and weighing heavily on the economy was the growing uncertainty about the dollar in world currency markets because of the United States' mounting trade deficits. At the beginning of 1978, Americans were still consuming a huge quantity of foreign oil and other imports. At the same time, foreign demand for more expensive American products remained weak, thereby driving down the need for—and price of—dollars. The first two trading days of January witnessed the largest sell-off of dollars since the early 1970s.

To prop up the demand for and price of dollars, the Federal Reserve Board (FRB) and the Treasury Department responded by making available up to $25 billion in foreign currencies to buy dollars. Two days later, the FRB, in cooperation with the president, raised its discount rate (the rate it charged member banks for its funds) from 6 percent to 6.5 percent, a move intended to attract foreign capital. News that the administration had intervened to support the dollar had the desired effect. At a cabinet meeting on 16 January, Treasury Secretary Blumenthal reported that the dollar had "held its own" against other currencies during the previous week and was continuing to do well in European markets. Nevertheless, business and financial leaders were unconvinced that the administration's action was enough to stop the dollar's protracted decline. "Intervention can change things for a day or a week," observed Henry C. Wallich, a Federal Reserve governor, "but it cannot make any permanent change."[14]

The president's economic program, therefore, came under attack by such disparate groups as representatives of urban interests, who accused Carter of not doing enough for urban areas and poor people, and the business and financial communities, who were worried about Carter's ability to sustain long-term economic growth. To make matters worse, the president decided not to reappoint Arthur Burns to a third term as chairman of the Federal Reserve Board, nominating instead G. William Miller, the chairman of Textron Inc. and a director of the Federal Reserve Board of Boston. Although Miller was well qualified for the position, he lacked Burns's credentials as an inflation fighter. Most business leaders simply did not know him and so did not know what to expect once he took Burns's place at the helm of the FRB.

In truth, Carter faced an economic riddle as he began his second year in office. He needed to deal at the same time with a catalogue of competing and inherently contradictory claims on government and his administration: to promote employment while halting inflation; to reduce taxes while meeting pressing social needs; to maintain business confidence without alienating traditional Democrats; and to stabilize the dollar abroad without undercutting his economic program at home. That the president understood the situation was evident at a January press conference, when he acknowledged that the success of his economic plan depended "on a very careful balance between different interests, between sometimes conflicting national needs, between doing too much, on the one hand, [and] doing too little on the other." He was also aware that he had to carry out this delicate task as a leader whose credibility, even among the Democratic faithful, was already badly tarnished. "In no case that I can think of do we have the kind of relationship that will be needed to command their enthusiastic support in 1980, and that includes many of the original Carter supporters," Hamilton Jordan told him in December. In an effort to win back the groups he had alienated, Carter had already begun to polish his presidential and political persona. His decision, for example, to stress unemployment over inflation in his budget message to Congress was intended to help heal the rift that had developed between his administration and organized labor.[15]

Meanwhile, Carter's standing in the polls continued to drop. A nationwide survey taken in mid-February by NBC and the Associated Press (AP) news service reported that only 34 percent of the American people thought he was doing an excellent or good job—a 21-percent decline in six months. Statewide polls taken by Peter D. Hart, an analyst for the Democratic party, revealed a similar drop in Carter's popularity ratings. Projecting toward the 1980 election, Hart found the results extremely disquieting. "One can only hope," he concluded, "that Shakespeare's line from *Measure to Measure*, 'The Best men are molded out of faults, and for the most, become the better for being a little bad,' applies to President Carter."[16]

Some of Carter's efforts at bridge building were undermined by events over which he had little or no control. A case in point was the coal strike of early 1978, which for a time threatened to paralyze the eastern half of the nation. The episode began on 6 December, when 165,000 members of the United Mine Workers (UMW) walked off the job after failing to reach agreement on a new contract with the coal operators, represented by the Bituminous Coal Operators Association (BCOA). At issue was the right of miners to engage in wildcat strikes in order to protest infractions of their contract or violations of safety standards. Although most observers anticipated a short walkout, by February it had surpassed the fifty-nine-day record set by UMW strikers in 1949. Meanwhile, coal production slipped from almost 15 million tons a week in January to less than 6 million tons by the middle of February. As coal stocks dwindled to emergency levels, power companies in the Midwest and Atlantic states asked their biggest customers to curtail their use of electricity. Diminishing supplies of coal also brought scattered layoffs, school closings, and shortened workweeks in the affected regions.

At first, the administration did not take much official notice of the coal strike, but as the walkout continued, pressure intensified on the White House to do something about it. According to Frank Moore, Carter's liaison on Capitol Hill, lawmakers were "in a panic" over the strike. In February, Carter responded finally by bringing the negotiators to the White House. By the end of the month, he had even decided to seek a Taft-Hartley injunction forcing the strikers back to work and legislation authorizing him to seize the mines. Just as he was about to announce these moves, the BCOA and UMW reached tentative agreement on a new contract. The truce was broken a few weeks later, when the rank and file rejected the contract by a two-to-one margin and sent the negotiators back to the bargaining table. Frustrated, the president declared on 9 March that he was invoking the Taft-Hartley Act, delaying for the moment any attempt to take over the mines. But not until 24 March was another agreement reached and then ratified by the miners, who had now been off the job for 109 days.[17]

During the strike, Tom Wicker of the *New York Times* and several other journalists had observed that the manner in which Carter responded to the walkout would have a significant influence on the way the American people viewed him. Even after it was over, Peter Hart noted that a "coal strike settlement could have been the catalyst to improve the President's standing with the American public." But as Hart's comments indicated and as an AP/NBC poll showed, the strike had just the opposite effect: Two-thirds of the people surveyed believed that Carter had performed poorly during the walkout.[18]

Actually, there was probably little more Carter could have done to shorten the strike or to mitigate its impact. Certainly he would have been imprudent not to have allowed collective bargaining to run its course before resorting to more drastic measures. Once arbitration was under way, he tried to use his office as a "bully pulpit," moving the negotiations to the White House and then applying considerable pressure on the BCOA to come to terms. At one point, he even let executives of big steel corporations with mining subsidiaries know that he would not assist the industry with its trade problems unless they were more forthcoming in their negotiations with the UMW. After it became clear that collective bargaining was not working, he employed the Taft-Hartley Act.

Nevertheless, Carter antagonized both sides in the strike by waiting almost four months before seeking an injunction against the miners and then by being the first president in more than twenty years to invoke Taft-Hartley. Indeed, the very fact he chose that measure, which was aimed primarily at labor, instead of seizing the mines, which would have chiefly affected the coal operators, made him seem antilabor to many union leaders. At the same time, his hard-line approach to the mine owners constraining them to settle with the UMW also made him appear antibusiness to many business leaders. Depending on one's perspective, therefore, Carter had done too little or too much, too late or too soon.

During the strike, the president also became entangled in the so-called Marston affair. David Marston had been working on the staff of Pennsylvania Senator Richard Schweiker when President Ford appointed him U.S. attorney for Philadelphia. After Marston refused to resign from what was normally a patronage post, Attorney General Griffin Bell fired him. That seemed to violate a pledge Carter had made at the Democratic convention in 1976, to appoint "all federal judges and prosecutors . . . strictly on the basis of merit." The attorney general—and later the president—tried to justify Marston's dismissal on the grounds that he had come to the job straight from a senatorial staff without any trial experience. But it was hard to fault the thirty-five-year-old Republican for his lack of ability when his office had vigorously and successfully prosecuted a number of powerful state legislators.

The circumstances under which Marston was fired, moreover, were suspect. Bell had waited until November 1977 before asking him for his resignation and had only acted after receiving a telephone call from the president, telling him to expedite Marston's ouster. Also, both he and Carter had been urged to dismiss Marston by Democratic Congressman Joshua Eilberg of Philadelphia, whose law firm was being investigated by Marston's office. In fact, the president had telephoned the attorney general immediately after talking to Eilberg. As it happened, neither Bell nor Carter knew about Marston's probe of Eilberg's law firm at the time they decided to dismiss the U.S. attorney. Even so, what made the Marston affair such an embarrassment to the administration was the *appearance* of impropriety. The president also performed poorly in his public comments on the controversy, at one point even denying that he had discussed the Eilberg case with Bell. He then erroneously told a group of Democratic congressmen that the Justice Department could not confirm that Marston was investigating Eilberg. He also refused to acknowledge that, with hindsight, he might have handled matters differently. As a result, new doubts were expressed about his commitment to high moral and ethical standards in government.

To the American people, however, the president's greatest problem remained the economy, particularly inflation. Throughout the autumn of 1977, the administration had considered a number of proposals for dealing with inflation, including an innovative concept recommended by Arthur Okun of the Brookings Institution to use tax cuts as an alternative to wage and price increases. But after much discussion, the administration rejected the idea because of its complexity and the difficulty of integrating it into the general tax cut the president was already seeking.

Instead, Carter called in his State of the Union message in January 1978 for a voluntary system of wage and price guidelines. Although he made every effort to underscore the fact that the program was not mandatory, most business and labor leaders were convinced that guidelines were a prelude to controls, which they strongly opposed. The very ambiguity of the proposal contributed to their fears. "It's like commanding the tides to stop moving," said Beryl Sprinkel, vice-president of the Harris Trust and Savings Bank of Chicago. Labor leaders were also concerned that wages would bear the brunt of government intervention. AFL-CIO chief George Meany termed the whole concept of voluntary wage and price guidelines as "wishboning."[19]

Over the next four months, inflation worsened. Rising food prices, larger than anticipated increases in energy prices, higher than expected labor costs, an accelerated depreciation of the dollar on world currency markets, and a jump in the wholesale price index of 1.1 percent in February, the highest in thirty-nine months, all contributed to the problem and dampened hopes of recovery. "The price outlook is deteriorating," Treasury Secretary Blumenthal and CEA Chairman Schultze advised the president on 15 March. Instead of the 6-percent inflation rate the CEA had forecast at the beginning of the year, it now estimated inflation for 1978 at 7–7.25 percent.[20]

Carter's advisers split over how to contend with inflation. Blumenthal and Schultze suggested a number of "anti-inflation initiatives," including holding pay raises for federal workers to 5 percent rather than the 6 percent provided for in Carter's 1979 budget and asking state and local governments to check their own pay increases while reducing sales and property taxes. But Eizenstat, Powell, and Jordan were worried about the political damage that implementation of the Blumenthal-Schultze proposals might cause. Well aware that Ford had tampered with federal pay raises just before the 1976 elections, they warned that the White House was playing with "political dynamite" and urged that the president make no decision on the proposals until he returned on 3 April from a trip to Africa and South America.[21]

Carter agreed to defer action on the inflation front, but once he was back in the United States, he adopted most of Blumenthal and Schultze's recommendations. In a speech on 11 April before the American Society of Newspaper Editors, he stated that he would "take the lead in breaking the wage and price spiral" by limiting pay raises for federal workers to 5.5 percent and freezing the salaries of 2,300 political appointees. He also asked all the governors and the mayors of major cities to hold down the wage increases of state and city employees and to consider lowering sales taxes. In addition, he renewed his plea to labor and industry to bring wage and price hikes below the average of the previous two years, and he announced that he was appointing his special trade representative, Robert Strauss, as his special counselor on inflation.

Knowing that his inflation program lacked vital support inside and outside his administration, the president could not have been taken unawares by the tepid, even skeptical, response to his speech. Business leaders expressed disappointment that the president had failed to address convincingly what they regarded as the prime causes of inflation—the ballooning federal budget deficit and the growth of the nation's money supply. Organized labor was angry that the White House was concentrating its efforts on fighting inflation rather than on stimulating the economy, and labor leaders were unwilling to practice wage deceleration without evidence of a slowdown in price increases.

By April, inflation was exacting a heavy toll on the administration. According to a *New York Times*/CBS poll conducted during the first two weeks in April, 63 percent of the people surveyed cited inflation as their greatest concern, and only 32 percent approved of Carter's record on the economy. By this time, too, Carter's domestic agenda for 1978 was in shambles. In both his budget and State of the Union messages in January, the president had pledged to revitalize the cities of the snowbelt region, bring down the rate of unemployment, reform the nation's tax structure, cut taxes by $25 billion, tame the rate of inflation, and sign into law his energy program. He had also tried to regain some of the support he had lost among urban leaders and organized labor while at the same time winning back the confidence of the business community.

Except for a drop in the unemployment rate, the president's efforts were largely unsuccessful. His administration still lacked an urban policy. His tax and energy programs were on hold, and sentiment began to grow on Capitol Hill to scale back the recent increases in social security taxes while reducing the size of the tax cut as a means of coping with inflation. Instead of mollifying organized labor, Carter had exacerbated existing tensions as a result of his anti-inflation program and his use of the Taft-Hartley Act to end the coal strike. Nor had he enlisted the business community, as many corporate heads still doubted the president's competency to deal with the hard economic times they thought lay ahead. It was not surprising, therefore, that an NBC/AP poll taken in late April gave the president only a 29-percent positive rating (his lowest yet) or that a Gallup survey, taken about the same time, showed Carter trailing Massachusetts Senator Edward Kennedy by a margin of 53 percent to 40 percent for the 1980 Democratic presidential nomination.

7

★ ★ ★ ★ ★

THE YEAR OF NEGOTIATIONS

Paralleling the disenchantment with Carter's handling of domestic policy was widespread dissatisfaction with his conduct of foreign policy. According to a Harris poll published at the end of 1977, only 38 percent of Americans approved of the way the president managed foreign affairs, while 51 percent disapproved. Events over the next six months did little to change this low public opinion of Carter as a world leader or to remove the sense of gloom and doom that now pervaded the White House. The president did achieve a major victory when the Senate, in the spring of 1978, ratified the Panama Canal treaties. However, even as late as the summer of 1978, most of Carter's other foreign policy initiatives were still in limbo, and the president's ratings in the polls stayed abysmally low.

From June 1977 to June 1978, the president continued to devote much of his time to the Mideast crisis. Carter had deplored Israeli Prime Minister Begin's decision in July 1977 to build additional settlements on the West Bank, and he had denounced them as illegal and obstacles to peace. But he did not allow Begin's action to interfere with his goal of reconvening the Geneva Conference on the Mideast, which had been dormant since 1973. On 19 September, Israeli Foreign Minister Moshe Dayan met with President Carter and Secretary Vance in the Oval Office and promised that Israel would delay settlements in the occupied territories for at least a year. Dayan even indicated that Israel might accept Palestinians at Geneva as part of a pan-Arab delegation. Leaving the White House after the meeting, Dayan said a Geneva meeting could be set up by year's end.

On 1 October, the administration took a step that even the secretary of state later acknowledged was counterproductive. It issued a joint communiqué with the Soviet Union formally calling for a new Geneva conference. Vance believed that as one of the cochairmen of the conference, the Soviets had to be involved in summoning the meeting and establishing its agenda. Nevertheless, the joint statement produced a storm of protest in Israel and the United States. From the hospital bed where he was being treated for a heart condition, Begin accused Washington of trying to force a settlement on Israel. In the United States, Jewish groups and other supporters of Israel picketed the White House.

Critics of the communiqué objected to it on three grounds. Most important, they protested against a reference in the statement to "the legitimate rights of the Palestinian people." Since these were code words used by the Palestinian Liberation Organization to justify their struggle against Israel, Washington had in the past always referred to Palestinian "interests" rather than "rights." Second, the communiqué made no reference to UN Resolution 242, which had been approved following the Six Days' War in 1967 and which recognized Israel's right to exist in secure borders. Finally, it seemed to invite the Soviet Union, which had been thrown out of the Mideast in 1973, back into the region, something that most Americans, as well as Israelis, were anxious to prevent.

As a result, the Geneva meeting never took place. The largest stumbling block remained PLO representation. Israel would not attend a Geneva meeting with the PLO; Syria would not go without it. As the movement toward Geneva became deadlocked once more, President Carter and Egyptian President Sadat grew increasingly frustrated. On 21 October, Carter wrote Sadat a personal letter asking the Egyptian leader for his help. On 2 November, Sadat replied by proposing a conference in East Jerusalem attended by the disputed parties and permanent members of the UN Security Council—an idea Carter believed was "doomed to failure."[1]

Much to Carter's surprise, the next time he heard from Sadat was in the second week in November, when the Egyptian president informed him he would be going to Israel. Earlier Sadat had let Begin know, through Secretary Vance, that he was eager to meet with the Israeli leader, and Begin had then invited him to come to Jerusalem. Distressed by the lengthy and tedious negotiations over calling a Geneva conference, the Egyptian leader accepted, hoping that in this way he might break the stalemate.

Sadat's dramatic three-day trip to Jerusalem and his address to the Israeli Parliament (the Knesset) drew worldwide attention. Thousands of Israelis, many waving Egyptian flags, turned out to welcome their former enemy. In his hour-long speech to the Knesset, Sadat captured the poignancy of the moment when he said he had come to Israel not to sign a peace but to break down "the barriers of suspicion, fear, illusion, and misrepresentation" that for so many years had kept his country and Israel from even talking about peace.[2] However, by his actions, the Egyptian leader incurred the wrath of much of the Arab world. As Carter and Vance had feared, Sadat's visit to Israel also ended whatever likelihood remained of a Geneva meeting. Returning home, the Egyptian president invited "all the parties to the [Mideast] conflict" to Cairo in order "to prepare for a Geneva conference." But not one of the Arab leaders—not even from such moderate states as Tunisia, Morocco, the Sudan, or Saudi Arabia—came to Cairo. Instead, representatives from such anti-Sadat nations as Iraq, Algeria, and Libya gathered in Tripoli, where they formed a "rejectionist" front and condemned the Egyptian leader.

Sadat's response was to announce that he would negotiate alone if other Arab leaders did not join him. In order to bolster his position in the Arab world, he sent Begin an urgent message asking him to make some positive statement on the Palestinian question and the occupied territories. The Israeli leader's reply was disappointing. Instead of communicating directly with Sadat, Begin came to Washington with an offer to withdraw Israeli forces from the Sinai in two stages over a three- to five-year period. He also proposed to grant Palestinians home rule in the West Bank and Gaza Strip for a five-year period, during which Israel would "hold in abeyance" its claim to sovereignty over the region. Israel would retain responsibility for public order and the right of military access throughout this time. After five years, Israel would decide whether to continue or modify the arrangement.

Carter and Vance found the plan not only unacceptable but dangerous. "I expressed my concern that his proposal was inadequate and that the inadequacy of it might cause the downfall of Sadat," the president recorded in his diary after conferring with Begin. He and Secretary Vance believed his proposal for home rule was an unsatisfactory substitute for Israeli withdrawal and Palestinian self-determination. They were also disturbed that there was no role provided for the Arab states and no clear indication whether Palestinian refugees and exiles would be allowed to return to their former homes. Finally, they wanted the five years proposed by Begin to be a transition period leading to a plebiscite and peace treaty between the Palestinians and Israel—in contrast to Begin's intention that the term be an experiment in local autonomy, which, if successful, might be made permanent.[3]

On the eve of the new year, therefore, fundamental differences still remained between Egypt and Israel. As if to underscore the gap separating the two countries, talks between Begin and Sadat that began on Christmas Day were unproductive. Meeting only with their advisers at the Egyptian town of Ismailia near the Suez Canal, Begin and Sadat could not agree on anything other than to form two committees to discuss political and military matters. Most of their time was spent arguing over Sadat's demands that Israel leave the occupied territories and grant Palestinian self-determination.

In the meantime, Carter embarked on a nine-day trip at the end of December 1977 that took him to Poland, Iran, India, Saudi Arabia, Egypt, France, and Belgium. Undoubtedly, the most memorable event of his journey was a toast he made in Iran to the shah, since it would later come back to haunt him. Addressing Iran's leader at a state dinner in his honor, Carter referred to the shah as an "island of stability in one of the more troubled areas of the world." Most reporters viewed the president's 18,500-mile journey as a great personal success. "Among friends overseas, Carter had established that his blend of populism and goodwill travels well," *Newsweek* commented afterwards.[4]

Yet the foreign policy issue that had absorbed the president during his trip—the Mideast crisis—seemed no nearer resolution after he returned to Washington than when he left. Indeed, his conversations with Arab leaders offered little reason for optimism. Sadat was still angry that Begin had not been more forthcoming during their recent talks. Although Carter had hoped to involve Jordan's King Hussein in the peace process begun by Sadat, the king made it clear he would not participate in negotiations until Israel withdrew from the occupied lands and agreed to Palestinian autonomy. The Saudis basically concurred.

Israel also pursued a hard line. In an interview, Israeli Prime Minister Begin revealed how distant a Mideast accord truly was. When asked if there were any conditions under which Israel could accept Palestinian self-determination, he replied there were not. When questioned about new Israeli settlements on the West Bank and Sinai Peninsula, he answered by referring to the "rights of the Jews to acquire land and settle in Judea, Samaria and Gaza."[5]

As a result, the administration concluded that the United States needed to become more involved in the negotiating process if Sadat's peace initiative was to succeed. Accordingly, the president decided to invite the Egyptian and Israeli leaders to Washington. Sadat would come first, so that Carter could reaffirm his support for Sadat's overtures and develop a common strategy for dealing with Israel's intransigence. This would give the appearance that the administration was siding with Egypt against Israel, but as Brzezinski later commented, "the bilateral Egyptian-Israeli talks were leading nowhere. Sadat now needed American help desperately in order to obtain an accommodation."[6]

The Egyptian president arrived in the United States on 3 February. In his discussions with Carter, he criticized Begin's "ridiculous" position regarding Israeli settlements in the Sinai and Palestinian self-determination, and he repeated his conviction that the Israeli prime minister did not want peace. He also expressed his disappointment that Washington was not playing a more instrumental role as mediator. Convinced that his initiative would collapse unless the United States compelled Israel to make concessions, he wanted Washington to resume its central place in negotiating a Mideast peace.

Carter agreed, but little progress was made over the next three months in obtaining an agreement between Israel and Egypt, much less in arriving at a comprehensive settlement. Indeed, as weeks passed without success, Carter became less and less concerned about a broad accord and increasingly more interested in a separate treaty between Egypt and Israel. But even that more limited objective began to seem beyond reach, partly because of worsening relations between Jerusalem and Washington. On 8 February, the day Sadat left the United States, Carter held a briefing for American Jewish leaders in which he accused Israel of being the biggest obstacle to a Mideast peace because of its position on the settlements issue. On the same day, Secretary of State Vance stated in a press conference that Israeli settlements in the Sinai were illegal, diminished the chances for peace, and should be dismantled. Prime Minister Begin lashed out at the administration, accusing it of "taking sides" against Israel. When he later learned that the White House had decided to sell fighter planes to Saudi Arabia and Egypt (part of a deal that also included the sale of jet fighters to Israel), he blasted the proposal as a threat to Israel's national security.

Concerned by this deterioration in Israeli-American relations, Moshe Dayan came to the White House for talks with President Carter. The foreign minister's mood was glum. He had arrived in New York on 8 February for a series of lectures scheduled months before. "I was immediately made to feel the cold wind in the wake of the 'Sadat festival,'" he later recalled. "The Israeli Government had been placed in the dock both by the American press and by some of the Jewish leaders." Indeed, a split had developed among American Jews over Sadat's peace initiative. Many American Jewish leaders had become persuaded that Begin's policy was a serious mistake and that the settlements should be torn down.[7]

On 16 February, Dayan met separately with Secretary Vance and President Carter. Neither discussion went well. Vance and Carter told him that Sadat felt King Hussein had to be brought into the peace process, but the Jordanian leader would not participate until Israel agreed to withdraw from the West Bank and Sinai. Dayan responded that Israel would welcome Hussein's involvement but not on the basis of advanced commitments. After leaving the White House, Dayan told reporters that "significant differences" still remained between Washington and Jerusalem. The president, equally disheartened, later wrote that "Dayan, in his highly critical mood, had not helped much to prepare us for the upcoming Begin visit."

The Israeli leader arrived in the United States on 20 March. Zbigniew Brzezinski subsequently described the president's two days of talks with the Israeli prime minister as "generally unpleasant." Carter was clearly in a fighting mood. Although he had been appalled by a PLO attack along the Israeli coast on 11 March in which 35 people were killed, he told Begin that Israel had overreacted: Its retaliatory invasion of southern Lebanon had left more than 1,000 dead and 100,000 homeless. He also insisted that under UN Resolution 242, Israel would have to remove its forces from all the occupied lands, including the West Bank. After five years, during which neither Israel nor Jordan would lay claim to the West Bank, the Palestinians living in that occupied territory should then have the right to decide for themselves whether to affiliate with Israel or Jordan or to continue under the so-called interim government.[8]

The president tried to reassure Begin that the United States would not permit the establishment of an independent Palestinian state on the West Bank. He also endorsed a modification of the West Bank's western boundary in order to give Israel greater security. But the Israeli prime minister refused to soften his stance on any of the issues he discussed with Carter. The president was so frustrated and angered by his talks with Begin that, after they were over, he did not even walk the Israeli leader to his waiting limousine. Meeting with congressional leaders, Carter stated that negotiations had reached an impasse, for which Begin was responsible.

For the next two months, Washington's role in the mediation process became largely one of messenger and facilitator, as Assistant Secretary of State Alfred L. Atherton, Jr., whom Carter had earlier appointed as a special ambassador to the Israeli-Egyptian political talks, shuttled between Jerusalem and Cairo exchanging notes. But there was no significant movement, either by Israel or Egypt, toward a settlement. Sadat did agree to slight border adjustments and the stationing of some Israeli units in the occupied territories, but Israel rejected any proposal that would return the West Bank and Gaza Strip to Arab control.

Meanwhile, as a result of his proposal to sell jet fighters to Saudi Arabia and Egypt, Carter's relations with American Jewish leaders reached a new low. American Jews continued to be seriously divided over Sadat's peace initiative and Begin's refusal to relinquish occupied territories, but Carter's plan to sell supersonic jets to Egypt and Saudi Arabia, followed by the PLO's terrorist attack on Israeli civilians, united American Jews against the administration. At a conference of the United Jewish Appeal in March, delegates booed and hissed when Mark Siegel, the White House's liaison to the Jewish community, tried to defend the administration's decision. Siegel resigned his White House position, saying he was no longer willing to "get his head beaten in for something he didn't believe in and couldn't influence."[9]

The clout of the American Jewish community was felt on Capitol Hill where the proposed sale to Saudi Arabia of sixty F-15 long-range bombers set off a fierce legislative battle. Eleven members of the fifteen-member Senate Foreign Relations Committee told Secretary of State Vance, even before the White House sent its bill to Congress, that the House and Senate would not approve the deal. Hamilton Jordan was equally negative, warning the president that "this is going to be a very tough legislative fight."[10] In Congress, lawmakers had to decide whether to allow the plan to go through or to block it through a resolution that *both* the House and the Senate had to approve. To win the support of pro-Israeli members, Carter offered twenty F-15s to Israel. Following ten hours of emotional, sometimes nasty debate and despite an intense lobbying effort against the transaction by Israeli backers, the Senate turned down a resolution that would have killed the sale, thereby handing the American Jewish lobby its most serious legislative defeat ever.

The president's surprising victory on the sale of the bombers had occurred on the heels of another success—final Senate ratification of the Panama Canal treaties. In a campaign carefully orchestrated by Hamilton Jordan and having all the trappings of a bid for public office, the White House had labored tirelessly throughout the fall of 1977 and early winter of 1977/78 to win the necessary two-thirds vote of the Senate. At first, it seemed the president's quest was hopeless. In a poll conducted in October by Pat Caddell, sentiment was running against the treaties by nearly a two-to-one majority. Senator Barry Goldwater of Arizona cautioned the president not to risk important political capital on such a lost cause. "I suggest to you, with all respect," Goldwater wrote Carter in September, "that you not get too excited about this Treaty. It is not something you originated."[11]

Thanks largely to the White House's lobbying efforts, however, opinion about the treaties began to turn around. According to a Gallup poll released on 1 February, 45 percent of the American people now favored the amended treaties with 42 percent opposed—the first time a plurality of Americans supported the agreements. On 1 March, the Senate ratified the neutrality treaty (the first of the two canal accords) after turning back a series of "killer amendments," which, if implemented, would have required the treaties to be renegotiated and resubmitted to the Panamanians for another referendum. However, the administration had gained approval of the neutrality pact with only two votes to spare (sixty-eight to thirty-two). There remained the canal agreement itself, transferring control of the waterway to Panama in the year 2000. Although the White House had momentum going for it, ratification of this second, more important treaty was far from certain.

Complicating matters was Panama leader Omar Torrijos's anger that the Senate had included in the neutrality treaty a "reservation" giving the United States the right to intervene militarily to re-open the canal if it should ever become necessary. But the Senate agreed to another stipulation in the second treaty explicitly prohibiting the United States from interfering in Panama's internal affairs. This seemed to satisfy Torrijos, and on 18 April, the Senate ratified the second treaty by the same sixty-eight to thirty-two margin.

Approval of the Panama Canal treaties was a great triumph for the president, in many ways his most important one since taking office. Over the months of debate before final votes, the president had contacted every senator at least once and some as many as eight times. He had also met privately with all but a few of the lawmakers and encouraged ambivalent senators to visit Panama in order to talk with military leaders and meet with President Torrijos. In addition, he had Vance, Mondale, Defense Secretary Harold Brown, and the Joint Chiefs of Staff spend much of their time on Capitol Hill lobbying for the agreement. Finally, he had won over undecided lawmakers by putting the prestige of the presidency on the line and by making support of the treaties a test of Democratic loyalty to his administration and of Republican support for a bipartisan foreign policy.

Political observers took note of Carter's achievements on Capitol Hill. Many commentators who had been highly critical of the president just weeks earlier now wondered whether they had jumped to a premature judgment. There was even talk in the news media of a "new Carter"—tougher and more in command of his administration, more flexible and pragmatic, more deferential to Congress, and more prepared to compromise on major issues than the "old Carter."[12]

Nevertheless, a Gallup poll published in May 1978 showed that registered voters preferred Senator Edward Kennedy over Carter as their 1980 presidential candidate by a margin of 53 percent to 40 percent. According to the latest Harris poll, the president's approval rating with the voters had sunk to 30 percent, a drop of 17 percent over the past four months. Even Carter's victories on the canal treaties and sale of F-15s to Saudi Arabia did not improve his prestige among American voters. "Ordinarily a president grows stronger by winning a hard political fight," the historian Gaddis Smith observed with regard to passage of the treaties. "But Carter's narrow triumph gained him no credit at home." Instead, ratification merely spurred public attacks and a more concerted political effort against the administration and against protreaty senators seeking reelection by the conservative right, which had led the fight to defeat the agreements. And the sale of the F-15s to the Saudis simply aggravated the administration's already tenuous standing among American Jews.[13]

Other foreign policy issues that also caused the president much consternation both at home and abroad included rapidly changing developments in Africa, relations with the Soviet Union, a growing controversy with NATO allies over a radiation-emitting neutron bomb, and the state of the international economy. Together, these concerns placed a huge burden on the president's schedule and strained the circuits of decision making in the Oval Office.

African problems centered on two regions: southern Africa and the Horn (the central eastern coast). In the former, the difficulty facing the president was how to assist a transition there from white minority to black majority rule that avoided a bloody civil war. No previous administration had championed the cause of black nationalism as much as the Carter administration, and a case in point was its policy on Rhodesia. In 1965, the United Nations had imposed economic sanctions against that country after its white-supremacist government declared its independence from Britain. The United States complied with the UN resolve until 1971, when lawmakers on Capitol Hill lifted the ban on Rhodesian chrome. But in 1977, the newly elected president was able to persuade Congress to restore the sanctions.

Since taking office Carter and his advisers had called repeatedly for black majority rule in southern Africa. Both UN Ambassador Andrew Young and Vice-President Walter Mondale had been criticized on Capitol Hill by right-wing Republicans such as Senator Jesse Helms for their comments about the minority white governments and apartheid policies of Rhodesia and South Africa. The conservative position was that the United States needed to support the friendly governments of these two African nations. In contrast, most black Africans showered the administration with praise. According to Zambian President Kenneth Kaunda, Carter had "brought a breath of fresh air to our troubled world."[14]

Opposing the Rhodesian minority white government was the militant black Patriotic Front. While the Front wanted immediate majority rule, Prime Minister Ian Smith insisted on a guarantee of white seats in parliament. In early 1978, Vance met with the leaders of the militant group, Robert Mugabe and Joshua Nkomo, in a failed attempt to reach a compromise. Smith then announced an "internal settlement" that provided for a new government and included black moderates. But Smith would remain prime minister and whites would be assured enough seats in parliament to prevent any constitutional changes. Predictably, the Patriotic Front denounced the plan and intensified its five-year guerrilla war against the Rhodesian government.

Smith's proposal for an internal settlement split the White House and exposed the growing estrangement between Secretary of State Vance and NSC Adviser Brzezinski. Vance believed Smith's plan was a subterfuge designed to keep whites in power; Brzezinski believed it offered a reasonable means of "let[ting] moderate Africans take over from Smith." Carter sided with his NSC adviser. Hoping that Smith's strategy would lead eventually to majority rule and under strong pressure from congressional conservatives to lift sanctions against Rhodesia, he ordered the American delegation at the UN to abstain on a resolution condemning the plan.[15] As a result, liberal lawmakers on Capitol Hill and black leaders at home and abroad became angered by what they regarded as the White House's tacit endorsement of Smith's internal settlement. Conservative senators were not much happier; led by Helms, they accused the president of lending implicit support to the Patriotic Front by opposing their efforts to lift sanctions against Rhodesia before a final settlement was reached.

Another, more serious international situation in that part of the world was the presence of Cuban troops on the Horn of Africa. Bordering on the Red Sea and Gulf of Aden and jutting out into the Arabian Sea, the Horn was one of the most desolate and economically destitute regions of the world—and, because of its location on the flank of the Middle East, one of its most strategically important. War had broken out in 1977 between the two occupants of the Horn, Somalia and Ethiopia, over irredentist claims by Somalia to the Ogaden desert in southern Ethiopia, which was inhabited largely by Somali nomads. At first Somalia, supplied by the Soviet Union, had the upper hand, nearly driving the Ethiopians out of the Ogaden region. But Moscow changed sides and began sending massive military assistance to Ethiopia's Marxist military regime. In addition, it airlifted 12,000 Cuban troops into the country. By early spring, Ethiopian and Cuban troops had driven the Somalis from the Ogaden and returned the territory to Ethiopian control. The Ethiopians, who had promised earlier that they would not cross into Somalia, then kept their word and stopped at the Somali border. As a result, the war wound down and the crisis ebbed. But Cuban forces, backed by the Soviet Union, remained in force on the African Horn.

The Cuban presence here and elsewhere on the continent was shaping Carter's African policy. On 11 May, a detachment of Cuban-trained exiles from Zaire's mineral-rich province of Shaba (formerly known as Katanga) crossed into Zaire from Angola. A year earlier, a similar force of Katangese exiles trained in Angola had invaded Shaba, but the administration had treated the attack as a local matter rather than as an issue in Soviet-American relations. This time, however, Carter took a more global view of the Angolan invasion by blaming it on the Soviets' Cuban proxies.

In a major foreign policy address at Wake Forest University on 17 March 1978, the president warned about an "ominous inclination on the part of the Soviet Union to use its military power ... with full logistical support and encouragement for mercenaries from other Communist countries." By this time, Carter had come to share NSC Adviser Brzezinski's bipolar perception of world politics, which pitted the United States in global conflict against the Soviet Union. His hardened policy toward the Soviet Union came about despite considerable progress over the last six months on the SALT II negotiations. As early as the spring of 1977, Washington had agreed to accept the Vladivostok ceilings on missiles as a basis for arms reduction, while Moscow indicated it would consider a modest reduction in the cap of 2,400 missiles. But the two sides had remained far apart on some major points, such as the number of MIRVs permitted to each of the two superpowers and the status of American cruise missiles and Soviet backfire bombers.

At the end of September, though, Moscow agreed to reduce the Vladivostok ceiling of 2,400 strategic missiles to 2,250 and made several other concessions, such as accepting the American position on the number of its submarine- and land-launched MIRVs. Although there were still differences over cruise missiles and the introduction of new ICBMs, the Soviet proposals represented a real breakthrough in the SALT talks. In effect, Moscow and Washington had reached agreement on the broad outlines of a SALT II compromise. Almost immediately political observers began to speculate on the possibility of a Carter-Brezhnev summit, perhaps as early as December or

January, to sign an accord. President Carter tried to curb that rumor, telling reporters that remaining disagreements on strategic arms "could take quite a long time to remove." But privately his administration began to plan for a meeting with the Soviet leader.

In no way, however, did this mean that the United States and the Soviet Union had entered into a new era of détente. The White House continued to flay Moscow for its repression of Soviet dissidents (although in less strident terms). Already angered that the United States was apparently backing away from a Geneva conference on the Middle East, the Kremlin still complained about Carter's obstinacy on human rights. And other issues bedeviled Washington's relations with Moscow, none more ominous from the Soviet perspective than the new attitude the White House was adopting toward the People's Republic of China (PRC).

Relations between the Beijing government and the Kremlin had been deteriorating since the 1950s; by 1977, war threatened over a disputed border along the Amur River. The White House was divided on how to respond to this mounting crisis between the two communist powers. Both Secretary of State Vance and NSC Adviser Brzezinski favored eventual normalization of relations with China, but Vance was more concerned about reaching a SALT II agreement with the Soviets, which he thought open courting of China would jeopardize. In contrast, Brzezinski, who chose to link a SALT II agreement to Soviet behavior in the African Horn and elsewhere, sought to pressure the Kremlin by playing the "China card"—that is, by making well-publicized overtures to Beijing, much as former President Richard Nixon had done in 1972. Indicative of Brzezinski's growing influence over Carter and of the president's own tougher policy toward the Kremlin, the president agreed to send his NSC adviser to China for talks with Beijing officials even though Vance opposed the trip.

Over the spring and early summer, relations between Moscow and Washington spiraled downward. Following the imprisonment by the Kremlin of leading Soviet dissidents Yuri Orlov, Alexander Ginsburg, and Anatoly Shcharansky, Carter cancelled several visits to Moscow planned by government officials and threatened to block the transfer to the Soviet Union of advanced oil equipment. In response to a military buildup of the Soviets' Warsaw Pact allies, the president also called for the strengthening of NATO defenses, noting that the Soviet Union "pose[d] a threat to [NATO] which far exceed[ed] their legitimate security needs."

Rather than hasten the SALT process as Carter had anticipated, Brzezinski's visit to China in May had the opposite effect. Moscow was offended when the NSC adviser referred to "the polar bear to the north" and accused the Soviets of supporting "international marauders" in Africa. After Brzezinski returned to the United States, Secretary Vance warned the president against "trying to play off China against the Soviets." But the president was now clearly committed to restoring normal diplomatic relations with the Beijing government before the end of the year.

By early summer, the situation between the United States and the Soviet Union had become so poisoned that some journalists were even writing about a "New Cold War." Carter set the tone for his side of the superpower dialogue in a key address to the graduating class at Annapolis in June. Advocating détente and continuation of the SALT process, he also accused the Soviets of waging "an aggressive struggle for political advantage" that could "escalate into graver tensions." "The Soviet Union can choose either confrontation or cooperation," he added. "The United States is adequately prepared for both."

The president saw no inconsistency between censuring the Kremlin on the one hand and pursuing SALT negotiations on the other. He also denied any linkage between the SALT process and what he considered Soviet misconduct. But his repeated attacks on Moscow created an atmosphere in which it was almost certain that such a linkage would be made. Even State Department officials acknowledged that Vance's decision in May to meet with Soviet Foreign Minister Gromyko in Geneva to continue SALT talks was one of the most difficult he had ever had to make. Likewise, Senator Robert Byrd commented that he saw no chance for ratification of a SALT agreement until the Soviets got out of Africa and improved their record on human rights.

The president had wanted a reasoned and measured policy toward the Soviet Union, one that balanced outrage at Soviet misconduct with the imperatives of ending the Cold War. What he achieved, however, was a policy strewn with contradictions and inconsistencies. As Jody Powell acknowledged, the president appeared to be sending two separate messages to two different audiences—a "soft" line for the Soviets (the offer of continued SALT negotiations) and a "hard" line for domestic political consumption (indignation at Soviet misbehavior). The result was a jumbled message read by both audiences, and neither the Kremlin nor the American public knew how to interpret or respond to it.[16]

Against this background, Vance met with Gromyko in Geneva in July to restart their discussions on a SALT agreement. Although the two negotiators made progress in dealing with the highly complex issue of modernizing strategic missiles, Soviet-American relations were strained through September. In the United States, the SALT talks also continued to be a bone of contention, with critics of the negotiations maintaining that they ignored the great progress the Soviets were making in terms of missile accuracy as well as the vulnerability of U.S. Minuteman missiles. Similarly, reports that Carter might declare a SALT II accord an executive agreement rather than submit it to the Senate for ratification angered lawmakers on Capitol Hill. As fall approached, then, the final outcome of the SALT negotiations was uncertain.

In the meantime, relations between the United States and its European allies had also become tense. West German Chancellor Helmut Schmidt, who had already collided with the president over his human rights policy and Germany's sale of a nuclear reactor to Brazil, even reproached the White House for not consulting its NATO partners in negotiating with Moscow. Schmidt's differences with Carter reached crisis proportions after the president decided not to go forward with the development of an enriched-radiation weapon (ERW) commonly known as the neutron bomb. Designed to deter a Soviet attack in Europe by enabling Western forces to destroy enemy tank concentrations without ravaging nearby population centers, the ERW was actually a nuclear warhead propelled by an artillery shell or a short-range missile. The warhead produced a surge of radiation, which would kill enemy forces without the blast, heat, and damage caused by other weapons emitting the same amount of radiation. Although a similar program had been cancelled in 1973, military planners were recommending in 1977 to begin full-scale production of ERWs.

Carter was faced with a difficult choice. On one hand, the neutron bomb offered a means to redress the military balance between NATO and the Warsaw Bloc without a long and costly buildup of NATO forces. Yet many Americans and Europeans regarded the concept of a weapon that killed people but preserved property as morally repugnant. Critics also maintained that deployment of ERWs would increase the chances of war since it implied an ability to wage, win, and recover from a nuclear attack. On 20 March, the eve of an important meeting of the NATO ambassadors, Carter spoke out for the first time against the weapon. The next day Brzezinski, Vance, and Defense Secretary Brown tried to persuade him to reconsider, arguing that it was essential for the cohesion of the alliance and for his own political standing that he go forward with the production and deployment of ERWs. But Carter remained adamant.

As the president's advisers had anticipated, Carter's announcement on 7 April that he was deferring production of the neutron bomb created a political tempest in the United States and throughout Western Europe. Americans and Europeans alike accused him of vacillation. As word leaked that his top advisers had urged him to reverse his decision, the furor grew even louder. On Capitol Hill, House and Senate leaders were flooded with angry telegrams from proponents of the bomb. Georgia Senator Sam Nunn warned that cancellation of the ERW program would "place in the minds of the Soviets the image of a timid and hesitant America which lacks the courage to confront the difficult choices ahead." Senate Minority Leader Howard Baker of Tennessee told reporters that cancellation would be "another in a long line of national defense mistakes" by the president: "First we gave away the B-1 bomber and now we are going to give away the neutron bomb." In Europe, Helmut Schmidt charged the president with betrayal, while other NATO leaders began privately to question American leadership.[17]

Much of the European uproar smacked of sanctimony. As the president told his advisers, one reason he put off a decision on the bomb was that none of the European powers had agreed to deploy the weapon on their own soil. Faced with strong left-wing opposition, European leaders sought to cut their political losses by making their support contingent on the failure of arms control. Chancellor Schmidt insisted that production of ERWs was "solely an American decision." Nevertheless, the president's action represented a significant setback in alliance relations that was not quickly resolved.

The fragile state of the international economy also took its toll on global amity. Following a brief recovery in late spring, the worldwide economic picture began to darken again over the summer. One recurring problem was the imbalance in world trade, particularly between the United States, Japan, and West Germany. In December, the Japanese had agreed to encourage more imports by stimulating their economy, but with an annual economic growth rate of 7 percent, they questioned whether there was much more they could do in this regard. Besides, they believed the United States' trade deficit was due primarily to the instability of the dollar and an inflation-driven demand for imports. Because Germany also blamed the United States' unfavorable balance of trade on its voracious consumption of oil, it too refused to expand its economy.

As the U.S. trade imbalance worsened, the free-fall of the dollar in foreign exchange markets resumed. When it became apparent that the trade deficit for 1978 would be larger than last year, a wild scramble began to unload dollars. By the end of June, the Japanese yen, the German mark, the French franc, and the British pound had all made substantial gains against the dollar, which forced those countries to intervene in foreign exchange markets in order to buy dollars and stabilize exchange rates.

The White House's primary strategy for dealing with the nation's trade and currency problems (aside from reducing oil imports) was to persuade its trading partners to do more to stimulate their domestic economies. That was the message the president took with him as he traveled to Bonn, West Germany, in July for another economic summit with world leaders. Since Carter's competence to handle domestic and global economic problems was under renewed attack at home and abroad, the administration attached great importance to the two-day conference in Bonn.

Results of the summit were mixed. Chancellor Schmidt agreed to recommend a tax cut in order to energize Germany's economy. The Japanese were also more forthcoming than the White House had expected. Just before the summit, Tokyo announced a $1-billion "emergency import" program to curb its massive export surplus. Yet no growth targets were set for the "locomotive economies" of the United States, Germany, or Japan (to use the metaphor Carter had employed at the London summit a year earlier). Nor were any solutions offered for redressing the world's trade imbalances or ending the turbulence in foreign exchange markets. The problems of sluggish economic growth, inflation, a weak dollar, excessive oil consumption, and trade protectionism continued to perplex and confound world leaders.

One example of a nagging economic predicament that refused to go away was revealed in the disappointing results of the multilateral trade negotiations (MTN), which, after almost five years, had just been concluded at Geneva. Although most of the five hundred negotiators from the ninety-eight countries represented at the talks termed this latest round a success, they failed to reach an agreement on such controversial issues as agricultural protectionism, agricultural and industrial subsidies, or the size of a tariff cut. Instead of providing for a new world trade system, which had been the original purpose of the MTN, the Geneva negotiations actually underscored the deep divisions still existing among the trading nations.

By the end of the summer, there was another run on the dollar. Some of the reasons for this latest attack on the American currency, such as the continuing trade imbalance and the deadlock on an energy bill, were depressingly familiar. But new ones included the perception that the summit had not come up with any dollar-strengthening proposals and persistent rumors that the petroleum-exporting nations were planning to stop pricing their oil in dollars, using instead a basket of strong currencies. More generally, the depreciating dollar was symptomatic of a continuing loss of confidence, even among the United States' closest allies, in its economic leadership. In terms of inflation, labor productivity, energy consumption, investment, and economic growth, Washington seemed incapable of managing its own economy, much less that of the world. As such, foreign investors were reluctant to gamble on the American dollar, causing it to drop and thereby undermining Carter politically at home.

By September, therefore, Carter faced mounting criticism internationally as well as domestically. Critics of the president took issue not only with his policies and programs but also how he conducted foreign affairs. To many Americans, including some who worked for him, Carter's foreign policy appeared inconsistent, directionless, and even contradictory. Neither the president nor his advisers as a group seemed to know what their foreign policy goals were. The division of authority between the State Department and the NSC was muddled, foreign policy issues were compartmentalized (for example, into arms control, human rights, détente, and Soviet policy in Africa) rather than integrated, and, in a change from Carter's first days in office, there was little sense of priorities. What applied, in other words, to Carter's domestic policy—lack of a coherent agenda tied to a series of clearly defined objectives—seemed to apply with equal force to the president's foreign policy.

8

★ ★ ★ ★ ★

WAR ON INFLATION

Domestically, inflation remained "public enemy number one" for the Carter administration as spring gave way to summer in 1978. All other endeavors were subordinated to winning the war against inflation, which surged by early summer to an annual rate of over 10 percent. Yet the results of the administration's efforts were not victory over inflation but the further alienation of Democratic constituencies that had voted for the president in 1976 and a continued deterioration of his rankings in the polls.

Overall, the economy grew nicely in the second quarter of 1978. Rebounding strongly from slow first-quarter growth, the GNP increased at an annual rate of 7 percent, industrial production at 15 percent, and retail sales at 25 percent. At the same time, unemployment held steady at about 6 percent, which was still under the rate of 6.2 percent projected by the CEA at the beginning of the year. Yet the White House and business and financial leaders were increasingly pessimistic about the economy. Although the administration and most private forecasters believed an outright recession (defined as two quarters of negative growth) was unlikely, many economists predicted a "growth recession," in which business would continue to expand, but so slowly (1 or 2 percent annually) that the unemployment rate would begin to rise.

By the end of the quarter, economic growth was already slowing down. Although the government's index of ten leading indicators, a major gauge of economic activity, still pointed upward, its performance was increasingly sporadic. Business and financial leaders were also disturbed by the cost of home mortgages, which had been advancing steadily and threatened the housing industry, and by a sharp jump in short-term borrowing costs when the Federal Reserve Board increased its discount rate from 6.5 percent to 7 percent.

No problem was more worrisome to the business community and the White House, however, than inflation. Even excluding higher mortgage rates and food prices, which had been climbing by more than 1 percent a month since the beginning of the year, inflation was still close to 7 percent and rising. In January, the administration had forecast an overall inflation rate of 6.2 percent for 1978 and 6 percent for 1979; it now refigured that rate to 7.25 percent for 1978 and 7.5 percent for 1979. By stepping on the monetary brakes, the FRB sought to curb inflation. But many economists, including the administration's own forecasters, feared that a too-restrictive monetary policy, coupled with a tight fiscal policy, could turn a mild slowdown into a full-fledged recession.

For that reason, the president was opposed to a growing movement on Capitol Hill to roll back his proposal for tax cuts and reforms amounting to $25 billion. Several polls had concluded that the American public, by an overwhelming margin, considered it more important to control inflation than to reduce federal taxes, even if meant a larger budget deficit. Lawmakers consequently argued for a smaller tax cut of $18 billion to $20 billion and the scrapping of most of the president's $10-billion tax reform.

Carter did not regard the size of the budget deficit as the major cause of inflation; rather, he attributed it to the "cycle of wage increases [and] price increases," which, he said, "kind of grow on one another." He further insisted that his program of tax cuts and reforms was needed to sustain economic growth and establish equity in a system that favored the rich. But there was such strong resistance to his tax proposals, even among Democrats on Capitol Hill, that he agreed to scale back his tax cut to $19.4 billion and to put off its effective date from 1 October to 1 January. In fact, he came to share the view prevalent on Capitol Hill that the tax cut should be trimmed in order to fight inflation, and in June 1978, he indicated that he would not object too strenuously if it was rolled back to $15 billion.

The White House remained convinced that the best way to deal with inflation was through voluntary wage and price controls, to keep wages and prices below the average of the previous two years. Responsibility for monitoring the program lay with the Council on Wage and Price Stability (COWPS) directed by Barry Bosworth, a thirty-five-year-old economist from the Brookings Institution. In a tactic known as "jawboning," COWPS and the White House applied public pressure on business and labor leaders to restrain price hikes and wage demands. A particular target of their campaign was hospital costs, which were rising at an annual rate of 15–16 percent, or about 5 percent more than the consumer price index (CPI). In April, the president proposed legislation to cap increases in hospital costs at about 11–12 percent, effective 1 October.

Almost immediately, the measure was attacked by the American Hospital Association, the American Medical Association, and other lobbyists for the health care and medical professions, who contended that the bill would lead to a decline in the quality of medical care. Even organized labor, which wanted to contain soaring health costs, feared that containment would come at the expense of hospital workers' wages. In July, a House committee gutted the legislation, endorsing instead a voluntary cost-cutting program suggested by the hospital industry itself. Defeated in the House, the president decided to carry the fight to the Senate, where the Human Resources Subcommittee had already reported out a bill drafted by its chairman, Senator Edward Kennedy, that was almost identical to the administration's proposal. But few political observers gave it much chance of reaching the Oval Office for Carter's signature.

The administration's drive for voluntary wage and price controls did not fare much better outside of Congress. Throughout the spring and summer, Carter, Bosworth, and other administration officials met regularly with leaders of business and labor in an effort to win their support for wage and price restraint. But prices and wages continued to rise. Business leaders accused the unions of making inflationary wage demands, while leaders of organized labor insisted that there had to be progress in holding down prices before they would agree to smaller increases in wages.

In August, Carter banished AFL-CIO President George Meany from the White House after Meany denounced a newly negotiated agreement with the postal unions that kept wages within the guidelines established by COWPS. Meany's attack on the contract guaranteed that the rank and file would turn it down when they voted on it the next week. The president was furious. "I don't want anybody else coming in here and telling me [Meany is] senile and didn't really mean what he said. He knows exactly what he is doing," Carter told aides after hearing of the labor leader's remarks.[1]

Some good news arrived from Capitol Hill at the end of July, when Congress approved a measure the president strongly favored: $1.65 billion in federal loan guarantees for New York City, so that the bankrupt metropolis could reenter public credit markets. Moreover, despite the opposition of labor unions representing government workers, the House and Senate also passed separate civil service reform bills incorporating Carter's proposals for a new merit system and more leeway for managers to fire incompetent employees. Lawmakers also failed to override the president's veto of a military procurement bill that included $2 billion for a nuclear aircraft carrier, which Carter maintained was not needed. That vote was particularly noteworthy because it was the first time the House and Senate had sustained a veto of a major defense authorization bill.

On taxes and other pieces of his legislative agenda, however, the president fought a losing battle with Congress. In August, the House approved a

$16-billion tax cut vigorously opposed by the administration. Stu Eizenstat referred to it as "the most regressive tax change ever proposed in Congress" because it catered to higher income taxpayers by reducing the capital gains tax (the tax paid on such assets as stocks, bonds, and real estate) from 49 percent to 35 percent.[2] The House also rejected most of the reforms Carter had proposed when he had first sent his tax program to Congress in January. Gone were his proposals for eliminating tax deductions, save for the disallowance of state and local gasoline taxes. Gone also was the president's recommendation for replacing the $750 personal exemption with a tax credit of $240. Instead, the House increased the personal exemption from $750 to $1,000, which, because of the progressive nature of the income tax, favored higher bracketed taxpayers.

Lawmakers also rejected what remained of Carter's proposals about welfare. Stonewalled on Capitol Hill, the president laid aside his plans for comprehensive reform. Instead, he signaled his support for a proposal that would make changes in existing welfare programs without overhauling the entire system. In June, the administration reached agreement with the House leadership on the broad outlines of legislation incorporating the principle of welfare reform within the existing welfare framework. But even this proposal failed to make it onto the House floor. Realizing the votes were not there for passage of the measure, House Speaker O'Neill announced he was putting off consideration of welfare reform for the remainder of the session.

In the midst of legislative struggles with Congress, Carter found himself drawn in the summer of 1978 into a bitter battle with Senator Kennedy over the explosive issue of national health insurance (NHI). While most Americans were covered by the Medicare and Medicaid programs or some form of private health insurance, 40 million Americans—mostly the working poor and the unemployed—still had little or no medical coverage when Carter took office. As a result, many Democrats, particularly organized labor, sought legislation that would provide insurance for all Americans. Seeking labor's support in his quest for the party's presidential nomination in 1976 and genuinely concerned about the inadequate health care of millions of Americans, Carter had called in April 1976 for a comprehensive and mandatory national health insurance system. Left unanswered, however, were such questions as how comprehensive the coverage should be, how it should be financed, and how it should be implemented.

Following his election, Carter's transition team identified two options for an NHI plan. The first provided for universal, federally financed health insurance; the second mandated private health insurance supplemented by federally financed coverage for catastrophic illness. Accompanying both plans were measures for curbing spiraling medical costs. Both options would also be phased-in over three years—and that was the rub. While the new president was committed to a comprehensive program, he wanted gradual implementation beginning in 1978, and then only as the budget would allow. But organized labor and liberal Democrats, especially Senator Kennedy, who for more than a decade had led the fight on Capitol Hill for NHI, wanted legislation enacted early in the new administration. In a major address in May before the annual convention of the United Auto Workers (UAW)— whose president, Douglas Fraser, was another leading proponent of NHI— Kennedy made clear his exasperation at Carter's decision not to introduce an NHI measure until 1978. "The American people," he said, "should not tolerate any delay on national health insurance."[3]

The president was caught between a rock and a hard place. He was scheduled to address the UAW the next day, and he was not eager to be upstaged by the Massachusetts senator or to sound as though he was reneging on his campaign promises. Moreover, he still needed and valued the support of Kennedy and other Democrats who had made NHI part of their liberal oath. Indeed, in the few months that he had been president, Carter had gone out of his way to consult with the senator, and Kennedy had responded by generally backing the president on such matters as tax reform and hospital cost containment.

Yet Carter's advisers distrusted Kennedy's liberal slant and political ambitions. "Kennedy is likely to represent the labor-liberal coalition on the ongoing NHI debate and to preserve differences with the Administration until late in the game," Hamilton Jordan warned the president. In addition, not only was the administration unprepared to submit a proposal to Congress at this stage, but the president was increasingly concerned about the inflationary impact of a comprehensive plan.[4]

Addressing the UAW, therefore, Carter promised "legislative proposals early next year," but he warned that any NHI program would be disastrous unless health care costs were tamed first. He also repeated his preference for a gradual phasing-in of health insurance, stated that the government could not "afford to do everything," and observed that the "achievement of all our goals depends on . . . a strong and growing economy." By the fall, however, Carter was contemplating not even introducing NHI legislation in the next session of Congress. His administration had made little progress in developing an insurance plan, and CEA Chairman Schultze had advised the president that, because of rising inflation and a sluggish economy, he should give NHI low priority when the House and Senate reconvened in January. The president reached the same conclusion. After discussing the details of a no-cost NHI program with HEW Secretary Joseph Califano, Jr., who was responsible for designing the proposal, Carter suggested to Califano that he (the president) might be able to satisfy advocates of NHI by pledging to have a bill ready by 1979.

This was wishful thinking. Kennedy, the UAW, and other proponents of NHI would not wait another year. Moreover, they disagreed with the White

House over some fundamentals of NHI; to discuss their differences, Carter called Kennedy to the White House. Although he promised that he would send an NHI measure to Congress late in 1978, the president stated plainly that he could not support the legislation favored by the senator and labor leaders, which provided for mandatory health benefits for all Americans paid for by payroll taxes and general revenues.

Over the next seven months, Kennedy met regularly with Carter, Califano, Eizenstat, and their staffs in an ongoing effort to resolve their differences. The president also met with UAW President Fraser and other union officials to discuss NHI options. But none of the principals involved were willing to compromise very much—certainly not the president, who had been told by congressional leaders that Congress would never agree to a substantial increase in federal spending or in the size of the federal bureaucracy to administer a national health plan.

Hitherto, relations between Carter and Kennedy had been amicable, but as the deadlock in negotiations continued, they became more critical of each other. According to Califano, at a meeting with Carter on 6 April, the Massachusetts senator "spoke in a tone so insistent that it was almost disdainful of the President." For his part, Carter rejected as "premature" Kennedy's proposal to establish a working group of administration officials, labor representatives, and members of his own staff to hammer out a bill.[5] The president recognized that he had to take some action on NHI this fiscal year, because, as Eizenstat reminded him, he could not back down from the pledge he had made to Kennedy and organized labor. But Eizenstat also warned him that proceeding with an NHI plan would be viewed on Capitol Hill as evidence of the administration's inconsistency—"talking about inflation and budget restraint one day and proposing what will be seen as an inflationary budget-busting scheme the next." Accordingly, he recommended to Carter that he state the principles on which national health care should be based but defer actual legislation until the next session. "It is one thing to honor a commitment," he said. "It is quite another to have the UAW and Kennedy dictate the date on which you send this proposal to us."[6]

Following Eizenstat's advice, Carter met with Kennedy in July in a final attempt to come to terms. The meeting was a disaster. In a concession to Carter, the senator indicated a willingness to accept a phasing-in of NHI *provided* the president agreed to a schedule for implementing a comprehensive plan regardless of economic or budgetary circumstances. Carter declined the offer. Meeting later with reporters, Kennedy accused the president of a "failure of leadership" that would cripple any national health care program from the start. The open split between Carter and Kennedy meant there would be no NHI legislation anytime soon. Given the state of the economy and the opposition to NHI on Capitol Hill, a consensus had already been building within the administration not to go forward with even a phased-in plan. The break with Kennedy and organized labor over the issue left the White House without any incentive to lobby for an idea whose time, it appeared, had passed.

The president's position on NHI was reasonable. Estimates for the comprehensive Kennedy-labor plan varied considerably, but even a modest version had a projected cost of at least $30 billion, which would have made a sham of Carter's endeavors to fight inflation. Even with the White House's backing, moreover, it was doubtful the House and Senate would have approved any plan, given its concern over inflation. Nevertheless, the Carter-Kennedy breach further divided the already fractured Democratic party and increased the likelihood of a Kennedy challenge for the party's nomination in 1980.

In other ways as well, the summer of 1978 appeared very much like the summer of 1977, when nothing seemed to go right for the White House. Dissatisfaction was rampant among traditional Democrats, and the president had to contend with two political brushfires involving members of his administration. First, UN Ambassador Andrew Young came under renewed attack for remarks he made during a newspaper interview. Referring to the trial of Soviet human rights dissident Anatoly Shcharansky, Young said there were "hundreds—perhaps even thousands—of people [in American prisons] whom I would call political prisoners." Barely a week later, Dr. Peter Bourne, Carter's chief health adviser and a close personal friend, was discovered to have prescribed Quaaludes, a powerful sedative, to one of his assistants who tried to fill the prescription using a fictitious name.

The White House did not allow storms to develop over these blunders—as it had in the past—but sought immediately to quell the public clamor Young and Bourne caused. Instead of rushing to Young's defense as before, Carter was persuaded by his staff to issue a release saying that statements on U.S. foreign policy "came from the President and the Secretary of State" and that Young's remarks did "not reflect the policies of this administration." Rather than stand by Bourne as he had stood by Lance earlier, the president accepted Bourne's resignation at once.

For those observers recalling the summer of 1977, however, there was a lingering sense of déjà vu—except that, a year earlier, Carter was still a popular president with an approval rating of between 60 percent and 70 percent. By 1978, only the South remained solidly behind him. In an ABC/Harris poll in August, 69 percent of the people surveyed did not approve of the job Carter was doing. Inflation remained the most compelling issue for the majority of Americans. Although the inflation rate declined from 11 percent in June to 6 percent in July as a result of a drop in food prices, the administration's own economists acknowledged that there was no significant price deceleration in any other area, nor was there much prospect of one in the months ahead. "Recent sharp increases in material costs will carry through subsequent production stages," Treasury Secretary Blumenthal informed the president in September.[7]

High taxes also claimed the attention of the American public. In fact, a taxpayers' revolt was taking place throughout the United States as largely white middle-class home owners called for cuts in property taxes and local government spending, both of which had burgeoned over the last decade. The taxpayers' revolt first attracted national attention in California, when Howard Jarvis, a successful seventy-five-year-old businessman, collected more than a million signatures to force a referendum on a proposal—Proposition 13—slashing property taxes by $7 billion and placing tight lids on the power of local government to raise revenues by other means. On 6 June, California voters stunned the nation by approving Proposition 13 by almost a two-to-one margin.

Movements began in other states to get similar proposals on the ballot. Potential presidential candidates, such as Republican congressman Jack F. Kemp of New York and Philip M. Crane of Illinois, tried to tap the tax revolt sentiment by mapping a national strategy firmly rooted in lowered taxes. The administration pointed to this taxpayer anger to validate its own commitment to budget cuts and tax reform. Ironically, by compelling Congress to pay greater attention to the tax-cutting demands of the middle class, Proposition 13 sealed the fate of the administration's tax reform and reduction proposals, aimed as they were toward low-income families.

Unquestionably, then, Carter faced a discouraging situation midway through his second year in office. Inflation had replaced economic recovery as the nation's major economic problem, but standard ways of handling inflation (higher taxes, higher interest rates, reduced federal spending, wage and price guidelines or controls) offended old-line Democrats. At the same time, the taxpayers' revolt—ostensibly a grassroots movement directed against local government—had national ramifications that made a more liberal fiscal policy politically untenable even had the president been so inclined.

Increasingly concerned about his declining political fortunes and his dwindling popular support, Carter took several steps over the summer to boost his public image. In July, he appointed Gerald Rafshoon, the successful Atlanta advertising executive who had earlier directed his media campaign for governor and president, as his assistant for communications. Rafshoon's express purpose was to change the public's perception of the president. Believing that the American people did not know Carter well enough, Rafshoon raised the president's visibility, even televising a "town meeting" from Berlin during Carter's visit to Germany in July. Denying that he was emphasizing image and style rather than substance, he nevertheless created a "public activity plan" for Carter and coached him on what he should say and how he should say it. "You should be serious, methodical, purposeful—working hard and *successfully,* on a *few* of the most important problems facing our country," he instructed the president soon after joining the administration. Rafshoon quickly established himself as one of Carter's top advisers along with Jordan, Powell, Eizenstat, and Moore.[8]

Rafshoon's arrival also signaled the end of the most extensive shake-up of the White House staff since Carter took office. As part of this shuffle, Midge Costanza, the administration's outspoken and often controversial advocate for the Equal Rights Amendment (ERA),[9] resigned after losing most of her staff. The president's appointments secretary, Tim Kraft, was moved to the senior staff and given the task of liaison to the Democratic party, itself a recognition by the administration that its relations with party regulars needed to be improved. As part of a similar and ongoing effort to repair relations with Congress, Frank Moore was assigned additional staff and authority, even though many congressional Democrats thought Carter's major problem on Capitol Hill was Moore himself.

By September, the White House reorganization and Rafshoon's public relations campaign appeared to be having some effect. Lawmakers returning from an August recess reported continued goodwill for Carter among their constituents despite lingering doubts about his competency. There was even concern expressed that criticism of the president had gotten out of hand. After visiting New England and the Rocky Mountain states, Haynes Johnson of the *Washington Post* relayed "an underlying sense of sympathy for the president." As a result of reports like these, the mood at the White House turned noticeably upbeat. "There's a feeling in the country," Rafshoon commented, "that the President is trying hard. . . . There's more understanding of his problems and how he's trying to deal with them."[10]

Attitudes at the White House changed from upbeat to downright euphoric when, just two weeks later, President Carter appeared before Congress to announce the successful conclusion of the historic Camp David accords between Egyptian President Sadat and Israeli Prime Minister Begin.[11] In the first few weeks after Camp David, it seemed as if the administration had been born again. The president's new popularity was evident in the polls, which leaped by as much as 15 percent in less than a month, and in his junkets on behalf of Democratic candidates seeking election in November. Traveling to New Jersey, the Carolinas, and the Midwest, an exuberant and exhilarated Carter was greeted by huge crowds wherever he went.

On Capitol Hill, the Senate finally passed the president's watered-down energy legislation, which he had submitted to Congress eighteen months earlier. The measure had been held up since the spring over the issue of natural gas deregulation. Although a conference committee had reached a compromise on deregulation in May, it took until the end of July for congressional staffers to translate the agreement into legislative language. It then took another month to sway enough votes in the conference committee so that it would send the beleaguered gas bill to the full House and Senate.

The battle that followed in the Senate was brutal, as senators on both sides of the issue droned on, repeating the same arguments day after day. Kennedy, who by now had broken with Carter over NHI and the administration's conservative fiscal policies, called the compromise "an absolute monstrosity." He was joined in opposition by such unlikely bedfellows as Republicans John Tower of Texas and Clifford P. Hansen of Wyoming. But at the end of September, the Senate approved the conference committee report.[12]

In the House, the struggle was nearly as intense. The crucial vote was on a rule to allow the House to consider the energy legislation as a single package. Throughout the long months of debate over energy, House Speaker Tip O'Neill had kept to the strategy of treating energy legislation as a unit rather than dividing it into separate measures, as the Senate had done. Accordingly, he wanted the House to vote on gas deregulation together with the other remnants of the energy program. But his tactic of a single-package vote had to be approved by the House Rules Committee and then by the full House. On 13 October, the committee passed the rule after a night of heated debate. Later that day, the full House followed suit by one vote, 207 to 206.

Once the House agreed not to split gas deregulation from the more popular parts of the energy package, the rest of the congressional debate was anticlimactic. In the Senate, retiring Democrat James Abourezk of South Dakota, a key critic of the gas bill, held up final action on the legislation with a three-day filibuster against the conference committee report. But he gave up when he realized that he was only angering colleagues anxious to return home to campaign. With the filibuster ended, lawmakers sent the five-part energy program to the president on 15 October, thereby ending its long odyssey through the halls of Congress.

The legislation that Carter signed into law was hardly "the moral equivalent of war" he described when he first sent his plan to Capitol Hill in April 1977. Nor was the Senate's last vote on gas deregulation "the most important decision" the Senate would make in the 95th Congress, as Carter said it would be when lobbying on behalf of deregulation. Most of the original proposals, which had been based on the principle of conservation through taxation rather than through deregulation and tax credits, had been either scaled back or, like the crude oil equalization tax, eliminated entirely.[13] Yet the final package was still a momentous accomplishment. By deregulating natural gas and establishing a single price structure for intra- and interstate gas, Congress made important strides toward conserving gas and distributing it more rationally. It also encouraged energy conservation and the expanded use of nonfossil fuels through various tax credits. Most significant, it attempted to grapple with a problem that only promised to worsen if left unattended.

Carter had been instrumental in maneuvering his energy program through Congress. To get the gas deregulation measure out of the conference committee, he had brokered a deal with Senator James B. McClure of Idaho.

In exchange for McClure's vote, the president agreed to soften his position on so-called breeder reactors. Because these nuclear reactors produced plutonium that remained radioactive for thousands of years, Carter had vetoed an authorization bill in 1977 providing $150 million in start-up costs for the construction of a demonstration breeder plant on the Clinch River, near Oak Ridge, Tennessee. Over the next six months, he continued to fight with Congress over the Clinch River project. But to obtain McClure's assent on gas deregulation, he agreed to withhold his opposition until a feasibility study was completed on a more modern breeder reactor using a fuel other than plutonium.

In lobbying for the energy legislation, Carter was ably assisted by the Democratic leadership on Capitol Hill. Yet it was his telephone calls and personal messages, his meetings and his staff's sessions with lawmakers and influential business, labor, and community leaders that made the difference. Almost all observers agreed that the conferees' crucial compromise on deregulation and the passage of the House rule would not have been possible without this patient but persistent intervention by the president and his staff.

The energy bill was only one of a rash of measures Congress approved just before adjourning in the middle of October. Another was an $18.7-billion tax cut. Like the energy bill, the tax legislation signed into law by Carter bore little resemblance to the tax reform proposals the administration had recommended at the beginning of the year; the House had turned down most of these in August. In September the Senate Finance Committee added insult to injury by approving cuts in capital gains taxes broader than those passed by the House and increasing the total tax reduction (by providing relief for virtually every taxpayer) to an estimated $22.6 billion—or about $3 billion more than the administration was now willing to accept. Nevertheless, by going head-to-head with Senate Finance Committee Chairman Russell Long and House Ways and Means Committee Chairman Al Ullman, the president was able to fashion a bill that provided greater relief for lower- and middle-income taxpayers than the measure approved by the House and, at the same time, cost well under $20 billion.

Going into the 1978 elections, few could doubt Carter's political momentum. Not only was he having considerable success on Capitol Hill, but his public image synchronized with the message the American people seemed to be sending to Washington—distrust of big and wasteful government, hostility to special interest groups, opposition to more and higher taxes, insistence on economic frugality and greater local responsibility, and an emphasis on personal values. The White House felt confident, therefore, that the November elections would be a triumphant referendum on Carter's presidency.

Carter's renewed political respectability, however, could not mask some grim realities. In particular, the president's brand of populism, while in line with the conservative drift of American voters, was not in accord with the views of key liberal Democratic blocs. In October, leaders from more than one hundred of these groups assembled in Detroit to counter the growing thunder from the political right and to hold Carter to his 1976 campaign promises. Although UAW President Fraser, who had been responsible for arranging the meeting, tried to reassure the White House that the gathering was not the birth of a "Dump Carter" movement, the labor leader had to work hard to squelch talk among the attendees of bolting the Democratic party or courting Kennedy for the Democratic nomination in 1980.

Carter's relations with one of the groups represented at the meeting, the Congressional Black Caucus, had become especially nasty. From the outset, black leaders had been critical of the president, complaining that he had abandoned blacks even though they had been responsible for his election in 1976. In fact, Carter had done nothing of the sort. During his presidential campaign, he had pledged to increase the number of black and other minority candidates for federal judgeships, and this he had done. By the time he left office in 1981, Carter had appointed more blacks (twenty-eight) and Hispanics (fourteen) to the federal judiciary than any other president before him, raising the percentage of black federal judges from 4 percent in 1977 to 9 percent in 1981. His administration also channeled more government contracts to minority firms, boosted substantially the amount of federal deposits in minority-owned banks, strengthened the Justice Department's enforcement of the voting rights statutes, and increased the effectiveness of the Equal Employment Opportunity Commission in settling job discrimination cases. But most of the president's efforts to assist blacks and other minority groups were undertaken through executive and agency action rather than through legislative initiatives, and their greatest impact was on mid- and upper-income minorities, not the poor.[14]

Consequently, the Congressional Black Caucus accused the administration of being unresponsive to the fundamental needs of most blacks and even attacked Carter's record on civil rights and federal appointments. In a lengthy document sent to the president at the end of September, the caucus listed some of their grievances with the administration. The lawmakers charged that there had been less federal funding for housing and economic development programs under Carter than under Nixon and Ford; that the administration's urban policy provided few direct benefits for poorer people or areas; that the administration had not done enough to create new jobs; that Carter had never given a major speech on civil rights; and that he had made only "limited Black appointments to top positions, [noting] particularly the absence of Blacks in top economic positions."[15]

In September 1978, leaders of the Congressional Black Caucus met with the president to discuss these issues but also to chastise Carter for not throwing his weight behind the Humphrey-Hawkins full employment bill. Carter had supported this measure, in which government provided "last resort" jobs if needed to guarantee full employment, when it was before Congress in the fall of 1977. But he did so only after considerable prodding from black leaders and organized labor. He also insisted on provisions that took into account the need to deal with inflation. In effect, the president sidestepped a frontal attack on unemployment through specific job-creating measures by the government.

Nevertheless, the black caucus made administration support for Humphrey-Hawkins, which had passed the House in March 1978 but was now tied up in the Senate, the test of its commitment to a black agenda. Carter and Vice-President Mondale told the group that the president had always regarded full employment as a "top priority" but that there were other urgent matters, such as producing an energy bill and curbing inflation. The caucus members warned that the White House would be blamed if Congress failed to pass Humphrey-Hawkins. When Carter and Mondale heatedly challenged that assertion, Congressman John Conyers of Michigan stalked out of the meeting in anger. After Conyers left, the chairman of the Congressional Black Caucus, Parren J. Mitchell of Maryland, and Ron Dellums of California took up the argument. According to Mitchell, he and Mondale engaged in a shouting match.

Surprised by what had taken place, both Mitchell and the White House tried to patch up their differences. Mitchell set up another meeting between black lawmakers and the president, at which Carter agreed to work harder for the Humphrey-Hawkins bill. In keeping with this promise, the president pressured Senate leaders to complete action on the legislation. At the same time, Hamilton Jordan arranged a White House conference with lobbyists from a number of black organizations to "demonstrate Administration activity" on behalf of the measure.[16]

On 15 October, the Senate approved the Humphrey-Hawkins legislation, but the final product was a bitter disappointment to its original proponents. Although the goal of reducing unemployment was intact, the Senate added another goal of lowering the rate of inflation to 3 percent by 1983 and eliminating it entirely by 1988. Backers of the bill feared that the inflation objective would undermine the measure's primary purpose of stemming unemployment. Many black leaders were grateful for the White House's assistance in forcing senatorial action on the bill, but there was also resentment that the administration had not worked earlier and harder on behalf of the legislation.

Likewise, feminist leaders were disappointed with the administration, even though Carter's record on most women's issues—as on many of the issues raised by black leaders—was actually good. As a presidential candidate in 1976, he had campaigned for the Equal Rights Amendment, which Congress had passed in 1972 but which still had to be ratified by four more states. As president, he supported legislation providing funding for a National Women's Conference in Texas in 1977 and then gave his firm endorsement to its agenda for achieving women's rights. In addition, he established an Interagency Task Force on Women and a National Advisory Council for Women and strongly backed an extension of the seven-year limit for passage of the ERA when it became apparent that not enough states would approve it within that time. Keeping his campaign pledge to appoint women to top positions in his administration, he not only selected Patricia Harris and Juanita Kreps for his cabinet but also named significantly more women to high-level posts, including federal judgeships, than any previous president had.

Moreover, Rosalynn Carter blazed new trails in assuming a major role in the administration. She frequently substituted for Carter at ceremonial affairs, advised him on important policy matters, and helped plan political strategy. In June 1977, she visited seven Latin American countries as an official envoy of the United States and conducted high-level negotiations with foreign leaders on such issues as the arms buildup in Peru, human rights violations in Brazil, and drug trafficking in Colombia. She also often participated in NSC briefings on foreign affairs. Domestically, she pushed aggressively for the Equal Rights Amendment, making dozens of calls to lawmakers in states where it was under consideration and traveling throughout the country to drum up support on its behalf. According to the president, both his staff and the news media understood that she could speak for him "with authority."[17]

Nevertheless, many of the women who had worked for Carter's election in 1976 accused the president of relying too much on his wife and daughter-in-law to secure ERA passage instead of doing his own campaigning. They were also angry at Carter's opposition to federal funding of abortion except in cases of rape, incest, or when a woman's life was in danger—a stance he had maintained even as a candidate. And, like many black leaders, they were concerned that the president was sacrificing economic and social programs that benefited the poor, including working mothers and single parents, in order to fight inflation.

Despite these differences with black leaders, feminists, and other liberal groups, the most serious political question for Carter in the fall of 1978 was how blue-collar workers, professionals, businesspeople, consumers, and farmers—that is, the millions of Americans who had voted for the president in 1976 precisely because he was not tied to traditional politics—viewed his administration's success in dealing with inflation. By every economic indicator, inflation was getting worse. From August to September, producer prices, which often set the stage for consumer prices, shot up at a yearly rate of 11.4 percent. Additional price hikes were announced by manufacturers of tractors and automobiles as well as producers of copper, lead, aluminum, and stainless steel goods.

Given the rate of inflation by October and the fact that even the administration's own economists did not anticipate much improvement in the coming months, the White House realized it had to reevaluate its system of voluntary wage and price controls, which were simply not working. Unwilling to abandon the program entirely, the administration switched to explicit numerical standards for wage and price increases and for specific government actions that would be triggered when the standards were exceeded.

On 24 October, the president went on national television to announce "phase two" of his anti-inflation program. Increases in wages and fringe benefits, he told the American people, would be limited to 7 percent, and prices would go no higher than .5 percent below a firm's average annual rate of increase for 1976/77. The budget deficit for 1979 would be held to $30 billion "or less." COWPS would announce specific price targets for the nation's major industries and would scrutinize the prices, wages, and profits of the nation's four hundred largest corporations. In what Carter described as "real wage insurance," workers whose wages were kept below 7 percent in a given year would get a tax rebate if inflation exceeded 7 percent during the year. Through these and other measures, the White House hoped to cut the rate of inflation to 6.5 percent in 1979.

Following his televised address, Carter appointed Alfred Kahn as the chairman of COWPS and his chief inflation-fighter. Kahn was a sixty-one-year-old former professor of economics at Cornell who, as chairman of the Civil Aeronautics Board, had made his mark on Washington by deregulating many airline operations and making the industry more competitive. Carter was attracted to him because of his own populist-progressive conviction that deregulation was a way to simplify government and unleash the efficiencies of the marketplace.

The administration arrived at its new anti-inflation strategy only after considerable debate among its top economic advisers over the size of the budget reduction required by the plan. That there had to be a major cut in the deficit was never in question. However, Treasury Secretary Michael Blumenthal wanted the president to state publicly that he intended to reduce the 1980 budget deficit to the $30-billion range. At the same time, Eizenstat and CEA Chairman Schultze feared that if the budget was cut too drastically (to around $30 billion), it could lead to a recession, which would actually increase the deficit. In the end, Blumenthal's fiscal conservatism prevailed.

In announcing his new assault on inflation, the president knew there would be an intense struggle among congressional Democrats over the size of the budget deficit and the programs that would be cut. But the reaction was worse than he expected, and it came not only from Democrats on Capitol Hill but also from business and financial leaders in the United States and abroad, who thought the program was still too weak and argued that the basic cause of inflation was not rising wages or prices but excessive demand for goods and services. Reflecting this displeasure, Wall Street was hit with a wild selling spree immediately after the president's speech, driving the Dow-Jones average down by almost 10 percent. Even more serious, the dollar plunged against gold and other currencies, as gold shot up $17 an ounce to $243 in five days. The continued slide of the dollar, Treasury Secretary Blumenthal warned in a news interview, would undermine any chance that phase two might succeed.

Taken aback at the dollar's fall, Carter summoned reporters to the White House press room on 1 November and announced that the cascading dollar threatened the world economy and that additional steps were being taken to prevent its collapse. Treasury Secretary Blumenthal then outlined the new measures, which included raising the discount rate by a full percentage point to 9.5 percent (the sharpest jump in forty-five years), reducing funds available to banks for loans by $3 billion, increasing reserves of foreign currencies by $30 billion, and stepping up monthly gold sales. By tightening credit, the White House hoped to convince investors that it was determined to stop inflation even at the risk of recession. By stockpiling foreign reserves and selling gold, it also intended to demonstrate its resolve to protect the dollar against unwarranted speculation.

In contrast to the president's address on 24 October, initial response to this plan was highly favorable. The stock market soared a record thirty-five points on a single day, while the dollar appreciated 7–10 percent against all major currencies. But the elation was short-lived. Although the dollar was still gaining ground, by week's end stock and bond prices had retreated. Within a few weeks, the dollar also began to come under heavy selling pressure. By the end of December, it had lost about half its November gains, and the administration had begun to cut into its $30-billion support fund.

Meanwhile, Carter was losing the fight against inflation. The year ended with an overall inflation rate of 9 percent. Food prices finished 10 percent higher than the year before, with the cost of meat up by over 18 percent. Although many economists expected inflation to slow in 1979, few believed it would dip below 7 percent. Moreover, any drop would be the result of tighter credit and a slowdown in the growth of the money supply, not the administration's guidelines. Accordingly, there was a consensus among business leaders that the economy would either be sluggish or actually drift into recession. Although the White House was generally more optimistic, the CEA raised its forecast for inflation in 1979 from 6.5 percent to 7 percent.

It was still far too early to evaluate the effectiveness of the administration's wage and price standards, which by year's end were only beginning to be implemented. But there were signs of trouble here as well, since some guidelines were already being bent. In December COWPS modified the 7-percent cap on wages to exclude automatic increases in health and pension benefits. Although COWPS hoped this action would make the rules more acceptable to organized labor, its decision threatened to open a Pandora's box of additional exclusions.

Even with the concession, many labor leaders remained adamant against the guidelines, none more so than AFL-CIO President George Meany. In November, Meany had written Kahn requesting a public hearing on the new wage and price standards, but he was turned down. Then Meany let the White House know that he wanted to discuss the wage and price strictures with the president. He indicated that he might support the program if the wage level exempted from the cap was raised from $4 an hour to $5 an hour. Kahn, Eizenstat, and CEA Chairman Schultze urged the president to meet with Meany, but the president first wanted assurances that the labor leader would support his anti-inflation measures. "Right now Meany looks like shit," he remarked, "and we look good and he knows it." Rebuffed, Meany became more obstreperous in his opposition to the wage and price standards.[18]

By year's end, Democratic liberals were also preparing to do battle with the administration over the budget. Even though Carter had pledged to hold the deficit for fiscal 1980 to $30 billion or less, he had also promised NATO allies in May to increase defense spending by 3 percent over inflation. This meant that most of the $15 billion in budget cuts would have to come from domestic programs. Reductions of that size could push the economy into recession. To liberals, therefore, the administration was offering an economic prescription that might well have been written by the Republican party. Not only could it lead to economic disaster, it would mean a renunciation of the Democratic party's commitment to minorities, the poor, and the underprivileged. Even the president's advocacy of deregulation as part of his anti-inflation strategy appeared to many Democrats as a convenient excuse for relaxing protection against job hazards, toxic emissions, and pollution of the land and waterways.

Election results from November 1978 offered little solace for Carter or for liberals on Capitol Hill. Although Democrats remained in firm control of both houses of Congress and the majority of gubernatorial offices, five Democratic liberals in the Senate—Dick Clark of Iowa, Floyd Haskell of Colorado, Wendell Anderson of Minnesota, Thomas McIntyre of New Hampshire, and William Hathaway of Maine—and one moderate Republican—Edward Brooke of Massachusetts—were defeated in their bids for reelection. Yet such right-wing Republicans as Strom Thurmond of South Carolina, Jesse Helms of North Carolina, and James McClure of Idaho were returned to office. Joining them were newly elected conservatives Roger Jepsen of Iowa, Gordon Humphrey of New Hampshire, William Armstrong of Colorado, and Thad Cochran of Mississippi.

Although the rightward shift by voters was likely to signal greater support on Capitol Hill for the fiscal restraint Carter wanted, it did not mean the end of his strife with Congress. The Democrats defeated in the Senate had generally supported the administration, and they were being replaced by some of the staunchest foes of the president's policies. In the previous Congress, Carter had been able to count on the occasional endorsement of Minority Leader Howard Baker, who had been indispensable to his victories on the Panama Canal treaties. Now Baker would find it politically more hazardous to come to the president's aid. "It's a new ballgame," one moderate Republican commented after the election. "It doesn't take much to change things around."[19]

As 1978 came to a close, the president's position was increasingly precarious. Attacked by Democratic liberals for being too conservative, he faced a new Congress that was more conservative and more partisan than the 95th Congress. Although his political future largely depended on his success in curbing federal spending, he could hardly to so without further embittering major Democratic constituencies. Even within the administration, there was considerable grumbling about the impending budget cuts. Labor Secretary Ray Marshall cautioned that the cuts should not fall too heavily on job-creation programs, because the administration would "have to prove that putting people on unemployment and welfare [was] less inflationary than giving them jobs." Stu Eizenstat's Domestic Policy Staff concurred, adding that it was "crucial to the Administration's credibility that youth funding not be cut in this year of rising unemployment." In a similar vein, HUD Secretary Patricia Harris sent a sharply worded memo to OMB stating that she could not live with proposed reductions in her department.[20]

It was no wonder, then, that many political analysts predicted a divisive contest over the president's budget when the 96th Congress convened in January and that others speculated openly about Carter's vulnerability to a Democratic challenger in 1980.

9

★ ★ ★ ★ ★

CRESCENT OF CRISIS

Jimmy Carter's most significant foreign policy success in his first two years as president occurred at Camp David during early September 1978, when President Anwar Sadat of Egypt and Prime Minister Menachem Begin of Israel agreed to a framework of peace for the Middle East that promised to end thirty years of hostilities between Israel and its Arab neighbors. Even more than the signing of the Panama Canal treaties, Camp David was hailed throughout the world as a monumental diplomatic accomplishment. For Carter, who had brought Sadat and Begin together and had then been instrumental in hammering out an agreement, the accords reached by the two Mideast leaders were a personal triumph and his administration's crowning achievement.

The administration's strategy for a Mideast settlement had been based on close collaboration with Sadat and separate negotiations with Begin, in the hope that Israel would soften its position on the occupied territories. The result was not compromise but impasse. Over the first six months of 1978, Carter tried to restart the negotiations, to no avail. Begin refused to guarantee the residents of the West Bank and Gaza Strip eventual autonomy even after Sadat agreed to allow Israel to maintain security forces in these territories during a transitional period. The Israeli leader's position had not altered one dot since December: limited home rule for the West Bank and Gaza Strip for three to five years, after which Israel would review the arrangement and evaluate how it was working.

Afraid of renewed conflict in the Mideast, Carter sought to bridge the chasm between Egypt and Israel. At the beginning of July, Vice-President Mondale visited Israel and then traveled to Alexandria where he conferred with Sadat. Both Begin and Sadat agreed to a personal request from Carter to send their foreign ministers to London later that month for a meeting arranged and presided over by Vance. However, the London session did not produce any concrete proposal for resolving the core issues separating Israel and Egypt. Then a secret meeting in Vienna between Sadat, Shimon Peres (the leader of Israel's opposition Labor party), and Israeli Defense Minister Ezer Weizman backfired. Although Begin had give his approval for the discussions, the Israeli cabinet censured Peres and Weizman for allegedly negotiating without authority and for using the peace process to further their own ambitions. Sadat was stung and retaliated by ordering out the nine-man Israeli military mission that had remained in Egypt since official talks had been broken off in February.

For Vance and his staff, the London episode confirmed that the United States would have to change its role in the search for a Mideast accord. "We felt that there was no use in continuing to try to mediate [an] Egyptian-Israeli agreement on the general principles of peace," the secretary later remarked. Instead, Vance began to think in terms of an American proposal for a comprehensive settlement that would include an Egyptian-Israeli peace and an autonomy plan for the West Bank.[1]

After Sadat's expulsion of the Israeli mission, Vance and President Carter decided that the secretary of state should go to the Mideast once more. Despite a vitriolic public exchange between Sadat and Begin, Sadat still seemed anxious to bring the United States back into the negotiating process. Faced with a cabinet sharply divided over the occupied territories, Begin also seemed to welcome a new American initiative. Although the President and Vance originally conceived of the Mideast trip as a "rescue mission" to breathe new life into the negotiations, Carter decided to take the bold move of inviting both Begin and Sadat to a summit meeting at Camp David. The president had concluded that the only way an agreement between Israel and Egypt could be reached was to bring the principals together for as long as it took to work out their differences. Once that was achieved, the door would be open to a general Mideast settlement.

Camp David was a gamble for the president. Although Begin and Sadat accepted Carter's invitation almost immediately, chances were that they would not see eye to eye on anything. Failure of the Camp David talks would only add to the public perception of an ineffectual president. In addition, Camp David violated a cardinal rule of summitry: Heads of state did not come together until after agreements had been worked out at lower levels of government, so that summits were largely ceremonial.

Carter prepared for the Camp David meeting with the same diligence and thoroughness with which he approached any major undertaking. Vance and Brzezinski thought the president's main task should be to persuade Begin to make concessions on the Palestinian question, but Carter believed that he should concentrate on achieving an Egyptian-Israeli accord without linking it to progress on this perennial stumbling block. Consequently, he directed the American team accompanying him at Camp David to "assume as our immediate ambition" a peace agreement between Egypt and Israel.[2]

Sadat and Begin arrived at Camp David on 5 September and were housed in separate cottages. The talks got off to an inauspicious start. There was little chemistry between Carter and Begin, whom the president described as rigid, unimaginative, and more concerned with particulars than with the larger picture of a Middle East settlement. Even his first session with his good friend Sadat did not go well, as Carter was disappointed by Sadat's insistence that no agreement was possible until Israel withdrew from all the occupied lands.[3]

In coming to Camp David, the Egyptian leader was at a disadvantage. Although Begin could leave the summit at any time without penalty, the Egyptian leader had incurred the wrath of the other Arab nations and risked his own political future by his peace initiative; he could not return home empty-handed. His hope was that Carter could force Begin into a crucial easing of Israeli demands. But Sadat underestimated the Israeli leader's ability to resist pressure even in face-to-face talks with the American president. Because Begin was a stickler for detail, he was also far less ready to compromise on specific issues than Sadat, who became bored by details and preferred to deal in more general terms.

At first, the president met with the two leaders together. But because they did not get along, he soon began conferring with them separately, thinking he might be able to break down the mistrust and animosity that had developed between them. But no progress was made until 12 September, when Carter presented Sadat with a four-page proposal for an Egyptian-Israeli peace treaty, the key sentence of which provided for restoration of "full Egyptian sovereignty . . . in the Sinai." The Egyptian leader considered the draft largely acceptable, but the next day, Begin flatly rejected it and stated that he would never agree to the removal of Israeli settlements from the Sinai.

The critical moment in the Camp David summit had arrived. Carter had brought Begin and Sadat to the pastoral surroundings of Camp David with the idea that the two leaders would come to trust and work with each other. Instead, they were not even on speaking terms. Then Sadat announced on 15 September that he was preparing to leave immediately for Egypt. Informed that the Egyptian delegation to Camp David was already packing its bags, Carter hurried to Sadat's cottage and warned him that the American people would hold the Egyptian leader responsible for the failure of the Camp David summit. Relations between the United States and Egypt would deteriorate, peacekeeping efforts would end, and his own administration would be discredited. Shaken by the force of Carter's argument, Sadat agreed to continue the negotiations.

Events then moved quickly. Israeli Defense Minister Weizman raised the possibility that Israel might give up its airfields in the Sinai if the United States would help build new airfields in the Negev Desert. The president indicated he would go along with such a deal provided Israel relinquished its settlements in the Sinai. Under tremendous pressure even from his own cabinet, Begin relented. On 17 September, during the twelfth day of negotiations, he told Carter that within two weeks he would have the Knesset vote on whether or not the settlements should be removed and that he would abide by its decision. Carter persuaded Sadat to accept this arrangement. The major obstacle to a Sinai agreement had now been removed.

Less successful were concurrent negotiations on other disputed issues, most notably the Palestinian problem and the Israeli occupation of the West Bank and Gaza. Egypt wanted a commitment from Israel to withdraw from the territories by a specified date and to grant the Palestinians in the West Bank and Gaza autonomy; Begin refused. Instead, he and Sadat finessed the matter by agreeing to an ambiguous "framework for peace," which Carter had prepared a week earlier when the summit seemed about to collapse. This second accord provided for a transitional period of no more than five years, during which Egypt, Israel, and Jordan would determine the final status of the territories based on "full autonomy" and a "self-governing authority" for the inhabitants of the two areas. Their negotiations would also be predicated on the principles of UN Resolution 242—though the pact did not spell out what that actually meant.[4]

After thirteen days, then, Carter was able to announce publicly that a consensus had been reached at Camp David calling for the signing of a peace treaty between Egypt and Israel and providing the basis for a Mideast settlement—a prize that had eluded peacemakers for more than thirty years. The signing of the Camp David accords, at a White House ceremony carried by all the major television networks, represented the high point of the Carter presidency. The summit was widely hailed as a shining triumph, and Carter was singled out for plaudits. Prime Minister Begin, President Sadat, the news media covering the summit, and the American public all acknowledged what the president had accomplished.

But even as Carter was being acclaimed, some observers expressed reservations about the pacts. Several commentators pointed out that nothing was said in the "framework for peace" about the building of new Israeli settlements on the West Bank and Gaza. In addition, the Camp David agreements assumed that Jordan and the Palestinians living in the occupied lands would participate in the negotiations over the West Bank and Gaza. Yet King Hussein had stated several times that he would not enter into the peace process until Israel returned East Jerusalem, a condition the Israelis would never accept. Furthermore, the two accords signed at Camp David were replete with ambiguous terms and provisions, which would make future talks extremely difficult. For example, the negotiators were expected to consider the "resolution of the Palestinian problem in all its aspects," as well as "other outstanding issues" concerning the West Bank and Gaza. But the documents did not specify what these other "aspects" or "outstanding issues" were.

In fairness to Carter, he had clearly accomplished his primary purpose at Camp David: to establish a basis for future negotiations. The Egyptian-Israeli accord was possible precisely because it did gloss over many of the most acrimonious issues blocking peace in the Middle East. Once these two enemies had agreed to a conciliatory framework, Carter hoped the other moderate Arab nations, particularly Saudi Arabia, would join the peace process. When that happened, he believed, the remaining obstacles to a Mideast settlement could be resolved. Perhaps the president was naive to think peace was attainable in that troubled region, but what better alternative was there?

The fact remains, though, that the Camp David agreements were dangerously vague, that they were based almost as much on faith as on a hard assessment of Mideast politics, and that, by papering over key differences between Egypt and Israel, they set up a diplomatic mine field that could very well explode in Carter's face. Amity required that the Arabs and Israelis proceed with more care and goodwill than they had previously displayed, and beyond the jubilation of the moment, there was hardly any reason to expect such a change in behavior. Despite their public professions, Sadat and his chief aides were keenly disappointed by the results of Camp David. Egypt had obtained an Israeli commitment to withdraw from the Sinai and its rich oil fields, but Israel had remained silent about the other occupied territories and the Palestinians. Sadat returned to Egypt, therefore, with little that would entice any of the other Arab leaders to a conference table with Israel.

By December, the fragility of the Camp David accords became apparent. Although Egyptian and Israeli negotiators had set 17 December as the deadline for a peace agreement between their two nations, talks soured very quickly after Israel announced the construction of new settlements on the West Bank. In an effort to meet the target date, Secretary Vance traveled to the Mideast and engaged in six days of shuttle diplomacy between Cairo and Jerusalem. But nothing came of this activity; in fact, Israeli leaders accused the White House of taking Egypt's side in the negotiations.

By early 1979, the Mideast peace process had broken down completely. In a lengthy memorandum to Carter, Hamilton Jordan attributed the depression again enveloping the White House to the Middle East stalemate. "Not only have the Israeli-Egyptian negotiations taken much of our time, energy, and resources," he told the president, "the recent growing concern that all that has been accomplished might somehow be lost has had a very negative effect on the attitude and morale of our foreign policy team."[5]

Yet as Carter realized, Egypt and Israel remained anxious to come to terms. Both Begin and Sadat understood that failure to sign a peace treaty would strengthen the hand of the hard-line Arab states (Syria, Iraq, and Libya) that had denounced the Camp David agreements. The problem was how to get both sides talking again. The president considered another summit, but he and Vance concluded that the risks of failure were too great. Instead, they held a series of high-level talks at Camp David with Egyptian Foreign Minister Mustapha Khalil and Israeli Foreign Minister Moshe Dayan. When these efforts also proved unproductive, Carter invited Begin to the United States for further negotiations.

The result was some of the most trying sessions ever held between the two leaders. Even before he left for the United States, Begin stated unequivocally that he would offer no new proposals. Arriving at Andrews Air Force base on 1 March, he announced that he would also not be pressured "into signing a sham document." Carter was hardly more diplomatic. At a dinner for the nation's governors on the eve of Begin's arrival, the president termed the inability of Egypt and Israel to reach a peace agreement "disgusting." His first meeting with the Israeli leader went so badly that he cancelled a second one scheduled for that afternoon.[6]

However, during the next day of negotiations, the atmosphere improved considerably. Perhaps chastened by the hasty impasse, the Israeli leader became less confrontational and more flexible on several key points. One issue was whether an Egyptian-Israeli peace treaty would take precedence over some defense agreements Egypt had with other Arab nations. The Israelis held it would, Egypt maintained it would not. Carter resolved the problem by stipulating in the draft treaty that the agreement would not supersede Egypt's other treaties nor would these other agreements supersede the Egyptian-Israeli pact.

The Israeli leader also seemed amenable to language proposed by Carter that would once more skirt the critical issue of linkage between a treaty and Palestinian autonomy. The formula Carter suggested *implied* linkage by stating that the treaty was part of the "framework for a comprehensive peace treaty signed at Camp David." Finally, Begin indicated a willingness to go along with ambiguous phrasing recommended by the president calling for a "goal" rather than a "timetable" of twelve months for arriving at an agreement on Palestinian autonomy but leaving unanswered what would happen if the "goal" was not achieved. After consulting with his cabinet, Begin informed Carter that his proposals were acceptable to Israel. Now the president had to sell them to Sadat.[7]

To finalize a pact, Carter decided to visit Egypt and Israel at the end of March 1979. After further discussions with Sadat and Begin, Carter was able to announce the conclusion of an Egyptian-Israeli peace treaty. Both sides had compromised. Egypt dropped its insistence on stationing personnel in the Gaza Strip preliminary to agreement on the fate of Palestine and also accepted the Israeli wording on a timetable for Palestinian autonomy. On its part, Israel gave up Begin's demand that Cairo guarantee to sell Israel oil from the Sinai fields being returned to Egypt. Israel also promised to remove its forces from the western half of the Sinai within nine months, as Sadat had requested. In return, Cairo would exchange ambassadors with Jerusalem one month after that phase of the withdrawal was completed.

Carter had achieved another diplomatic coup to match the Camp David accords. Once more, he was greeted with a tremendous outpouring of public acclaim for his achievement—hailed as a statesman who had gone the extra mile and grasped the impossible. At Andrews Air Force base, several thousand invited spectators maintained a midnight vigil to welcome him home.

Like the Camp David accords, however the Egyptian-Israeli agreement was reached only by avoiding the two crucial obstructions to a meaningful peace in the Mideast: Palestinian autonomy and Israeli withdrawal from the occupied territories. Arab reaction to the treaty was swift and negative. "An act of treason," proclaimed the Algerian government. "Humiliating concessions," broadcast Syria's state-run Damascus radio. "We do not turn the other cheek," declared PLO leader Yasser Arafat. Jordan's King Hussein, whose support was essential to any settlement involving the West Bank, held an emergency meeting of his cabinet and then called for implementation of economic measures against Egypt.[8] From Saudi Arabia, which could have attempted to topple Sadat by denying Egypt the financial support on which it depended, there was cryptic silence. Although some commentators interpreted this as acquiescence in the pact, no evidence corroborated that view. In fact, Sadat had become so totally isolated in the Arab world, and his political future so mortgaged to a comprehensive Mideast settlement, that any further diplomatic tremors could unravel the Egyptian-Israeli agreement.

At this juncture, developments in the Iranian Revolution intervened. The reasons for the revolution, led by Islamic fundamentalists, were complex and long-standing, but key factors included the repressive nature of the shah's regime, particularly the activities of his notorious secret police, SAVAK, and the shah's efforts at modernization, which the Islamic right wing found much too liberal. By August 1978, Iran was experiencing revolutionary convulsions. That month a fire at a cinema in Abadan left 377 people dead. Although no one knew the perpetrator, Iranians held the shah responsible. Riots and protests, some with over 100,000 people, took place throughout the country. The shah declared martial law and banned demonstrations. When a group of protestors tried to defy the ban by assembling in Tehran's Jaleh Square, government troops fired on them, killing as many as 700. For the first time, multitudes clamored for the shah's ouster—even his death—and appealed to the army for assistance.

During the next four months, the situation went from bad to worse. Huge demonstrations became routine and more violent. Although the shah was able to stall the revolution through the army's support, a new wave of bloody protests swept the nation in December. Iranians defied the military government in scattered clashes that left hundreds dead. On Ashura, Iran's holiest day, more than 1 million anti-shah demonstrators marched through Tehran. From Paris, seventy-eight-year-old Ayatollah Ruhollah Khomeini, spiritual head of Iran's 32 million Shiite Muslims and the emerging leader of the rebels, called for a general strike and the overthrow of the shah. Iranians responded by shutting down the oil fields for the second time in little more than a month. Increasingly, Americans became targets of the protesters.

Still trying to hold on to his throne, the shah freed 122 political prisoners, relaxed an evening curfew, and did not try to block the traditional street processions that marked the holy days. As strikes continued to paralyze the country and oil production fell to a trickle, he named Shahpour Bakhtiar, an outspoken critic of the shah's regime and a leader of the opposition National Front, to head a new government. He also agreed to leave Iran for "rest and recuperation"; when he returned, he would become a constitutional monarch who would reign, not rule.

On 16 January 1979, the shah boarded a Boeing 727 for Egypt. Although he claimed his departure was temporary, most believed the Iranian monarch would never return. As news spread of the shah's exit, Iranians took to the streets, celebrating in joyous abandon. Within hours, virtually every public square and boulevard once named for the shah had been renamed for Khomeini. On 9 February, Khomeini arrived in Iran and received a tumultuous welcome from crowds so huge that the route of his motorcade became impassable and he had to take a helicopter into Tehran.

To consolidate his power, however, the Ayatollah had to secure the loyalty of the military, whose leaders were generally promonarchist. At first, there were real fears of a civil war between Khomeini's millions of supporters and the military backing the Bakhtiar government. But although some fighting did take place, the military very quickly declared its neutrality in the country's political battles. Stranded, Bakhtiar resigned, leaving the civilian government to his replacement, Mehdi Bazargan. Although Bazargan, an adviser to Khomeini, had broad political experience, the country's power shifted to Khomeini.

The Carter administration had been slow to respond to the mounting crisis in Iran, sometimes even seeming oblivious to what was happening there. Despite growing evidence of SAVAK's brutality, including its use of torture, and despite his own commitment to human rights, the president had continued to permit the sale of huge amounts of military equipment to Iran. Over the objections of Assistant Secretary of State for Human Rights Patricia Derian, the administration even sent the shah tear gas and other weapons for crowd control. Never did Carter seek to open lines of communication to the shah's political opponents, particularly to the Ayatollah Khomeini.

The administration's actions respecting the Iranian Revolution left many unanswered questions. Why did the White House persist in supporting the shah? Why did it not attempt to establish a dialogue with Khomeini or with some other more moderate faction in Iran? What else could have been done to bring about a resolution of the crisis that was more favorable to American interests in the region? These issues were later picked over in a spate of memoirs published by former State Department and White House officials who had been principals in the events culminating in the shah's overthrow. Although most of these accounts have an ax to grind, they do explain much about how foreign policy was made and unmade in the Carter White House.

On one point there is consensus: The administration accepted the thesis formulated during Richard Nixon's administration that the shah merited American support because under his rule Iran had become the bulwark of American interests in the Middle East. In later years, Vance described the country's strategic importance for the United States: "Iran was seen as the major force for stability in the oil-rich Persian Gulf. Its military strength ensured western access to gulf oil and served as a barrier to Soviet expansion. Its influence in [OPEC, the Organization of Petroleum Exporting Countries] made it important to the American economy." NSC Adviser Brzezinski echoed these views, as did President Carter, who also pointed out the important role of Iran in supplying oil to Israel.[9]

Although the shah had been a "friend" of the United States in the Mideast, it was not clear his enemies would be. In fact, the administration had trouble developing an accurate profile of his opposition, with the result that the White House did not grasp the full extent of Khomeini's support until sometime in November. Even then, officials were as worried about leftist infiltration of the militants as about Khomeini's own power base. The White House also lacked accurate information about the military—the factions within the army and the degree to which the military leadership would remain loyal to the shah.

The State Department's handling of the Iranian crisis certainly warranted criticism. Vance was so preoccupied with the Camp David process that he was never a principal actor in the unfolding drama in Iran. Nor did the department itself give developments in Iran the attention they deserved. "I could detect neither high-level concern nor any comprehensive attitude toward the events that were in progress," Ambassador William Sullivan later complained. In fact, the State Department did not set up a working group on Iran until after the Jaleh Square massacre, by which time the march of events was well under way.[10]

Khomeini was a mystery to the administration, beyond his stated determination to overthrow the shah and to establish an Islamic republic. Although many government officials shared the shah's perception of the Ayatollah as a right-wing obscurantist who would turn his country back from modernity, others thought he would be reasonably progressive on economics issues and certainly anticommunist. They also believed he would have to turn to the West because of Iran's need for trained personnel to manage its oil production and industries. Unlike the analysts who preferred a military government—even a military dictatorship—to rule by Khomeini, these people favored making contact with Khomeini's forces in anticipation of the shah's fall.

Ambassador Sullivan, for one, strongly urged an approach to the Ayatollah. Since becoming the U.S. representative in Tehran in 1977, he had established a good personal and working relationship with the Iranian monarch. But when he realized in the autumn of 1978 that the shah was in trouble, he opened communication with various opposition groups in case the shah should be ousted. In November, he wrote a long telegram to the State Department pressing the government "to think the unthinkable," to act as if the revolution would succeed, and to prepare for the transfer of power from the shah to a coalition government of Khomeini followers and the military.[11]

Sullivan's warnings fell on deaf ears. At the White House, Brzezinski and his NSC staff asserted that the United States should support the shah even if he used violent military measures to put down the opposition. They dismissed as appeasement the idea of a coalition government. Believing that the Bakhtiar government would not survive, Brzezinski favored a military coup as its successor—and he continued to advocate a coup right up to the military's declaration of neutrality following Khomeini's return to Iran.

The loudest critic of Sullivan, however, was not Brzezinski but Gary Sick, the NSC staffer responsible for Iranian affairs. Sick accused Sullivan of undermining the shah's will to resist when he should have been encouraging the monarch to take a firm stand against the militants. He also charged the ambassador with misleading the White House by his optimistic reporting on the country's situation and then with abandoning the shah by opening contact with the Islamic zealots seeking to overthrow him.[12] Sick was basically correct in his accusations. Instead of conducting diplomacy in accordance with administration policy—that is, to support the shah against the Islamic fundamentalists—Sullivan pressured the shah to leave the country, exaggerated the moderation of Khomeini's followers, and urged them to become part of a coalition government. As a result, the Iranian monarch and his military commanders were confused about what the American response would be if they suppressed the opposition with military force. In the process, the ambassador diminished the prospects for an alternative to Khomeini, including a civilian government with strong military backing.

By December 1978, President Carter had lost confidence in Sullivan, whose recommendation "to think the unthinkable" he found totally unacceptable. Instead, he sent to Tehran Gen. Robert Huyser, deputy commander of U.S. forces in Europe, who knew many of Iran's military leaders. Huyser's assignment was to bolster the military and convince them to stay in Iran should the shah beat his retreat, but this task put him at cross-purposes with Sullivan. While the general was trying to rally the military behind the Bakhtiar government, the ambassador denigrated the government's chances of survival and continued his overtures to Khomeini's followers. Not sure the United States would support military action and holding Sullivan personally responsible for the shah's decision to leave Iran, the military allowed the Bakhtiar government to fall.

Yet it is far from clear that military intervention was ever a viable option. Uncertainty about the American position was only one reason why the military did not launch a coup or otherwise seek to stop Khomeini. Before his departure, the shah had advised against a military overthrow because it would lead to further bloodshed. The generals also feared that draftees, who composed half the army, might not cooperate in military action against the Ayatollah. In addition, there was the risk that an unsuccessful coup might unleash economic and political chaos, which could then be exploited by the Soviet Union—the real enemy, in the generals' view.

In retrospect, it seems likely that by the time the United States became fully aware of the seriousness of the situation in Iran, it was probably too late to change the course of events. The real failure of Washington's Iran policy was the unequivocal support the government had previously given the shah. The decision in 1972 to rely on the Iranian monarch for the security of American interests in the Middle East and the virtual blank check he received to buy American military hardware fed the shah's inflated vision of his own importance and blinded him (and the United States) to the growing opposition to his rule among all strata of Iranian society. The dearth of intelligence about Iran compounded the errors.

Finally, the manner in which President Carter responded to the crisis pointed to one of the fundamental problems of his entire administration. Throughout the turmoil in Iran, the White House had not provided clear leadership. Given that the Iranian status quo was in flux by the fall of 1978, the president had two policy options: support the shah against the rising tide of revolution (as his NSC favored), or work toward some kind of coalition government, which would have to include Khomeini's followers (as the State Department preferred). Carter chose instead to waffle. "We were not willing to make the shah's decision for him but he was told in unequivocal terms that we would back him in whatever action he found necessary," the White House later explained. But except for the Huyser mission, the president did little to demonstrate the substance of his administration's backing.[13]

One reason why the president failed to arrived at a well-defined Iran policy was the internecine warfare occurring within the administration. Secretary of State Cyrus Vance's preoccupation with the Egyptian-Israeli talks allowed the NSC to take charge of relations with Iran. But this did not mean that Vance was uninterested in developments there or that the administration spoke with one voice. Within the state Department, the head of the Iran desk, Henry Precht, and a number of his colleagues urged the White House to establish contact with Khomeini's followers as Ambassador Sullivan had recommended. However, believing that these officials were motivated by personal animus toward the shah, Brzezinski and his staff gradually cut them out of the decision-making queue. The national security adviser even told Undersecretary of State George Ball not to talk with Precht.

A type of guerrilla warfare ensued in which stories were leaked from the State Department highly critical of White House policy. On the basis of one such leak, NBC and CBS reported on 5 February that American officials did not believe that the Bakhtiar government would last more than two days and that the administration was preparing to withdraw its support for the regime. At the White House, Hamilton Jordan and the president were irate. "If the leaks continue," Jordan advised Carter, "you will have no choice but to ask Cy to make a series of major changes at the State Department."[14]

American troubles in Iran and in other parts of the Muslim world seemed only to multiply in the first few months after the overthrow of the shah. On 14 February, Iranians stormed the American embassy in Tehran and temporarily detained Ambassador Sullivan and his staff. The siege lasted a few hours and was lifted by followers of the Ayatollah Khomeini. Afterwards, Khomeini sent a personal emissary to Sullivan to apologize, but the incident amounted to a violation of American sovereignty.

On 15 February, the U.S. ambassador to Afghanistan, Adolph Dubs, was killed. Dubs had been kidnapped the eventful day before by unidentified gunmen; at the time, Afghanistan was governed by Marxists who had taken power less than a year earlier after a bloody coup. The White House pled for restraint in the handling of the situation, but the Afghan police staged a "rescue mission," during which Dubs was killed. The administration suspected—but could not prove—that Moscow had either conspired in, or knew beforehand, about Dubs's kidnap and murder.

Developments such as these made the first few months of 1979 seem an especially dangerous time to many Americans. Indeed, Zbigniew Brzezinski coined the phrase "crescent of crisis" to describe the area stretching along the Soviet Union's southern flank from the Indian subcontinent to Turkey and then southward along the Persian Gulf to the Horn of Africa. Calling the region of "vital importance" to the United States, the NSC adviser warned that its fragile social and political structures had already led to power vacuums that "could well be filled by elements hostile to our values and sympathetic to our adversaries."[15]

As Brzezinski's comment suggested, the regional turmoil was part of a broad clash of interests between Moscow and Washington and a general deterioration in Soviet-American relations. The tension was exacerbated when

President Carter decided to grant full diplomatic status to the Soviet Union's major adversary in the communist world, the People's Republic of China. The American public first learned of Carter's decision during a hastily arranged television speech on 15 December 1978, in which he also announced the forthcoming visit of China's deputy prime minister, Deng Xiaoping. The news even surprised lawmakers on Capitol Hill. The Chinese had insisted that before full diplomatic relations could be restored, the United States had to terminate its defense pact with Taiwan and not sell Taiwan any more arms. The administration responded that it could not abrogate the agreement without a year's notice and that it would continue some military sales to the Taiwanese after the treaty expired. Anxious to attract American capital to help modernize China's economy and seeking additional security in a period of growing estrangement between Beijing and Moscow, Chinese leaders accepted Carter's terms.

Although normalization of relations with the Beijing government was applauded in the United States as a major diplomatic breakthrough, the president still faced the difficult task of convincing skeptics that he had not sold out Taiwan and that his gambit had not been a mistake. He was not entirely successful. In the Senate, Barry Goldwater of Arizona termed the president's decision on China "one of the most cowardly acts ever performed by a President of the United States." In both the House and Senate, bills and amendments were introduced incorporating language that would have been unacceptable to Beijing—including a formal American commitment to protect Taiwan in case of an attack by mainland China. Although the administration defeated most of these measures in committee, the final legislation that Congress approved at the end of March provided for stronger guarantees of Taiwan's independence than the White House had wanted.[16]

At the end of February, China's invasion of Vietnam confirmed the worst fears of everyone who had denounced diplomatic recognition of the Beijing government. Six weeks earlier, Vietnam had attacked Cambodia, driving its odious ruler Pol Pot and his Khmer Rouge forces into the mountains and then renaming the country Kampuchea. China was determined to punish Vietnam for its invasion of Cambodia. During his visit to the United States in January, Deng Xiaoping told the president of his plan for a punitive strike across China's border into Vietnam. Carter tried to dissuade him, maintaining that such military action would refute one of the administration's best arguments for normalization—that it would contribute to peace and stability in Asia. But Deng rejected his advice; Vietnam had to learn that it could not attack one of its neighbors with impunity.

The Chinese offensive held to its retaliatory purpose: The forces drove twenty-five miles across the border and withdrew after only seventeen days. But Republican Senator Charles Mathias of Maryland expressed the sentiments of many Americans when he condemned the administration for "misplaying the China card." To such critics, China's attack across the border was no different than Vietnam's aggression against Cambodia and was proof that the Chinese leopard had not changed its spots.[17]

By its turnabout on China, the White House provoked the Soviet Union. Although President Carter tried to reassure the Soviets that normalization was not directed against Moscow, Kremlin leaders were disturbed by Carter's willingness to allow Deng to speak out against the Soviet Union while in the United States. Moreover, in a final communiqué, the president joined the Chinese leader in denouncing "hegemony," a Chinese code word for Soviet expansionism. The public statement raised visceral Soviet fears of a Sino-American alliance that would tilt the strategic balance in favor of the United States.

These events prompted Cyrus Vance to observe years later that "the sudden surge of Soviet inflexibility [on SALT] in the winter of 1978–79 was due primarily to developments relating to China."[18] Despite the uneasy relations between the United States and the Soviet Union, their negotiators had made so much progress on a SALT II treaty that both sides expected to reach a final agreement by the end of 1978. A SALT pact with Moscow, followed by a January meeting between Carter and Brezhnev to sign the document, seemed so close at hand that the White House alerted the TV networks to an impending announcement by the president that they would want to broadcast. Brezhnev was expected to make a similar announcement from the Kremlin.

The synchronized statements were never issued. Instead, Vance and Soviet Foreign Minister Gromyko informed reporters that success had eluded them again. "A lot of work has indeed been done," Gromyko explained, "but there is still work that needs to be done." Vance agreed, leaving reporters and government officials alike to puzzle over what had gone wrong.[19]

Part of the explanation for the abrupt standstill was simply the complexity of the issues holding up a final pact. The Soviets and Americans could not agree, for example, on a definition of new types of ICBMs. Without such a definition, existing missiles could be modified without violating the SALT I restriction that allowed each side one new ICBM system. Similarly, they could not resolve the highly technical problem of "telemetry encryption"—the encoding by the Soviets of electronic signals from their missile sites in order to keep information about their missiles secret. The U.S. needed access to these codes to assure that Moscow was complying with an agreement.

However, the main reason why a SALT agreement was not concluded in December was the diplomatic rapprochement between Washington and Beijing. Even though Brezhnev had told Carter that he approved of normalization, he had also remarked that it was natural for Moscow to be concerned about China's antagonism toward the Soviet Union. In an interview with reporters from *Time* magazine in January, he had warned that there were "some in the U.S. and in other western countries who have found the hostile course toward the Soviet Union followed by the present Chinese leadership so much to their liking that they are tempted to turn Peking into an instrument of pressure on the world of Socialism." Under these circumstances, Brezhnev was not inclined to be flexible in the final stages of the SALT talks.[20]

Carter and his advisers, in other words, had underestimated the intricacies of the points still unresolved and overestimated Moscow's readiness to sign a treaty. Carter's apparent approval of Deng's attacks on Moscow during the Chinese leader's visit then delayed a SALT II agreement even more. Indeed, it appears that Deng's purpose in coming to Washington may have been to undermine the negotiations. In an interview just before leaving for home, he belittled the SALT talks, remarking that "such agreements [as SALT] are neither as significant nor as useful as the normalization of relations between China and the U.S." Rather than the United States playing its "China card," as NSC Adviser Brzezinski had intended when he went to the PRC in the spring, perhaps China had successfully played its "American card."[21]

By the early spring of 1979, therefore, the United States appeared to many observers as a hapless giant in an increasingly unfriendly world. Moreover, the "crescent of crisis" delineated by Brzezinski now seemed to vault the Atlantic to include the small Central American country of Nicaragua. A civil war had been raging there for two years between the forces of the country's dictator, Anastasio Somoza, and leftist guerrillas, known as the Sandinistas, who were seeking to overthrow him. Throughout the fighting in Nicaragua, the administration followed a zigzag course—criticizing Somoza's human rights violations, deploring even more the Sandinistas' Marxist leanings and Cuban support, but advocating a mediated end of the war. At the same time, the president's inconstancy alienated both the Nicaraguan dictator and his opposition.

As the Sandinistas grew militarily stronger and gained popular support, the White House applied more pressure on Somoza to give up the reins of power. Believing that his continued presence increased the chances of a radical takeover, the White House finally terminated military aid and most economic assistance to Nicaragua and reduced the size of the United States embassy in Managua. Still, the president continued to vacillate; there was even a report in the *Washington Post* that the administration was considering a resumption of some aid to Nicaragua. Although this did not happen, it seemed to demonstrate that Carter was incapable of a resolute response to a deteriorating situation even in the United States' own backyard.

Another episode that reflected poorly on the president occurred during his state visit to Mexico in February 1979. Although Mexico's president, Jose Lopez Portillo, had been the first head of state to pay an official visit to the Carter White House, several developments strained Mexican-American relations—most notably, the efforts to prevent Mexicans from illegally crossing into the United States to find employment, and the cancellation by the administration of a $2-billion agreement to buy natural gas from Mexico. Lopez Portillo used Carter's visit to broadcast his displeasure with Washington's stance on both these matters. "Among permanent, not casual neighbors," he remarked during a toast to the American president, "surprise moves and sudden deceit or abuse are poisonous fruits that sooner or later have a reverse effect." Two days later, he again lashed out against the United States, referring to it as a nation able "to buy" Mexicans "who have to sell themselves."[22]

Carter ignored the barbs, and in his three days of meetings with Lopez Portillo and other Mexican leaders, he tried to improve the diplomatic climate. He pledged, for example, to reopen negotiations over natural gas purchases and to deal with undocumented workers "as fairly and humanely" as possible. But his visit left a sour taste from the humiliating spectacle of an American president having to endure in silence a public scolding by a lesser power's leader.

As a result, Carter came under attack by many of the same people who just a few months earlier had praised his statesmanship and diplomatic skills. The president's high marks for getting Egypt and Israel to sign a peace treaty were overshadowed by the growing perception of national impotence, which was attributed to Carter's inexperience, his indecisiveness, and his inability to define and achieve his foreign policy goals. According to an AP/ NBC poll taken in late March, immediately after the president's successful peacemaking trip to the Mideast, only 29 percent of the American people surveyed approved of his conduct of the presidency. Although the low figure had more to do with Carter's handling of the economy than with any other issue, less than half of the respondents (44 percent) applauded his direction of foreign policy. The president's role as peacemaker, while widely praised, had done little to improve his overall approval rating with the American people, which was up only 1 point from February.

In the realm of domestic policy, however, the paralysis of leadership seemed most pronounced and the president most vulnerable; consequently, it was there that the strongest attacks were made against Carter's administration.

10

★ ★ ★ ★ ★

A GROWING SENSE OF CRISIS

Each year, the proposed federal budget sets forth the assumptions and priorities of an administration for the next fiscal year. Once approved by Congress and signed into law, it determines who will be that year's principal beneficiaries of the government's largesse. Although the budget is predicated on economic assumptions about the state of the economy, therefore, it is a political document as much as an economic one, with substantial winners and losers whom no administration can ignore except at grave political risk.

President Carter understood well this elemental fact about the budgetary process. To his credit—and against the recommendations of some of his closest advisers—he nevertheless tried to subordinate political considerations to his fight against inflation in preparing his budget for fiscal year 1980. His primary weapon in this war was budgetary austerity, but the politics of austerity encroached upon his economic program and further eroded his support among traditional Democrats. More important, it added to a growing sense of crisis and to the image of a president incapable of keeping his own house in order, much less managing the affairs of state.

The battle lines between the president and his more liberal foes within the Democratic party were drawn at the party's second midterm conference held in Memphis in early December 1978. At the gathering, Carter's forces clashed with opponents over the size and priorities of the budget for 1980. In his October speech on inflation, the president had stated his intention to present Congress with a lean budget that limited the deficit to around $30 billion; he repeated this pledge in Memphis. But because of automatic adjustments for inflation in certain programs and a previous commitment the president had made to NATO for an increase in defense spending of 3 percent over inflation, there would be only a small pool left for projects dear to the hearts of many Democrats—health, education, housing, jobs, and aid to the cities.

Led by UAW President Douglas Fraser, liberal delegates attacked Carter's appeal for frugality. Although the administration was able to beat back this challenge, the three-day meeting underscored the depth of the fissures within the Democratic party. Indeed, the warmest reception was given not to the president but to Senator Edward Kennedy, who, in contrast to Carter's bland defense of his administration, stirred the emotions of the convention hall with his evocation of historic Democratic values.

During the conference, Hamilton Jordan and the president made clear their intention to run the 1980 campaign much as they had the 1976 one—as outsiders appealing to the broad mainstream of American voters rather than to Democratic loyalists. This was demonstrated by their reaction to the vote on the administration's budget resolution, which had been subjected to a floor fight by the liberal contingent. But Jordan made light of the 40 percent who voted against it, remarking that the "make-up" of the meeting was not representative of the Democratic party. Carter shared this view, telling his cabinet later that delegates at such gatherings typically came from the most liberal wing of the party and that he had never been their man.[1]

Other members of the administration were less sanguine. Eizenstat, Vice-President Mondale, Labor Secretary Ray Marshall, HUD Secretary Pat Harris, and a number of White House aides were deeply worried about the divisive impact of the administration's budget on the Democratic party. They were also concerned that the proposed budget was a retreat from the president's commitment to social justice. Carter responded to their fears by restoring about $2 billion in budget cuts in the areas of education, health, jobs, and urban aid. But he still remained firmly wedded to economic austerity. In his budget message to Congress on 22 January 1979, he called for total expenditures of $532 billion, which included a projected deficit of $29 billion, or $12 billion less than the 1979 deficit. Although total spending was about 8 percent over that for the current fiscal year, the bulk of the increase was due to the 3-percent growth in defense spending and the automatic hikes previously legislated by Congress.

Reaction to the president's budget proposals was predictable. Reporters dubbed the anticipated struggle as the "battle of guns vs. butter." The Reverend Jesse Jackson compared the president's anti-inflation program to a "domestic neutron bomb." "It does not destroy any buildings—only people who are less organized and therefore less able to defend themselves from such an attack." Such liberal bastions as Americans for Democratic Action, the Congressional Black Caucus, and organized labor closed ranks to fight the president's plan. Union leaders, mayors, minorities, senior citizens, and feminists descended on Washington, while House Speaker Tip O'Neill indicated to the president that he would fight the administration on a number of the social programs targeted for cuts.[2]

Inevitably, speculation mounted about a Kennedy challenge to the president in 1980, fueled particularly by their great differences over budget priorities. At the Memphis conference, Kennedy had accused the White House of ignoring traditional Democratic constituents—the needy, the elderly, workers, and minorities—and had called Carter's austerity plan "seriously defective." But his most severe disagreement with the president continued to be over NHI. In the budget he submitted to Congress, Carter postponed the unveiling of his own health insurance plan. Instead, he limited his recommendations on health to modest increases in Medicare and Medicaid coverage for low-income children and pregnant women. He also urged lawmakers to pass legislation defeated last year that would have contained hospital costs, which he believed to be the largest contributor to inflation. Kennedy, who sought passage of a comprehensive NHI program, condemned the president's health funding as unacceptable.[3]

Although Kennedy stated on numerous occasions that he would support Carter in a bid for reelection, political pundits continued to predict, and Democratic liberals to hope, that the senator would oppose Carter in 1980. In such a contest, Kennedy remained the odds-on favorite. A *Los Angeles Times* poll in January 1979 showed the president trailing the Massachusetts lawmaker by 23 points in a national election and by 51 points in a New Hampshire primary, the site of the first scheduled primary contest in 1980.

If there was no recession in 1979 and inflation abated without increased joblessness, Carter's political advisers were confident they could defeat a Kennedy challenge. Pointing to the conservative mood of the country, they maintained that budget austerity was not only good economics but also good politics. However, a number of leading economists were already questioning whether Carter could hold the budget deficit to under $30 billion without bringing on a recession and more unemployment. Alan Greenspan, who had headed President Ford's CEA, thought that a recession was indeed likely and that it would probably cause a deficit of $40 billion to $50 billion.

Figures for the first three months of 1979 seemed to justify these pessimistic forecasts and to expose the fallacy of the White House's own predictions, particularly on inflation. The White House had estimated that its endeavors would push the inflation rate down to 7.4 percent in 1979 and 6.6 percent in 1980. But by the end of March, it was clear that inflation was defying the administration's projections. Over the last six months, the consumer price index had increased at a 10.4-percent annual rate compared with 9.4 percent during the previous six-month period.

The upturn in fuel costs was especially sharp. Because of the revolution in Iran, oil production in that country nearly stopped, ending a worldwide glut of oil that had kept oil prices stable for more than a year. The oil-exporting countries responded by raising the price of their oil by as much as 17 percent, causing oil prices to skyrocket. But food costs, up a staggering 18 percent from a year ago and 4.5 percent in February alone, also drove the CPI higher. Even excluding fuel and food, the CPI was still growing at an annual rate of 9 percent.

Not surprisingly, all the polls continued to indicate that inflation was the most urgent national problem for Americans and that many people felt the president was not doing enough to address rising prices. The White House's program of wage and price standards was singled out for criticism. Despite price controls, corporate profits had soared by as much as 25 percent between the first quarters of 1978 and 1979. This led labor leaders to demand higher wage hikes than what was permitted under the administration's guidelines. Even Alfred Kahn, the president's chief inflation-fighter, recognized that the system of wage and price controls was coming unglued. After learning of the jump in business profits, Kahn's verdict was, "A catastrophe."[4]

Discontent also spread against the president's strategy of curbing inflation by means of a tight budget. Black lawmakers on Capitol Hill and other black officials were particularly strident in their criticism of the White House. Statistics for February revealed that unemployment among black teenagers had increased during the month from 32.7 percent to 35.5 percent. The administration argued that its jobs programs were being targeted to the hard-core unemployed. But in Washington, stores were broken into and looted after hundreds of black teenagers reported for snow-shoveling work only to be told that the jobs had already been filled. Similar disturbances also occurred in Baltimore. Many local leaders, including black elected officials, blamed the unrest on the president's austerity program. "They do not buy the linkage between the battle on inflation and the need to cut job programs," Louis Martin, Carter's assistant for minority affairs, told the president.[5]

Although the economy was the administration's principal domestic concern in the early winter of 1979, the White House also had to contend with a scandal involving the Libyan connections of the president's brother. Billy Carter's personality was very different from that of his older brother, and he was commonly lampooned as a redneck with a beer belly. But his good-natured humor and his willingness to laugh at himself were so well-received by the American public that he became a popular guest on talk shows and was in great demand on the lecture circuit. This situation changed dramatically after Billy returned to Georgia in September 1978 from a trip to Libya, where he had been the guest of the Libyan government. In January, he helped host a lavish reception in Atlanta for a "friendship delegation" from Libya. Asked why he was involved, he replied, "The only thing I can say is there is a hell of a lot more Arabians than there is [sic] Jews." He also said that the "Jewish media [tore] up the Arab countries full-time," and he defended

Libya against charges of state-sponsored terrorism, remarking that a "heap of governments support[ed] terrorists and [Libya] at least admitted it."[6]

The public outcry was immediate and loud. President Carter tried to disassociate himself from his brother's statements. In an interview with NBC news, he expressed the hope that the American people would "realize that I don't have any control over what my brother says [and] he has no control over me." Billy later apologized for his comments, claiming that they "were not intended to be anti-Semitic." But the incident publicly embarrassed the president and touched some raw nerves, particularly among American Jews, whose relations with the president were already troubled. "If [Billy]'s not working for the Republican Party, he should be," quipped the *Atlanta Constitution* in summarizing the political damage done to the administration.[7]

The formal signing of the Egyptian-Israeli agreement at the end of March provided some political relief for Carter but not for long. Shortages of oil hit the West Coast especially hard, and by mid-May, long lines of cars were waiting for an hour or more to reach the gas pumps. Fights broke out at numerous gas stations, and weapons ranged from fists to guns, knives, and broken beer bottles. Across the nation, gas stations were closing on Sunday or shortening weekday hours in order to have enough gas on hand until the next deliveries.

As president, Carter had repeatedly warned of impending energy shortages and had proposed a comprehensive energy plan whose fundamental premise was energy conservation through both a wellhead tax on domestic production and a tax on industrial users of oil and gas. Instead, Congress had approved legislation with no provisions for oil pricing. As a result, efforts to conserve fuel were hampered because fuel prices remained substantially below world prices. The cost of domestic production, which in March 1979 still accounted for 52 percent of American consumption, was determined not by the international market but by the Energy Policy and Conservation Act of 1975 (EPCA)—a complex piece of legislation that set different prices for old and newly discovered oil. About 70 percent of all domestic crude oil production was subject to EPCA price ceilings. Although the world oil price was around $15.20 per barrel, price ceilings ranged from about $5.50 a barrel for old oil to $12.65 for new.

As oil shortages became more serious and OPEC countries started to raise their prices, the White House struggled to find new ways to conserve oil. As required by the EPCA, the administration submitted a standby gasoline rationing plan to Congress. But the administration had little enthusiasm for rationing, which would be cumbersome to execute and politically unpopular. Another idea was to unleash gasoline prices by removing EPCA controls on domestic oil. Under current legislation, all price controls on oil were to be lifted in October 1981, but the president could phase in decontrol at an earlier date. This would have the desired effect of raising prices, but the oil producers would reap higher profits. Even though the oil companies argued that such revenues were needed for exploration and discovery of new petroleum deposits, considerable opposition arose on Capitol Hill to decontrol, which many lawmakers asserted would be inflationary and benefit only the oil industry.

After reviewing various alternatives for dealing with the energy predicament, including immediate decontrol, the president decided at the end of March to implement a phased elimination of oil price controls. On 5 April, Carter outlined his "phase two" energy plan in an address from the Oval Office, telling the American people that they would have to use less oil and spend more for it and announcing that he was phasing out all controls on oil by 1 October 1981. Since the oil companies stood to gain some $13 billion when domestic prices rose to world levels, the president also called for a "windfall profits" tax, which would return about half the new profits to the government. The tax would be used to fund the development of alternative fuel sources, help poor families pay for the rising cost of fuel, and stimulate the construction of energy-efficient mass transit systems.

Carter could not have chosen a more opportune time to address the American people on the importance of energy conservation. Just one week earlier, the worst accident in the history of nuclear power to that time occurred at a plant on Three Mile Island near Harrisburg, Pennsylvania. For six days, Americans contemplated in horror the possibility of a nuclear meltdown or an explosion that would send lethal radioactive gases into the atmosphere. Although that did not happen, the accident undermined claims about the safety of nuclear energy. During the same week, OPEC ministers meeting in Geneva agreed to raise their prices for the second time in a little more than three months—this time by 9 percent.

By dramatizing the limited options for the United States, these events should have generated support for Carter's new energy program. That they failed to do so was in part the president's own fault. Assuring the American people that the energy crisis was "real," he nevertheless delivered a harsh indictment of the oil industry, which seemed to assign them sole responsibility for higher oil prices and dilute the urgency of the situation. "Just as surely as the sun will rise," he stated, "the oil companies can be expected to fight to keep the profits they have not earned."

Moreover, there was a basic miscalculation in Carter's energy plan. At a time when the greatest concern of the American public was inflation, the president proposed to handle energy shortages by allowing energy prices to rise even higher. From a conservation viewpoint, this made sense, but politically it was a disaster. Democratic lawmakers reacted forcefully against the president's decision to decontrol, and they maintained that the windfall profits tax was still too generous to the oil companies. Calling Carter's program "seriously flawed," Senator Kennedy claimed that the oil lobby had intimidated the president "into throwing in the towel" on decontrol without even "entering the ring." He urged the president to continue controls at least until a windfall tax had been passed. Having tried and failed with that approach over the wellhead tax, Carter was determined to decontrol first and to make Congress responsible for the tax. So angry were Democrats with the president's actions that they began a legislative drive to take away his power to lift controls.[8]

Amid the storm over decontrol and windfall profits, the White House was also battered by other dour economic news. Figures released in May revealed that inflation was growing at an annual rate of about 14 percent and that the economy had entered a slump. Meanwhile, the administration's wage and price standards now faced judicial challenge. At the end of May, a federal district court judge ruled that the president had exceeded his authority in promulgating guidelines and then threatening to withhold federal contracts from companies violating them.

There were assaults on other fronts as well. In the May *Atlantic Monthly*, former presidential speechwriter Jim Fallows, who had become disenchanted with Carter's policies and had left the White House, delivered a scathing attack against the president in which he accused him of being "ignorant" of how power could or should be exercised. A few weeks later, a grand jury in Atlanta indicted Bert Lance for his loan practices as president of the National Bank of Georgia. The charges came after a lengthy investigation, and there had been allegations that part of the proceeds of a loan to the Carter family peanut business had been illegally diverted to the presidential campaign in 1976. Although the president and his brother Billy, who ran the company, were exonerated, the indictment nevertheless reopened an old scandal that the White House would just as soon have forgotten.[9]

By this time, a crisis of confidence in the White House had developed within American society. A Yankelovich poll found that only 23 percent of the people questioned believed that things were going well in the country. In contrast, 64 percent believed that the nation was "in deep and serious trouble," up from 41 percent a year earlier. Although the main concern of the interviewees was still inflation, a more general feeling of pessimism seemed to be spreading throughout the country. In a lengthy memorandum, "Of Crisis and Opportunity," Pat Caddell warned the president that if he could not effectively deal with inflation and restore the confidence of the American people, he would lose the election in 1980.[10] As public disenchantment with Carter grew, pressure intensified on Kennedy to oppose him in 1980. The Massachusetts senator continued to deny any plans to seek the Democratic nomination in 1980. His office even tried to halt a pro-Kennedy meeting in Iowa, which drew more than one hundred labor leaders disgruntled with the administration. Despite his disavowal of presidential ambitions, Kennedy as legislator remained at odds with Carter on a number of issues, and their most serious dispute continued to be over national health insurance.

In March, the White House unveiled a proposal for NHI, which staked out a middle ground between Kennedy and Russell Long of Louisiana, whose own plan provided only for catastrophic insurance. As Stu Eizenstat described it, "We offer Kennedy our opposition to a catastrophic-only bill and our commitment, in principle, to a comprehensive plan. We offer Long our support of first-phase legislation [Medicare and Medicaid reform and catastrophic coverage] . . . which has a credible chance of passing." But Kennedy rejected the White House compromise. Instead, he announced in May his own comprehensive national health plan and called on the president to support it, warning that he would do "everything" he could to defeat the president's scheme.[11]

The White House was annoyed by the senator's threats and personal barbs, but it also fretted over the prospect of Kennedy in the 1980 race. The latest Gallup poll in May showed Kennedy beating the president among Democrats 54 percent to 31 percent. And a New York Times/CBS survey published in June placed the president's personal rating (as opposed to his job rating) in the negative for the first time—that is, only 33 percent of the people interviewed rated him favorably while 45 percent rated him unfavorably. Pat Caddell termed this result "staggering." "Almost no candidate whose personal rating has been negative has survived reelection," he told the president. As the economy unraveled and Carter's slide in the polls continued, the president's cool restraint foundered. He became increasingly agitated and short-tempered. At a White House dinner with a small group of lawmakers in June, he boasted that if Kennedy challenged him in 1980, he would "whip his ass."[12]

However, during the spring, most of the president's malice was directed at Congress, which was busy mauling his legislative agenda. Early in April, lawmakers on Capitol Hill killed his wage insurance plan by slashing $2.5 billion slated for the program from the budget. The next month, they defeated standby gasoline rationing, which the president was mandated to submit to Congress. At the end of May, Democrats on Capitol Hill sent a message to Carter by voting in caucus, 139 to 69, to reinstate controls on oil. All this left Carter utterly frustrated. "What do you suggest that I do?" he asked Democratic Congressman James Hanley of New York. "Ignore the [energy] problem and hope it will go away? Find a scapegoat?"[13]

The president also bore the brunt of trends over which he had no control. As James McGregor Burns, a leading student of the presidency, observed, Congress sought to assert itself in the post-Watergate era, but "its essential power [was] that of obstruction and negation." Presidential programs were chewed up by a vast array of committees and subcommittees and undercut by well-financed and politically active interest groups. "When a new kind of problem comes along," complained Butler Derrick, a third-term Democrat, "we just add some new sort of committee, a 'select committee.' We've got committees, select committees, [and] permanent 'select committees.'" In addition, party loyalty had been steadily breaking down, as lawmakers gained and held office more by building personal organizations than by being loyal Democrats.[14]

Certainly Carter attempted to mobilize support for his policies, which he also hoped to convert into votes in 1980. He tried to improve his accessibility by bringing Gerald Rafshoon into the White House. In addition, he regularly invited to the White House leaders from the public and private sectors and lobbied them on his proposals. But while he devoted a great deal of attention to building coalitions on specific issues, he did not provide the vision or spirit of comity necessary to cement those coalitions. In fact, he often seemed to be running with the fox while chasing with the hounds—appealing to traditional Democratic constituencies in the language of a Republican.

The White House also seemed incapable of sending out consistent signals. Was there a gas shortage? The president said there was, and most economists agreed that supplies in the spring were short 5–20 percent. Yet Carter seemed to downplay the crisis when he emerged from a meeting with California Governor Jerry Brown and suggested that federal assistance was not needed to solve the state's gasoline shortage. At Carter's side, Energy Secretary James Schlesinger declared that "it would be safe to say that we hope the worst is over." During a speech in Iowa, the president also indicated that he would not veto a bill extending controls if it was passed by Congress. His statement came as a shock even to his own staff. "This gives the impression of an absence of leadership," Eizenstat told Carter. "This gives the impression of waffling on a critical issue."[15]

Likewise, administration officials and White House aides complained that while Carter had identified inflation as the nation's most serious domestic problem, he had still not developed a coherent strategy for dealing with it. "We have not shown a clear direction to our policy," Treasury Secretary Blumenthal told the president in March. "We have spent too much time debating options, when action was more important than substance"—a rather startling statement for a Treasury secretary to make.[16]

Carter himself was dissatisfied with the quality of the economic advice he was receiving and with the chorus of voices claiming to speak for the administration. However, the situation could largely be traced to the president's own refusal to focus on one economic counsel and to the internal quarrels among his advisers. Alfred Kahn, whose loose tongue on such topics as decontrol (which he first publicly opposed and then supported) was becoming an irritant at the White House, did not get along with his own director of COWPS, Barry Bosworth. Eizenstat and Schultze were also often at odds with Blumenthal; politically more liberal than Blumenthal, they were generally more reluctant than he to cut social programs or raise interest rates.

By the summer of 1979, the Carter administration confronted a widespread sense that the nation had come to a critical pass—and nothing that happened over the summer and fall alleviated that feeling. Indeed, the economy seemed out of control. For June, the CPI went up 1 percent, less than the 1.1 percent increase in April and May but still a disturbing annual rate of 12.5 percent. Although the slowing of prices gave Carter's economic advisers some hope that inflation might be easing, that optimism was shattered by the announcement that wholesale prices had jumped in July at the alarming annual rate of 13.7 percent.

As inflation raged, pressure on the dollar again mounted in international money markets. In a rescue effort, Carter named Paul Volcker as his choice for chairman of the Federal Reserve Board. Volcker would replace William Miller, whom the president had appointed Treasury secretary following the resignation of Michael Blumenthal.[17] The new FRB chairman had served as undersecretary of the Treasury under Richard Nixon and was president of the Federal Reserve Bank of New York at the time of his appointment. In these positions he had gained an international reputation as a brilliant monetary technician and diplomat. His selection was widely praised on Capitol Hill and in international financial and banking circles.

Volcker's solution for inflation, however, was to increase interest rates and tighten the money supply even though this meant lower economic growth in an already sluggish economy. Between August and October, the FRB raised its discount rate from 10 percent to 12 percent, and it reduced funds available for loans by substantially increasing reserve requirements. The nation's major banks responded by raising their prime rates, first to 13 percent and then to 14.5 percent. Many analysts predicted the prime rate would go even higher by year's end, possibly throwing the economy into recession.

While the FRB sought to counter the economy's woes through monetary policy, the administration's approach was to tinker with its program of wage and price controls and renew its struggle with Congress for hospital cost containment legislation. Its wage and price guidelines did have some mitigating effect. Overall wage increases in major union contracts declined from 8.2 percent in 1978 to 7.5 percent through June 1979. But the moderation in salaries was not uniform. Such powerful unions as the Teamsters and the UAW won raises of more than 30 percent over three years, while 1979 salaries of top business executives increased by nearly 15 percent. As for the president's proposal to restrain hospital costs, it was again rejected emphatically by the House (234 to 166) after Carter ignored warnings by House leaders that he did not have the votes to win. Instead, the House approved a substitute motion creating a national commission to study hospital expenses, a measure that Jody Powell called a "joke" because it merely delayed legislative action on the issue.[18]

Meanwhile, inflation marched on. Wholesale prices for August jumped 1.2 percent, much higher than most economists had predicted. Conditions were worsened by further increases in the cost of oil and growing uncertainty about future oil prices. In September, Nigeria put into effect a $3 to $5 per barrel surcharge, while Venezuela announced that it was cutting its oil exports by 7 percent, thereby putting additional upward pressure on oil prices. Although OPEC was not expected to discuss another general rate increase until its December meeting, Saudi Arabian Oil Minister Ahmad Zaki Yamani warned that the OPEC nations would not tolerate a continuing erosion of their purchasing power.

On commodity markets, international traders and speculators again drove up the price of gold. In September, gold reached a record $340 an ounce. In one day alone, it soared $27; two days later, it jumped another $16. Tighter money, rising inflation, and concern about oil prices also led to pandemonium on Wall Street as stocks, which had been climbing most of the year, nose-dived. In just five days in October, the Dow-Jones average plunged 58.62 points, the second steepest one-week decline ever, ending the week at 838.99.

Clearly, then, much of the American public's discontent with the Carter administration in the fall of 1979 was the result of a deteriorating economy, particularly rising inflation and the energy crisis. But what distressed Americans almost as much as the economy was their perception of presidential ineptitude. This malaise intensified in July following a sequence of unusual events—a presidential speech on energy was postponed without explanation; leaders from a broad cross section of American society trekked to Camp David for discussions with the president; and five members of Carter's cabinet resigned.

The catalyst for these incidents was the June announcement by OPEC, while the president was attending the Tokyo summit, of its fourth and largest price surge in five months. Even before OPEC's notice, American drivers were exhibiting their frustration and anger. In Levittown, Pennsylvania, truckers barricaded expressways and set off the nation's first energy riot, resulting in two nights of violence that left 100 injured and led to more than 170 arrests. In North Carolina, Governor James Hunt mobilized 900 National Guardsmen to avert a blockade of fuel deliveries in Greensboro and Charlotte.

The latest OPEC increase only exacerbated the sense of rage already being manifested by Americans. Following the advice of his top aides, Carter hurried back from Tokyo, skipping a planned vacation in Hawaii, in order to address the nation on energy. Work began on the speech in flight, and the White House asked the television networks for time on 5 July for a major presidential address. But just thirty hours before he was to go on the air, the White House canceled the speech without offering any reason.

For the next eleven days, the president remained at Camp David conferring with prominent people from business, government, labor, and the academic and religious communities. He also made secret helicopter flights to the homes of two "average middle class" families in Pennsylvania and West Virginia. Again, no explanation was given for these meetings other than a statement by Jody Powell that the president was consulting people in and out of government on "major domestic issues . . . which include, but go beyond, the question of energy."[19]

In truth, Carter was dissatisfied with the various drafts of the speech he had received; each reflected the opinion of one clique of advisers concerning the proper content and tone for the message. Eizenstat wanted the president to identify OPEC as the chief culprit of the energy crisis and to emphasize his commitment to a synthetic fuels program. He and Energy Secretary James Schlesinger also pushed for a more optimistic tone, while media coordinator Gerald Rafshoon thought the president should make a more realistic (and pessimistic) assessment of the situation. Hamilton Jordan argued for a message stating concrete solutions for the nation's problems; Pat Caddell believed the president needed to embrace a broader theme than energy. As a result of these differences among his own people and his personal conviction that Caddell was right, Carter decided to delay his speech and undertake instead a complete reevaluation of his administration.

The president's overhaul covered a wide range of topics from the energy crisis to presidential style. In a meeting with a small group of influential public figures, including Clark Clifford, Lane Kirkland, Jesse Jackson, and John Gardner of the consumer group Common Cause, the president was sharply criticized for his lack of leadership. In discussions with his own advisers, Pat Caddell again made the point that the president had to address the crisis of spirit, which he maintained was the most serious problem affecting the nation.

Vice-President Mondale strongly disagreed, stating that what bothered most Americans had little to do with a crisis of spirit but a lot to do with energy problems, inflation, and economic stagnation. The president's other advisers supported this pragmatic view. Carter needed to display leadership, Rafshoon argued, not sermonize on the failings of the American people. But the president ignored this counsel. When he finally came down from Camp David and gave his long-delayed speech on 15 July, he subordinated the energy crisis and the nation's other economic ills to the "crisis of spirit"—the country's most pressing problem, according to the president. Carter never defined exactly what he meant by this phrase, but it was interpreted by the news media to denote a pervasive mood of despair about the nation's future.

Although the president did not use the term *malaise*, it rapidly became the catchword for his message.[20]

As he presented additional recommendations for dealing with the energy situation, the president continued to emphasize this intangible undercurrent plaguing the American people. Carter called for limits on oil imports, cutting them by one-half, or 4.5 million barrels per day by 1990. He also proposed the establishment of an Energy Security Corporation to help finance the development of synthetic fuels and an Energy Mobilization Board to cut through the red tape that often strangled nascent projects. Resolving the energy crisis, he said, was crucial to the health of the American economy, but it was also important because it involved a test of American will—a test the American people had to pass if the United States was to remain a vibrant nation. "We are at a turning point in our history," he declared. "All the legislation in the world can't fix what's wrong with America. What is lacking is confidence and a sense of community. . . . Energy will be the immediate test of our ability to unite this nation."

The president's speech was well received. After eleven days in seclusion, rumors abounded about his physical and mental health; that assured a large audience for his address, and most Americans who heard him were impressed by his presentation. Following Rafshoon's advice, he used short, crisp sentences; seemed to make sense out of complex issues; appeared candid and sincere; spoke with passion and eloquence; and inflected his voice for dramatic effect better than he had at any time before. Finally, and most important, he appeared strong, decisive, and ready to take on the enemies of the consumer—even the oil giants and the OPEC cartel.

Yet a few days later, Carter undermined his improved standing with the American people by accepting the resignations of five members of his cabinet: Treasury Secretary Michael Blumenthal, Attorney General Griffin Bell, HEW Secretary Joseph Califano, Energy Secretary James Schlesinger, and Secretary of Transportation Brock Adams. The president had been considering a purge of his cabinet since returning from Tokyo. A group of his top advisers, including Vice-President Mondale, Jody Powell, and Hamilton Jordan, had told him that if he was going to reassess his administration, he should be prepared to make changes in his cabinet. In particular, the White House staff said, Schlesinger, Califano, and Blumenthal should be replaced because they did not work well either with the staff or with Congress. At first, Carter argued against the idea, but senior Democratic leaders whom he consulted at Camp David gave him much the same advice. He had also been disturbed for some time by embarrassing leaks and by what he regarded as disloyalty among top administration officials. He concluded, therefore, that a shake-up of his administration was warranted.

At a cabinet meeting on 17 July, he asked all his cabinet secretaries and the senior members of his staff to submit "pro forma resignations"; he would then decide which ones to accept. "I have one and one-half years left as President," he said, "and I don't deserve to be re-elected if I can't do a better job." The next day he announced that he had accepted the resignations of Schlesinger, Blumenthal, and Califano; then, a day later, those of Bell and Adams. Of the five cabinet secretaries, only Bell had intended to resign (although Schlesinger had earlier offered to leave).[21]

Certainly the president had just cause for taking this action. As he had been told at Camp David, Schlesinger, Califano, and Blumenthal had longstanding difficulties with Congress and the White House staff. Schlesinger's arrogance had infuriated lawmakers on Capitol Hill, and they also held him responsible for the country's energy mess. While Califano was highly regarded in Washington for his intelligence and management of the government's most complex agency, he could also be insufferable, and White House staffers, including Hamilton Jordan, suspected he was the source of a number of leaks on such issues as welfare reform and NHI. Because of his more conservative economic views, Blumenthal frequently clashed with Eizenstat and Schultze on fiscal policy; like Califano, he was not regarded by the White House as a "team player." As for Brock Adams, he was forced out mainly because of his unbridled tongue and his refusal to follow a directive from the White House to fire his top assistant.

Even so, many lawmakers on Capitol Hill were incensed by both the suddenness and the sweep of the cabinet dismissals. In particular, liberal Democrats were outraged by the firing of Califano, since he claimed he was removed at the insistence of the Georgia coterie influencing the president. Carter himself admitted later that he handled the cabinet changes poorly. "I . . . should have announced immediately," he wrote, "that Treasury Secretary Mike Blumenthal and HEW Secretary Joe Califano had resigned, and that I had accepted the resignation, which I had been offered many months ago by Jim Schlesinger." Instead, his gambit of asking for mass resignations made it appear that the government was falling apart.[22]

As part of his shake-up, moreover, Carter named Hamilton Jordan as chief of staff and instructed the rest of the White House staff to obey Jordan's orders "as if they were the President's own." Critics of the administration had long maintained that Carter needed someone to run the White House's day-to-day operations and limit intrusions on his time, but the president's appointment of his young and controversial aide—a sometime target of the gossip columns—was unsettling. Then, as one of his first acts as chief of staff, Jordan distributed a questionnaire to every senior member of the administration asking them to grade their own senior subordinates on their work habits, interpersonal relations, and loyalty to the White House. The questionnaire not only was insulting in tone but made it seem that another bloodletting—this time reaching into middle management—was imminent and that allegiance to the administration would be at least as important as competence in deciding who was fired.

Carter was able to undo some of the damage from the purge by selecting highly qualified people to fill the vacant slots. To head the Department of Energy, he named Charles Duncan, a Pentagon official and former executive with Coca-Cola who was respected for his managerial expertise. To replace Blumenthal, he appointed FRB Chairman William Miller. As HEW secretary, he moved Patricia Harris over from HUD. As Harris's successor, he named Moon Landrieu, a former mayor of New Orleans and past president of the U.S. Conference of Mayors. For transportation secretary, he appointed Neil Goldschmidt, mayor of Portland, Oregon, who, at age thirty-nine, had already made a name for himself because of his knowledge of urban affairs and his focus on mass transit. Finally he replaced Attorney General Bell with Bell's trusted lieutenant, Benjamin Civiletti, who had been assistant attorney general in charge of the criminal division.

In the weeks that followed, Carter and his new chief of staff also undertook a major reorganization of White House personnel to calm the "semi-hysteria" that Jody Powell said the cabinet changes had caused. In the process, the last pretense of the cabinet-level autonomy promised by Carter when he first took office was extinguished.[23] Aware that he was not popular on Capitol Hill—that, indeed, House Speaker O'Neill regarded him with open contempt—Jordan also tried to improve his relations with lawmakers by visiting them in their offices and soliciting their views. In a meeting with O'Neill, he apologized for past indiscretions. "You have really opened the door for me on the Hill," he wrote the Speaker afterwards, "and I realize the great mistake I made in not establishing some relations there the past two years."[24] Nevertheless, the cabinet shake-up was a disaster for the president. By summarily firing four members of his cabinet and accepting the resignation of a fifth, the president destroyed both his administration's efforts to restore his image as a forceful leader and the goodwill created by his 15 July address. An AP/NBC news poll, taken after the dismissals, gave Carter a "good-to-excellent rating" of only 23 percent, which was two points lower than his rating at the time of his address to the nation.

Carter had also been unwise to choose the energy crisis as the tinder on which to rekindle the American spirit, for there was no more divisive issue in 1979 than energy. Nothwithstanding the proposals Carter outlined to the American people in July, a windfall profits tax, which the president had first submitted in April, remained the core of his program. In June, the House had approved a measure providing for a 60-percent tax on decontrolled oil, which was expected to generate revenues of $277 billion before being phased out by 1990. Capitulating to a public outcry after reports of record earnings for the oil industry, the Senate passed its own tax measure; weaker than the House bill, it was still supposed to raise $178 billion in taxes by 1990. In committee, House and Senate conferees agreed to a compromise $227-billion target but had not yet worked out other differences by year's end. Regardless, a final bill, passed by both houses and ready for the president's signature, seemed assured soon after Congress convened in January.

In addition to the windfall profits tax, lawmakers also approved a standby gas-rationing bill and seemed ready to concur on the establishment of an Energy Mobilization Board, to speed up the construction of energy-related facilities, and an Energy Security Corporation, to spearhead the development of such synthetic fuels (synfuels) as liquids and gas from coal, oil from shale, and alcohol from grain.

By the close of 1979, therefore, the president was on the verge of gaining congressional approval for the most comprehensive energy legislation in the nation's history. But as in any bruising fight, especially one with such high stakes, the costs of victory were also high. Instead of winning broad support for his effort on behalf of an energy plan, the president alienated even groups whose support might have seemed beyond question. Environmentalists usually found themselves on the same side as Carter on such legislative issues as the protection of millions of acres of Alaskan land from commercial development.[25] However, they vigorously opposed the creation of a powerful Energy Mobilization Board, which they feared would ignore laws protecting the environment as it sought to facilitate the licensing and building of new energy plants. Similarly, they fought against the administration's proposal for an Energy Security Corporation, concerned that synfuel production would pollute the air and make heavy demands on scarce water supplies.

Representatives of low-income Americans who, as Stu Eizenstat reminded the president, spoke for "substantial segments of the Democratic party's basic constituency," also condemned the administration's energy program. Looking at the energy situation in terms of higher prices rather than as a test of the American will, they did not like what they saw. Aware of the opposition to the president's energy plan even within the Democratic ranks, Eizenstat warned Carter that Americans could only be persuaded to pay the price of his energy program on the basis of clear economic and political arguments—such as Iran's cutoff of oil—not by obscure references to an American angst.[26]

In other words, Eizenstat told Carter in November what Vice-President Mondale had contended in July—that Americans were not suffering from some emotional collapse and in need of catharsis. What disturbed most Americans were real and tangible conditions. It was not so much a crisis of spirit as the president's apparent inability to do anything about inflation, the energy problem, and rising unemployment that made his administration seem so ineffective. This perception was reflected on a leadership scale used in a Yankelovich/*Time* magazine poll conducted in October 1979. In contrast to Kennedy, who received the highest rating, Carter received the lowest of all potential presidential candidates, including such Republicans as former Treasury Secretary John Connally, former California Governor Ronald Reagan, former CIA Director George Bush, and Tennessee Senator Howard Baker. In commenting on the survey, Pat Caddell explained to the president that "the [American public] see too much of what has troubled them the last two years—*that events dominate us, that we react to, not lead events.*"[27]

The last half of 1979, then, was an extremely difficult period for the Carter presidency. To many political observers, the president was on the ropes and about to go down for the final count. Even some notable victories on Capitol Hill—such as passage of a $5.7-billion welfare reform program, approval of a $3.5-billion aid package for financially strapped Chrysler Corporation, and adoption of a measure establishing a new Department of Education (which candidate Carter had promised the National Education Association in 1976)—were unable to improve his standing with either the American people or traditional Democratic constituencies. Liberals continued to criticize him for his "first-phase only" national health insurance strategy. Urban leaders persisted in their complaints about inadequate help for the cities. Black leaders remained unhappy with the administration's efforts on behalf of the poor and the unemployed.

The black community was also deeply upset by the forced resignation in August of UN Ambassador Andrew Young after it was revealed that Young had held an unauthorized meeting on 26 July with a representative of the PLO, Zehdi Labib Terzi. Two hundred black leaders assembled at a meeting called by the National Association for the Advancement of Colored People (NAACP) to vent their anger. Since American Jewish leaders had led the call for Young's dismissal, the session was punctuated by anti-Semitic outbursts. Eventually cooler heads prevailed, and both Jewish and black leaders attempted to heal the rift that had developed between them. But even Carter's appointment of another black, Donald McHenry, to replace Young at the UN failed to lessen the bitterness that many blacks felt toward the administration as a result of Young's firing.

The president was also hurt in August by charges that Hamilton Jordan had used cocaine while visiting a fashionable discotheque in New York and might have used cocaine at other times as well. A special prosecutor was appointed by the Justice Department to investigate the charges leveled against Jordan. The department decided the case was without merit, but the accusations themselves were enough to taint the administration with scandal.

Ready to replace the president at the head of the Democratic ticket in 1980 was Ted Kennedy, who ended months of speculation by announcing in November that he would challenge Carter for the Democratic nomination. All the opinion polls showed Kennedy the first choice among Democrats, leading Carter decisively in every region of the country except the South, where the president maintained a slim lead over him. Yet the White House and some perceptive observers sensed that Kennedy's support was wide but not deep and that he was vulnerable on a number of counts. In fact, the administration entered the primary season confident that the president would best Kennedy. What it could not have anticipated, however, was how much developments in Iran and in the little-known country of Afghanistan would boost Carter's chances.

11

★ ★ ★ ★ ★

FOREIGN POLICY, PATRIOTISM, AND POLITICS

In contrast to such domestic matters as inflation, budget austerity, and oil and energy policy, there was no burning foreign policy issue or set of issues before 1980 that aroused the American people against the White House. In fact, on most foreign policy considerations, Americans agreed with the president. Carter had, after all, won their approbation for his efforts in the Middle East, which resulted in the signing of the Egyptian-Israeli peace treaty. Also, by a margin of better than two to one, both Democratic and Republican voters who knew enough about the SALT talks to form an opinion viewed them favorably; even a substantial number of conservatives approved of SALT. Similarly, a clear plurality (46 percent) of Americans surveyed supported the president's decision to increase military spending even at the expense of domestic programs. Sixty percent agreed with Carter's diplomatic recognition of the People's Republic of China.

The paradox was that while most of them did not fault Carter on any specific issue—indeed, praised him enthusiastically for the Camp David accords and the Egyptian-Israeli treaty—their overall assessment was negative. Moreover, many Americans in the spring and early summer of 1979 had serious concerns about the implications of the president's conduct of foreign policy. Fifty-four percent of the people polled by Pat Caddell thought the United States' position in the world was only "fair" or "poor," while 44 percent believed it was "excellent" or "good." More important, only 13 percent of the interviewees thought the nation's position in the world was "growing stronger"; 62 percent believed it was "becoming weaker."[1]

There were a number of factors that supported this feeling of national weakness. The country's growing dependence on oil imports and the declining value of the dollar left it more exposed to the whiplashes of the international economy. Despite the SALT negotiations, the Cold War remained as frigid as when Carter first took office thirty months earlier. Indeed, some Soviet specialists forecast a period of great instability in Soviet-American relations when the visibly ailing Soviet leader, Leonid Brezhnev, stepped down or died. Considerable uncertainty also surrounded developments in Rhodesia, where the election of a black prime minister failed to stop the escalation of guerrilla forces, and in Nicaragua, where the dictatorship of Anastasio Somoza was about to be toppled by the leftist Sandinistas. But the most serious situation facing the president was occurring in Iran, where anti-American sentiment, encouraged by the Khomeini regime, was reaching dangerous proportions.

Both the world energy crisis and the weakened dollar had already revealed the nation's vulnerability in the world economy, as did its unfavorable balance of trade. Carter rejected claims by American producers for relief from foreign competition through higher tariffs, allowed by the Trade Act of 1974, even though such action would have been politically popular on Capitol Hill. Instead, he sent to Congress in January 1979 a massive trade bill based on an agreement of intent reached at the multinational trade negotiations in Geneva (MTN) the previous summer. Six months later, the House and Senate approved the legislation, which sharply restricted nontariff barriers to free trade, ranging from government subsidies to product safety standards. Nevertheless, economic relations between Washington and its trading partners became increasingly strained as protectionist sentiment spread in the United States and abroad. By April, it had become so strong that some columnists predicted an impending trade war.

Protectionism, however, was only the tip of the iceberg of world economic problems. As the Joint Economic Committee of Congress warned the president in June 1979, inflation, unemployment, and excess industrial capacity were increasing worldwide, productivity was languishing, and the "energy picture [was] becoming more troubling."[2] At the end of the month, the president attended the Tokyo economic summit hoping that the United States and its trading partners would stand together against the oil cartel—perhaps even establish an international corporation to fund the development of alternative fuels. Instead, the meeting underscored significant differences among the world's strongest industrial powers and OPEC's largest customers. Although the seven leaders in Tokyo ratified an American proposal to set specific country-by-country ceilings on oil imports, they did so only after a bitter exchange between Carter and West German Chancellor Helmut Schmidt. According to the president, "Schmidt got personally abusive," claiming that Washington's interference in the Middle East was responsible for the oil crisis.[3]

Moreover, the agreement reached on oil imports was not impressive. At

the end of the summit, Carter announced that the United States would re-
strict its imports of oil to 8 million barrels a day. But this was slightly more
than current levels and considerably more than the year before, when Alaskan shipments had held down imports. As if to accent the danger of such
energy dependence, the OPEC countries, meeting at the same time in Geneva, jacked up the world price of oil to between $20 and $21 a barrel—up 15
percent from the previous week, 50 percent since the first of the year, and
1,000 percent from the $1.80 price at the beginning of the 1970s. More and
more, it seemed that Carter was becoming a prisoner of events he could not
control.

Even the signing of a SALT agreement in June furnished few political
benefits to the beleaguered president. Although Moscow and Washington
had been close to an accord since the end of 1978, disagreement on technical
issues, along with Soviet concern about improved Sino-American relations,
had delayed final action on a pact. Months of secret negotiations between
Soviet Ambassador Anatoli Dobrynin and Secretary of State Vance resolved
the last remaining points: The Soviets acknowledged the need for some
telemetry in rocket testing for verification purposes, and they accepted the
American definition of new ICBMs (any missile type differing from an existing missile by more than 5 percent in length, width, total weight, or throw
weight).

Concluding a SALT agreement, however, was only half the fight; winning Senate approval of the treaty promised to be just as arduous. The battle
lines over SALT had been forming for two years. Opponents claimed that it
gave the Soviets significant military advantages over the United States, that
it would foster a false sense of security among the American people, and that
with the loss of important "listening posts" as a result of the Iranian Revolution, Soviet adherence to its provisions could not be monitored. The administration argued that the treaty should be considered on its own merits and
not on the basis of ongoing Soviet-American differences, that it would place
important limits on the strategic arms race, and that there was enough intelligence overlap to verify Soviet compliance without the Iranian listening
posts.

At the end of June 1979, the White House began an extensive public relations campaign to mobilize public support for the SALT agreement, just as
it had for the Panama Canal treaties a year earlier. But foes of SALT II were
equally vigorous in their efforts to defeat a treaty. Their most effective tactic
was to link the pact to other issues touching on Soviet-American relations
(such as the Cuban presence in Africa and Soviet violations of human rights).
Senate Minority Leader Howard Baker, whose backing was essential if a
SALT agreement was to be approved, stated that the administration and the
Soviets should recognize that "linkage is a fact of life."[4]

Republicans were not alone in opposing the agreement. In the Senate, defense hard-liner Henry Jackson kept up an unremitting drumfire against SALT, on the grounds that it weakened the United States' defense posture. In contrast, Democrats William Proxmire of Wisconsin and George McGovern of South Dakota, who normally supported arms control measures, informed the president that they might vote against SALT II because it did not go far enough in restricting the strategic arsenals of the two superpowers. Proxmire, McGovern, and a number of other lawmakers also thought the president was making too many concessions to win over the opposition. In particular, they objected to Carter's decision to develop the MX mobile missile system. Meant to give the United States the same capacity to launch a first strike against Soviet ICBMs as the Soviets were believed to possess against the United States, the MX would be the one new missile system permitted to the United States under the terms of the SALT treaty. The president chose this course with great reluctance. "It was a nauseating prospect to confront, with the gross waste of money going into nuclear weapons of all kinds," he recorded in his diary on 4 June. But NSC Adviser Brzezinski persuaded him that without the MX trade-off, a SALT agreement had no chance on Capitol Hill.[5]

A few days after making his decision on the MX, Carter traveled to Vienna to meet with Brezhnev for the signing of the SALT II accord. The American president used the occasion to discuss a range of issues, including human rights, Iran and the Middle East, Africa, and Southeast Asia. Brezhnev, obviously failing in health and needing assistance even to walk down a few steps, warned the president not to seek to manipulate the Soviets through its new relationship with Beijing. But instead of rancor and browbeating, there was considerable goodwill between the two leaders.

Within two hours of his return from Vienna on 18 June, Carter was on Capitol Hill urging the Senate to ratify the SALT treaty he had just signed. Hard-liners remained unpersuaded. Republican Jake Garn of Utah told the president that the upper chamber was not likely to approve the SALT pact in its present form. A short time later, Minority Leader Baker, whose vote the White House had counted on, shocked the administration by announcing that he too would reject the agreement unless significant changes were made, including a requirement that the Soviets dismantle all their huge SS-9 and SS-18 missile launchers.

In testimony before the Foreign Relations and Armed Services committees, administration officials proved highly adept at defending the treaty against critics who charged that it gave the Soviets an advantage because they were not required to scrap their heaviest land-based missiles, which had far greater destructive capability (throw weight) than American MIRVed launchers. Turning that argument on its head, Vance pointed out to the Armed Services Committee that the heaviest Soviet missiles could be armed with as many as 30 warheads—in contrast to the maximum of 10 warheads allowed under SALT II. What mattered, asserted Brown and Vance, was the total number of warheads permitted to each side. Under the SALT treaty, the Soviets would have between 10,000 and 12,000 warheads, or about the same as the United States.

As the hearings on the treaty continued into August, the debate over SALT turned from the details of the accord to the size of the military budget. At the end of July, Georgia Senator Sam Nunn, widely respected on Capitol Hill as an expert on arms control, declared that he would not vote for the SALT treaty without a commitment by the president to increase the defense budget by 5 percent after inflation. A week later, he, Jackson, and Republican John Tower of Texas sent the president a letter asking him to "make public" his administration's plan for defense spending for the next five years. Former Secretary of State Henry Kissinger made a similar request, asserting that the United States could only achieve an enduring peace by having the world's strongest military force.[6] By shifting the debate over SALT to broad questions of the military balance of power and the size of Carter's defense budget, Nunn and Kissinger effectively tied approval of the treaty to the type of arms race liberal Democrats like McGovern and Proxmire opposed—an arms race that was also bound to have an adverse impact on Carter's efforts to slash the deficit. The president would have to accede to a larger budget or cut domestic spending.

As the administration contrived to win ratification of the SALT treaty, Senate Foreign Relations Committee Chairman Frank Church of Idaho announced at the end of August that a Soviet combat brigade had been discovered stationed in Cuba. The issue had first surfaced in July when the major news organizations quoted senior administration officials as conceding that they had received intelligence that the Soviet Union was setting up a high-ranking command structure in Cuba, which would be able to handle a brigade-size unit. Stepped-up reconnaissance over the next month confirmed that the Soviets had a force of between 2,000 and 3,000 men who appeared to have been in Cuba since at least 1975 or 1976 and who had recently participated in combat field maneuvers. The force was small and did not violate any agreement between Washington and Moscow. In fact, a Soviet brigade had been in Cuba since before the Cuban missile crisis of 1962. During that incident, President John F. Kennedy had asked Moscow to remove the troops; receiving no response, the subject had been dropped.

Fighting to keep his Senate seat in 1980 against a formidable right-wing challenge, Church attacked the White House for allowing the Soviet troops in Cuba. On 5 September, Secretary of State Vance held a news briefing in which he tried to mimimize the significance of the Soviet brigade by noting that the Soviet troops had been in Cuba for many years—perhaps even since the 1960s. But he also stated that he would "not be satisfied with the maintenance of the status quo," and his remarks were echoed by the president two days later. Carter and Vance later acknowledged that their statements sounded harsher than they had intended. Although they seemed to be insisting on removal of the brigade from Cuba, what they really wanted, they said, were changes in the functions and structure of the brigade so that it would not be a combat force. But the Soviets refused to alter the composition of the brigade or to discontinue its field operations.

Meanwhile, opponents of the SALT treaty used the issue to attack and delay ratification of the SALT agreement, claiming that the presence of the troops demonstrated the Soviets' untrustworthiness and threw into question the quality of U.S. intelligence. Senator Tower stated categorically that the agreement would not be approved so long as Soviet combat troops remained on the island. Even Church, a treaty-backer despite his instigation of the controversy, believed that there was "no likelihood whatever that the Senate would ratify the SALT treaty" until after Soviet forces left Cuba.[7]

Vance and Carter had taken an inconsistent stance: Asserting that the Soviet troops were not a new phenomenon[8] and so posed no military threat, they simultaneously demanded changes in the status quo. What were the Kremlin, lawmakers on Capitol Hill, or the American public to make of this contradiction? In particular, how were the Soviets to react to what seemed to them an artificially created crisis over the presence of a Soviet brigade in Cuba that had been there for years? Clearly the Kremlin was suspicious and angered by the whole situation, and even veteran foreign policymakers in the United States were critical of the administration's conduct. Believing that the White House was being indecisive, White House Counsel Lloyd Cutler and Senior Adviser Hedley Donovan, former editor in chief of *Time*, persuaded the president to invite sixteen senior statesmen to offer their views on the issue of the Soviet brigade. Dubbed the "Wise Men," the diverse group included such well-known Washington figures as George W. Ball, McGeorge Bundy, Henry Kissinger, John J. McCloy, W. Averell Harriman, Dean Rusk, and Clark Clifford. Their overall conclusion was that the brigade had been in Cuba since the 1960s, that it was not a threat to the United States, and that the administration had mishandled the affair.[9]

On 1 October, President Carter delivered a speech from the Oval Office in which he tried to put the controversy behind him. He still called the brigade "a political challenge to the United States" and announced that he was increasing American surveillance over Cuba and strengthening the American presence in the Caribbean. At the same time, he conceded that "the greatest danger to American security [was] not the two or three thousand troops in Cuba [but] the breakdown of a common effort to preserve the peace and the ultimate threat of a nuclear war."

Carter succeeded in defusing a potential explosion in Soviet-American relations, but his message failed to disarm critics of the SALT II treaty. Not until the end of October was the Democratic leadership on Capitol Hill able to refocus the debate over SALT by asking the president again to inform Congress of its defense spending plans for the next five years. The following month the Foreign Relations Committee gave a nod to the agreement, but portents for its ratification by the full Senate were not good. The vote in committee was nine to six, less than the two-thirds that would be needed for final passage.

Aside from the debate on the SALT treaty, the president also had to deal with problems in three different parts of the world—Rhodesia, Nicaragua, and Iran—which vied for news media attention during 1979 and tested his ability as a crisis manager. In Rhodesia, the issue facing Carter was whether to lift sanctions against the country following the April election of Rhodesia's first black prime minister, Bishop Abel T. Muzorewa. Although the voting appeared to have been conducted fairly, the Patriotic Front and most African countries denounced it as a sham. In the United States, black leaders showed their support for the Patriotic Front by arguing against lifting the sanctions.

And Carter agreed. On 7 June, he stated that he would continue to impose sanctions indefinitely. Although the elections "were reasonably free," Carter noted that they still fell short because blacks were not allowed to vote on the new constitution and because whites continued to occupy too many top government positions. On Capitol Hill, congressional supporters of Rhodesia lashed out at the president. The Senate even attached an amendment to a Defense Department authorization bill requiring the immediate removal of sanctions. Lobbying hard against the provision, the administration was able to work out an acceptable compromise, whereby the president would lift sanctions against Rhodesia by 15 November unless he determined it was not in the interests of the United States to do so.

Meanwhile, the British succeeded, after promising genuine black-majority rule in Rhodesia, to get the Patriotic Front to sit down in London with Muzorewa. In September, the two sides agreed to a new constitution, general elections, and a cease-fire. On 15 December, President Carter responded to this development by withdrawing the sanctions against Rhodesia (renamed Zimbabwe Rhodesia). No longer a foreign policy concern, the question of sanctions had nevertheless left its contentious mark on the relations between the White House and Capitol Hill.

Also dividing the Congress and leading to harsh attacks on the White House was the administration's policy toward Nicaragua. At the beginning of 1979, the president had imposed sanctions against that country after Somoza refused to hold elections supervised by the Organization of American States (OAS). By late spring, it had become apparent that Somoza's days as Nicaragua's strong man were numbered. At the end of May, the Sandinistas launched their "final offensive," seizing Leon, the country's second-largest city, and capturing a string of towns both north and south of the capital. The

Sandinistas also established a five-member junta to serve as head of a provisional government.

In the United States, the president came under conflicting pressures from foes and friends of the Somoza regime. Opposition to the dictator mounted after a correspondent for ABC news, Bill Stewart, was forced to lie down with his face on the ground and then was shot in the back of the head by a member of Somoza's National Guard. The execution, shown on national television, shocked and infuriated the American public. Thousands of letters and telegrams poured into the White House demanding immediate reprisals of some sort. But Somoza had his own backers in Congress, who argued that the Sandinistas were Marxists and that their victory would create another Cuba in the Western Hemisphere. On 13 June, more than 120 members of the House signed a letter urging the president to stop the reported flow of arms from Cuba and Panama to the Sandinistas.

The White House was also worried about the leftist leanings of the Sandinistas and their ties to Cuba. In order to prevent the Sandinistas from simply seizing power after toppling Somoza, the State Department proposed to establish an OAS peacekeeping force and an interim government of national reconciliation. On 21 June, Vance outlined this plan to the OAS, but the idea was doomed from the start. Neither the Sandinistas nor the other members of the OAS were prepared to accept a proposal that did not recognize the right of the Sandinistas to install a temporary government pending elections.

In truth, the administration's policy toward the Nicaraguan revolution was shortsighted. The State Department had anticipated that its plan might be rejected, yet it had no acceptable alternative. As a result, the administration had little diplomatic leverage when Somoza fled the country in July and the Sandinistas assumed control. To the president's credit, he tried to work with the new government—establishing formal relations on 24 July, sending emergency food and medical assistance, and asking Congress for $75 million in economic aid. But while the junta agreed to a cabinet dominated by moderates, the Sandinistas had their own agenda, which involved accepting Cuban military aid and moving the country politically more to the left.

The outcome to the revolution trapped the administration between two sets of critics. Certainly the Sandinistas objected to Washington's earlier assistance to Somoza and its later efforts to direct the course of the revolution, as did a number of lawmakers on Capitol Hill. At the same time, the president incurred the wrath of Somoza supporters by not doing more to save him and by allowing the Sandinistas to take over. As reports circulated in Washington that the Sandinistas were lending their support to leftist elements in El Salvador, Guatemala, and Honduras, the censure of Carter became ever more strident.

Of the foreign policy problems that Carter faced as president, however, none absorbed more of his time or had a greater impact on his administration than the ongoing upheaval in Iran. Eventually, his management of this crisis in Iranian-American relations would make him look weak and ineffective and contribute to his defeat for reelection. But in the late winter and early spring of 1980, it had just the opposite effect, boosting his popularity among the American people and propelling him ahead of Ted Kennedy in the quest for the Democratic presidential nomination.

In the months after the February storming of the American embassy in Tehran, relations between the United States and Iran had actually returned to a semblance of normality. Despite the bitter anti-Americanism of the Ayatollah Khomeini, the administration reasoned that the religious leader, having achieved and won his revolution, would quickly recede into the political background. Washington would then be able to maintain diplomatic relations with the Tehran government through Mehdi Bazargan, a loyal follower of Khomeini but also a leader of the major moderate political group in Iran, the Liberation Movement.

What the White House and most Middle East experts failed to realize was that Khomeini was bent on founding a Islamic theocracy in Iran; that in order to achieve this he had to discredit the moderates; and that he would use their contacts with the United States, whom he referred to as the "Great Satan," for this purpose. The administration also did not fully apprehend the religiosity of the vast majority of Iranians and their devotion to Khomeini as their spiritual *and* temporal leader.

Not until a group of Iranian militants seized the American embassy in Tehran on 4 November, taking sixty American hostages, was the fallacy of U.S. policy starkly revealed. The storming of the embassy was precipitated by the president's decision at the end of October to allow the shah to enter the United States for treatment of cancer. Carter was aware that this action would place the embassy in jeopardy. Following the first attack on the embassy in February, he had rescinded an invitation for the deposed Iranian leader, who was then living in Morocco, to reside in the United States, because Vance had warned him that if the shah was allowed into the country, American lives in Iran would be endangered. Instead, the administration arranged for Mexico to grant him asylum.

By October, however, the shah's health had begun to deteriorate. Two of his loyal and influential friends, Henry Kissinger and New York banker David Rockefeller, informed the White House that he might die unless he received medical treatment in the United States. Vance was still reluctant to admit him, fearing the Iranian reaction. Carter was also concerned about another assault on the embassy, but he decided to permit the shah entry after the Tehran government indicated it would take no retaliatory action if he came only for medical treatment.

For several days nothing happened, and it seemed that the deposed monarch might be able to complete his treatment without incident. But then militant Iranians, claiming to be students, seized the embassy, took hostages in the name of Khomeini, and demanded that Washington send the exiled shah home to face "revolutionary justice." Apparently they acted without the knowledge of Khomeini and never expected to retain the embassy and the surrounding compound for any length of time. But the Ayatollah sensed an opportunity to get rid of Bazargan and other moderates and to solidify Islamic control over Iran. When the Iranian prime minister ordered the militants to withdraw from the embassy and release the hostages, Khomeini refused to back him and instead encouraged the militants to hold fast. In despair, Barzagan resigned.

In the United States, Iranian students demonstrated in support of their country—parading in New York, Houston, and Columbus, denouncing the White House, and demanding the shah's immediate extradition. The demonstrations prompted a violent backlash across the nation. The worst incident occurred in Beverly Hills: A group of Americans, some wearing hard hats and carrying baseball bats, beat Iranians staging an anti-shah march. American workers also refused to unload Iranian ships or service Iranian airliners. On Capitol Hill, resolutions were introduced to prohibit Iranian students from protesting against the United States and even to expel all Iranian students from the country.

For President Carter the taking of the embassy was a nightmare. Reviewing his options, he ordered preparations for military action but quickly ruled out an immediate strike as impractical; the United States simply lacked the military capability to rescue the hostages. Instead, he decided to work for their release through diplomatic channels, hoping that pressure from the international community and Iran's middle class would persuade Khomeini and the militants to yield. Vance set the desired tone, telling reporters that it was "time not for rhetoric, but for quiet, careful and firm diplomacy."[10]

To halt the violence against Iranians that might lead to retaliation against Americans in Iran, the president asked the Justice Department if there was a legal way to limit demonstrations. On 12 November, he ordered the cessation of all oil purchases from Iran; two days later, he froze all Iranian assets in the United States. Primarily, he engaged in various diplomatic efforts to gain the release of the hostages—such as sending to Iran former Attorney General Ramsey Clark, who had been an outspoken opponent of the shah's regime and had even met with Khomeini in Paris earlier in the year.

The American public gave Carter high marks for the calm and deliberate manner in which his administration reacted to the crisis. As Americans watched Iranian crowds taunt the United States, the president's prestige soared. According to a Gallup poll, in the four weeks since the hostages had been seized, public approval of Carter's presidency jumped from 30 percent to 61 percent, the sharpest gain ever in a Gallup survey of presidential popularity. Seventy-seven percent of the people questioned specifically approved of the president's handling of the crisis.

President Carter's resurgence in the polls was reflected in his bid for re-election in 1980. In one of the most remarkable turnabouts in American political history, the president, who had been trailing Ted Kennedy badly in presidential preference surveys just a month earlier, suddenly found himself in December 1979 with a commanding lead over the Massachusetts senator. According to most polls, moreover, Carter led Kennedy in every section of the country, among all age groups, and even among those who called themselves liberal Democrats. In trial heats against the leading Republican candidates, the president also enjoyed comfortable leads, including a fourteen-point edge over former Governor Ronald Reagan, his closest rival in the polls.

Although Kennedy did not announce his candidacy for president until November, he had been toying with the idea for at least a year. However, Carter had always believed the senator was vulnerable on several fronts, including his liberal voting record, the traditional stigma of a challenge to an incumbent president from one's own party, and widespread doubts about his character because of the Chappaquiddick incident ten years earlier.[11] Once Kennedy officially entered the race, the president's advisers were confident his huge lead in the polls would evaporate. A matchup in Florida on 13 October gave an early indication that their instincts were correct, as a referendum to select county representatives to the state Democratic convention presaged the relative strength of the candidates. Unwisely, leaders of a draft-Kennedy movement in the state declared that they would win from 35 percent to a majority of the delegates. Instead, the Carter organization outspent and outblitzed the Kennedy camp, sending into Florida such heavy artillery as Rosalynn and Lillian Carter, Vice-President Mondale, and former Ambassador Young. When the votes were counted, Carter's supporters had beaten the Kennedy slate by two to one.

Over the next few weeks, the campaign between Kennedy and Carter intensified. The president continued to take advantage of his incumbency to dispense patronage, announce federal grants, and respond to local concerns wherever he traveled. By the end of October, the polls showed the president gaining on the senator. Then, on 4 November—the day the White House received word that demonstrators had overrun the American embassy in Tehran and taken hostages—CBS aired an interview that Kennedy had taped earlier with news correspondent Roger Mudd. In what might have been the worst public appearance of his political career, Kennedy seemed unable to give a direct answer to any of the questions Mudd asked him, such as why he was running for president or how his administration would differ from Carter's if he was elected. Halting and rambling, he also faltered when queried about Chappaquiddick. Political observers agreed that Kennedy had hurt himself badly.

Even so, at this point the president remained the underdog in the campaign, trailing Kennedy in all the national polls. Working against Carter were the state of the economy, the pending fight in the Senate over ratification of SALT II, and the leadership issue, at which Kennedy was already hammering hard. At best, Carter would do well in the South while the senator would be strong in New England, with the final outcome for the nomination being decided in such states as New York, Pennsylvania, and California—states likely to go for Kennedy, according to the analysts.

Iran's seizure of American hostages in November completely changed the election calculus. Almost immediately Hamilton Jordan sensed the implications Iran's action might have for politics in the United States. Anticipating that the situation would be resolved quickly, Jordan nevertheless instructed Phil Wise, the president's appointment secretary, to be circumspect with the press. "Don't forget," he told Wise, "the press will be looking at this in the context of the campaign. It'll be over in a few hours, but it could provide a nice contrast between Carter and our friend from Massachusetts in how to handle a crisis."[12]

Meanwhile, Kennedy continued to run into problems. Responding to a reporter's question about the possibility of allowing the shah of Iran to live permanently in the United States, the senator assailed the former leader for heading "one of the most violent regimes in the history of mankind." How could the United States justify taking in the shah, he asked, "with his umpteen billions of dollars he'd stolen from Iran?" Kennedy was instantly criticized by the administration and the press for his remarks. Furious, Carter told a bipartisan congressional delegation, "I don't give a damn whether you like or do not like the shah. The issue is that American hostages, fifty of them, are being held by kidnappers—radical and irresponsible kidnappers."

Kennedy's ragged start boosted the president's own candidacy, which he announced officially on 4 December. In a brief televised statement, he addressed the leadership issue, since the Kennedy forces were trying to make it the campaign's theme, and described his own style as calm, strong, and effective. But then he surprised his listeners by stating that he was postponing any stumping. "While the crisis continues," he remarked, "I must be present to define and lead our response to an ever-changing situation of the greatest security, sensitivity, and importance." Two weeks later, Carter also decided that, because of the hostage crisis and the recent invasion of Afghanistan by Soviet forces, he would cancel a planned debate in Iowa with Kennedy and California Governor Jerry Brown—another presidential candidate but not one regarded as a major factor in the race.

The Soviet Union's decision in December to send 85,000 troops into Afghanistan caught the president off guard even though he had been warned by NSC Adviser Zbigniew Brzezinski that the Soviets might invade the country. Before the invasion, Moscow had already deployed between 5,000 and

10,000 military advisers in Afghanistan and provided other military aid to the Marxist government of Hafizulah Amin. But Amin was no more able than his predecessor, Nur Muhammad Taraki, to suppress the insurgency against the Kabul government. Distrustful of Amin, the Soviets executed him and installed a puppet regime headed by Barbrak Karmal.

At the same time the Soviet Union invaded Afghanistan, much of the Islamic world, including the vital Persian Gulf, was in turmoil. The fervor of Islamic revolution begun in Iran appeared to be spreading throughout the region. In Saudi Arabia, a small but fanatic Muslim sect seized the Grand Mosque in Mecca, Islam's holiest shrine, holding hundreds of pilgrims as hostages. After two weeks of bloodshed, in which as many as 200 pilgrims and 300 guerrillas may have died, Saudi forces were finally able to regain complete control of the shrine. In Pakistan, 20,000 Muslim rioters stormed and burned the American embassy in Islamabad, shouting, "Kill the American dogs," and murdering two Americans after rumors circulated that the United States and Israel had been responsible for the raid on the Grand Mosque.

With so much of the Middle East in upheaval, the president feared that unless he took a firm stand against the Afghan invasion, the entire region would be vulnerable to Soviet attack. "A successful takeover of Afghanistan," he later wrote, "would . . . pose a threat to the rich oil fields of the Persian Gulf area and to the crucial waterways through which so much of the world's energy supplies had to pass." On 3 January 1980, therefore, he asked the Senate to table indefinitely its consideration of the SALT II agreement. Speaking to the American people the next day, he announced that the Soviet Union would be barred access to high technology or other strategic items and that he was placing an embargo on U.S. grain sales to the Soviets. He also raised the possibility that the United States might boycott the 1980 Summer Olympics scheduled for Moscow. "We will deter aggression, we will protect our nation's security and we will preserve the peace," he declared to the nation.[13]

Imposition of a grain embargo on the Soviet Union had been the most contentious issue within the administration. Mondale and Eizenstat strongly opposed the ban on the grounds that it would cause great injury to American farmers. "Food is not, in my opinion, an appropriate weapon to use in the international political arena," Eizenstat told the president. With the Iowa caucuses only a few weeks away, there was also real concern at the White House about the embargo's political impact on that heavily agricultural state. Although President Carter was sensitive to these arguments, he also believed that a stoppage of grain, coincident with an agreement by other nations not to replace the supplies withheld by the United States, was the most powerful leverage Washington could use against Moscow. He was also prepared to compensate farmers for the losses they might suffer as a result of the embargo.[14]

The response to the president's speech was generally favorable. According to Hamilton Jordan, telephone calls to the White House ran two to one in support of the president. Moreover, in the Iowa caucuses on 21 January, Carter beat Kennedy decisively, carrying ninety-eight of ninety-nine counties and even defeating the senator in blue-collar and Catholic areas where he was supposedly popular. At least as important as Kennedy's own failings as a candidate was the fact that patriotism prevailed over politics for Iowan Democrats. Farmers did not like the grain embargo, but they decided to back the president in a time of international emergency.

Buoyed by the results in Iowa, Carter delivered his State of the Union address two days later. In his toughest attack on the Soviet Union since taking office, he enunciated what became known as the "Carter Doctrine." "Let our position be absolutely clear," he told a joint session of Congress. "An attempt by any outside force to gain control of the Persian Gulf region will be regarded as an assault on the vital interests of the United States of America, and such an assault will be repelled by any means necessary, including military force."

To show that he meant business, Carter proposed that all men between the ages of eighteen and twenty-six be required to register for a future draft. He also asked for five annual increases of 5 percent in real military spending rather than the 3 percent that had been his goal since 1977, and he requested $400 million in military and economic aid to Pakistan, which bordered Afghanistan. Furthermore, he announced that his administration would negotiate for the use of naval and air facilities near the Persian Gulf and expand the American military presence in the Indian Ocean, and he expressed his view that the United States should not participate in the Summer Olympics in Moscow.

Although he only hinted at it in his State of the Union address, Carter was also determined to draw militarily and politically closer to China. Ever since the United States had instituted diplomatic relations with the PRC at the beginning of the year, NSC Adviser Brzezinski had been pushing for closer military ties with Beijing irrespective of—indeed, precisely because of—the ramifications for U.S.–Soviet relations. Until the invasion of Afghanistan, Secretary of State Vance, who wanted a more balanced relationship between the United States and the two communist powers, was able to persuade the president not to sell arms to the Chinese or to allow military linkages with China.

That changed, however, as a result of the Soviet aggression on Afghanistan; Brzezinski quickly proposed, with the support of Defense Secretary Brown, the establishment of a "U.S.–Chinese defense relationship." The Chinese, not wishing to be a pawn in the geopolitical rivalry between Washington and Moscow, balked at the idea, but they did take advantage of permission to purchase military hardware and high technology items whose export to the Soviet Union was now prohibited. In addition, they were granted most-favored-nation trade status, which was also denied to the Soviets.

Pique rather than prudence dictated Carter's response to the Afghan invasion. Indeed, he may have acted as much out of frustration over other differences between Moscow and Washington and a more generalized despair over the Iranian hostage crisis as out of foreign policy considerations. If his purpose was to force the Soviets out of Afghanistan, he and his secretary of state utilized a questionable strategy. In the first place, there was no intelligence to indicate that a grain embargo, a boycott of the Olympics, or any other action the president proposed would deter the Soviets from their aggressive course. Rather than narrowing down a list of options, moreover, the president fired a volley of measures at the Soviets, which were meant to punish them as much as convince them to leave the country they had just invaded.

Even Brzezinski, who seized the opportunity to convert the president completely to his view of the Soviet Union as a global menace, questioned Carter's tactics. Although he regarded the invasion as part of Moscow's hegemonical foreign policy, he recognized the need for a more temperate response—one that would be punitive but also allow for dialogue and take into account future relationships with the Soviet Union.

The president was not insensitive to such arguments, but because he was bent on chastening the Soviets, he adopted virtually every punitive measure suggested to him regardless of its immediate or long-term consequences. "I was sobered . . . by our strained relations with the Soviets," he later acknowledged, "but I was determined to make them pay for their unwarranted aggression without yielding to political pressure at home."[15] As a result, U.S.–Soviet relations became mortgaged to the Soviets' withdrawal from Afghanistan, dealings between Moscow and Washington became even more strained, and ratification of a SALT II agreement, which had been one of Carter's highest priorities since taking office, was indefinitely postponed. Finally, the United States had made a commitment to the Persian Gulf without giving serious thought to the military or foreign policy implications of that move.

In Europe, NATO allies were deeply troubled by the U.S. response to the Soviet invasion. Although they condemned the Soviet action, they refused to become involved, arguing that the attack did not necessarily mean aggressive designs on other nations outside the Soviet orbit. Of Europe's leaders, only Britain's new prime minister, Margaret Thatcher, fully backed Carter's tough line toward Moscow. In contrast, Chancellor Helmut Schmidt was harshly critical of the president, complaining again that Carter conducted foreign policy without considering its impact on Western Europe.

Within the White House, there was uncertainty about the underlying principles and premises of the administration's foreign policy. How had it changed as a result of the Iranian Revolution and the Afghan invasion? What was left of détente? How should the impending military buildup proposed by the president be shaped to give maximum support to the nation's long-range strategic objectives—and what were those objectives? How did human rights now figure into foreign policy considerations?

For the moment, Carter was able to capitalize politically from the developments in Afghanistan and Iran, but Carter's own advisers were already wondering how long this could continue. If the hostage crisis dragged on, the American public might begin to blame the president. Moreover, it was difficult to gauge the depth of the people's concern about distant and alien Afghanistan—or whether they would hold the president responsible if the Soviets refused to withdraw. At some point, Americans might even wonder if these developments could have been avoided—if the president bore the brunt for a nation incapable of responding to violators of international law. Should that happen, it would be campaign fodder for the president's political opponents.

12

★ ★ ★ ★ ★

ECONOMIC PAIN
AND POLITICS

In response to the Iranian hostage crisis and the invasion of Afghanistan by the Soviet Union, the American people had rallied behind President Carter. As a result, the president was able to run an effective Rose Garden campaign for renomination against Senator Kennedy. Ultimately, however, the outcome of the 1980 election—which, in April, was more than seven months away—would be determined by public perceptions of Carter's overall performance. Large elements of the Democratic party, and even larger segments of the American public, still were not satisfied with his presidency. Americans were troubled by lengthening unemployment lines, by prime interest and inflation rates nearing 20 percent, and by skyrocketing prices for gold and other precious metals. As the economy seemed to be spinning out of control and the hostage situation reached an impasse, Carter's ability to lead the nation came into question once more.

Inflation remained the White House's most serious domestic problem. During January 1980, the CPI rose 1.4 percent, or an annual rate of about 18.2 percent—the highest in six years. Wholesale prices for January climbed at an annual rate of 21 percent as prices for finished goods, which had actually declined the previous month, began to escalate once more. Wage increases failed to keep up with the inflation rate, so that the purchasing power of an average urban employee declined 1.4 percent for February alone. Most unnerving of all, some economists predicted that double-digit inflation would persist throughout the 1980s.

While the White House tried to grapple with inflation through voluntary wage and price guidelines, fiscal restraint, and tighter credit, unemployment rose dramatically. The Labor Department reported that during April the nation's jobless rate had ballooned to 7 percent and the number of unemployed workers had jumped to 7.3 million, the largest increase in overall unemployment since January 1975.

Interest rates also continued to advance. By the beginning of March 1980, the prime rate for most banks had increased to 16.75 percent; by the end of April it stood at about 18.5 percent, and some business leaders were even predicting it might hit 20 percent or more. As both the inflation rate and interest rates climbed, housing starts fell, dropping 6 percent in January to 1.4 million, the lowest level since July 1976. The free-fall in housing, which continued throughout the first quarter of 1980, had a ripple effect, causing housing-related industries to close down or lay off workers.

Responding to the worsening economy, the nation's financial and commodity markets experienced some wild gyrations. On the one hand, financiers believed that the president was finally acting with decision and direction because of his response to the hostage crisis and the Soviet invasion of Afghanistan. Anticipating an increase in defense spending, Wall Street investors drove the Dow-Jones average up by almost 85 points in January and February, closing on 13 February at 904. But as fear grew within the business community that inflation was getting out of hand, stocks began to spiral downward, closing in the third week of March at 785—its lowest level since April 1978.

Seeking a safe haven for their money, investors speculated in precious metals, so that the price of gold zoomed to over $850 an ounce. When billionaire Nelson Bunker Hunt attempted to corner the silver market, the price of silver jumped from $6 per ounce in early 1979 to $50 an ounce by February 1980. But this level could not be sustained, and by April, silver prices had fallen to around $10 an ounce. The price of gold also dropped to around $450 an ounce.

Meanwhile, in a February *Newsweek*/Gallup poll, almost half of the people interviewed (48 percent) identified inflation as their primary worry (up from 39 percent a month earlier). This anxiety—which encouraged consumers to spend now in anticipation of higher prices later—was also evident at the White House. "I believe we truly are on the verge of an economic crisis which is as severe for the country as the foreign policy crises you have been dealing with over the last several months," Stu Eizenstat told the president on 26 March.[1] In the same February *Newsweek*/Gallup poll, 52 percent of the respondents supported government limits on wage and price increases as a way to cope with inflation. Ted Kennedy attacked Carter relentlessly for not imposing controls or freezing oil prices. Even politicians and economists opposed to controls insisted that the president needed to take new steps to deal with economic problems.

Although still reluctant to deviate from the program of fiscal and monetary restraint that he and Paul Volcker were pursuing, Carter recognized that he would have to address some of the economic and social concerns of traditional Democratic constituencies in order to keep Kennedy at bay and win reelection in November. In his 1980 budget proposal, therefore, he called for substantial expansions in such highly visible areas as housing and jobs, including a new $2-billion youth employment program. Revenues for this spending would come from the additional income tax receipts resulting from inflation, the windfall profits tax, and increased social security taxes.

The proposed budget was received with skepticism, even cynicism. Because of inflation and the economic slowdown, the projected $29-billion deficit for fiscal 1980 had to be revised upward to $40 billion, and few economists or financial leaders believed that the prediction of a $15.8-billion deficit for 1981 would remain constant. In fact, a few short weeks after Carter sent his budget to Capitol Hill, the White House realized it would have to reconsider the economic assumptions on which it was based. The recession proved to be much more tenacious than most economists had foreseen. The nation's two most important industries, housing and automobiles, virtually collapsed. Housing starts in March were down 42 percent from a year earlier after suffering the sharpest monthly decline in twenty years. Car sales were also off 24 percent from the previous year. Unemployment in Detroit reached a staggering 24 percent. Either because of or in spite of the administration's economic policy, the nightmare of "stagflation"—higher prices, severe unemployment, and a stagnant or declining economy—had come true.

The president responded to this economic crisis by conducting a scaled-down version of the previous summer's Camp David domestic summit. Seeking a national consensus around what he hoped would be a bipartisan economic plan, he held a week-long series of meetings in March with more than three hundred Democratic and Republican lawmakers from Congress, business and financial leaders, and representatives from various farm, labor, and civic groups. The upshot of the sessions was a call to balance the budget as a first, visible step toward fighting inflation. Working closely with the congressional leadership, the White House then molded a new economic program predicated on balancing the budget through another round of cuts. As did lawmakers on Capitol Hill, the president's advisers agreed that in order for the program to be credible, the reductions had to be across-the-board even though this meant curtailing programs for such groups as the elderly and the poor.

On 14 March, the president announced his new economic plan to the American people. Asserting that inflation threatened the nation's security, he stated that his major goal would be to balance the $612-billion budget for 1981. He would also curb credit-financed spending which "fed" inflation, expand the monitoring activities of COWPS, impose a "gasoline conservation fee" on imported oil of about ten cents per gallon, and develop specific recommendations for revitalizing the U.S. economy. These actions would not produce "a quick victory" over inflation, he warned. But they would bring inflation under control by year's end and "put an end to the fear about the future that afflicts so many of our own people and so many of our institutions."

Yet the program Carter unveiled to the nation fell short of delivering the shock treatment many economists thought was needed to break the whirling inflationary cycle. In the first place, total federal spending for 1981—even if Congress approved the president's recommendations—would still be about $43 billion more than current levels. Furthermore, the reductions would not by themselves balance the budget; that would require approval of other, revenue-raising measures, including the ten-cents-a-gallon fee on imported oil. Again, passage of such legislation was far from certain. Although Carter did not itemize the specific budget cuts he would make, it was widely—and correctly—reported that he would not touch such entitlement programs as social security, veterans' benefits, and unemployment relief even though these were the fastest growing portions of the budget.

Even Eizenstat was surprised by the indifferent response to the president's inflation-bashing endeavor. "Despite the effort which went into your anti-inflation announcement," he told the president, a recent survey indicated that "a significant majority of Americans are unaware of it." Referring to the "growing national sense that things are out of control," he urged the president to leave the White House and travel the length and breadth of the country, meeting the American people and explaining to them his economic program. "You need not debate Kennedy or even 'campaign,' " he said. "The key is to get out and let the people know you are the general in charge."[2]

The president refused, however, to alter his political strategy—even though Democratic voters manifested their frustration with the administration by giving Kennedy a clear primary sweep in New York and a victory in Connecticut on 25 March. Carter's defeat in New York was a serious setback for his campaign. Heretofore, the fight for the Democratic presidential nomination had seemed to be a mismatch, as the president, stubbornly ensconced in the White House, beat the Massachusetts senator in his own backyard of New Hampshire. The polls also showed Kennedy losing support in the rest of the country, particularly in the South and Midwest. On 11 February, Pat Caddell reported to the president that Kennedy's negative rating in Illinois had climbed to 60 percent, higher even than in any southern state. According to his analysis, "Unless the mid-Atlantic is surprisingly better—New York and Pennsylvania—it is hard to see where Kennedy goes without a major shift in fundamentals."[3]

Speculation even began over how much longer Kennedy would stay in the race. With contributions starting to dry up and money running out, it was clear he had to score a substantial victory soon and that upcoming primaries in Illinois and New York were his last chance to do so. All the polls predicted that he would lose in Illinois, and even in New York, he appeared to be in trouble.

In March, however, the administration made a colossal diplomatic blunder, which might have saved New York for Kennedy and kept him in contention. At the UN, the United States voted in favor of a resolution calling on Israel to dismantle civilian settlements in occupied Arab territories, including Jerusalem. Twice before in 1979, the United States had abstained on similar votes, and at the end of February, Carter had instructed the American delegation to do the same on this variant. However, Vance and the president wanted Israel to know of their displeasure with the continued building of Israeli settlements on the West Bank. On 1 March, the secretary of state informed the president that reference to Jerusalem had been deleted from the UN resolution, and he asked that the United States be allowed to vote in favor of it. The president agreed, and it carried unanimously.

The Israeli government and American Jewish leaders were infuriated by the vote and by the fact that the references to Jerusalem had erroneously not been deleted. When the president learned of the mistake, he issued a statement saying that the vote had been cast as a result of a "failure of communication" and that he had approved the resolution "with the understanding that all references to Jerusalem would be deleted." In other words, Carter reaffirmed his administration's support for the resolve—which most of the American Jewish community regarded as anti-Israeli—and admitted error only in the inclusion of Jerusalem. New York's large Jewish population reacted by voting in overwhelming numbers for Kennedy, who defeated Carter by 16 percent.

But the Jewish vote was not the sole reason for the margin of Kennedy's victory or for his win in Connecticut. By all indications, in going to the polls, Democratic voters were casting their ballots as much against the administration as in support of Kennedy. For the first time, according to a *New York Times*/CBS survey, more voters trusted Kennedy over Carter (49 percent to 46 percent). Also for the first time, the Iranian hostage crisis and the Afghan invasion worked against the president. More than half of the people questioned believed the president was being "too soft" with Iran, and only 17 percent thought his conduct of the Afghan crisis had improved the United States' global image. "The East wind that chilled the Carter candidacy this week was made up of four I's—Inflation, Iran, Israel and Ineptitude," commented *New York Times* columnist William Safire following the New York primary.[4]

Kennedy's chances of beating the president at the Democratic convention remained slight, since the senator would need to win 62 percent of the remaining delegates. That prospect was unlikely because the contest now shifted to the South, Midwest, and West, where Kennedy had little popularity, organization, or money. Nevertheless, the president's political advisers were shocked by what his defeat in New York and Connecticut exposed: the size of the anti-Carter protest vote. A Yankelovich poll taken a week later confirmed their worst fears. The survey found that 70 percent of the people questioned thought it was time for a change in the Oval Office. Eighty-one percent of the respondents thought the United States was in serious trouble. For the first time, Republican front-runner Ronald Reagan moved ahead of Carter in the polls, 44 percent to 43 percent. Only 18 percent of the surveyed group rated the president "a very strong leader," compared with 38 percent for Reagan and 27 percent for Kennedy.[5]

Despite Carter's growing political vulnerability, he beat Kennedy convincingly in the Wisconsin primary and Kansas caucuses on 1 April and drove Jerry Brown out of the race entirely. But in Wisconsin, which permitted crossover balloting (that is, Democrats voting for Republicans and vice versa), thousands of Democrats voted in the GOP primary. As a result, Republicans outdrew Democrats for the first time in twenty-five years, and Ronald Reagan, the Republican winner over George Bush, received a larger total than the president.

By this time, the president also had to contend with the possibility of a third-party challenge from Republican Congressman John Anderson of Illinois. Anderson had entered the presidential race as a liberal alternative to the other Republican candidates. Although few political observers took his campaign very seriously, he began to attract support because of his willingness to take politically unpopular positions, such as advocating a fifty-cents-a-gallon tax on gasoline as a conservation measure. Although no one could be certain whether Carter or Reagan would be hurt more if Anderson appeared on the ballot in November, it seemed more likely that he would woo liberals away from the president than capture moderate Republicans.

What Carter apparently expected was for Kennedy to acknowledge that he could not win the nomination, withdraw from the race, and endorse the president. Only then could he begin the healing process within the Democratic party that was required for a win in November. "Fritz [Mondale] and I needed several months to pull together our badly divided party to prepare for the general election," Carter later commented. But instead of withdrawing, the Massachusetts senator announced that he was staying in the contest all the way to the convention.[6]

As of the first week in April, then, Carter's campaign advisers were more confident than ever that the president would be renominated in August, but they also remained greatly concerned about the obstacles posed by Kennedy, Reagan, and Anderson. Even though Kennedy could not win, he could keep the party divided and undermine Carter's chances in November. Former governor Reagan was proving to be a much more formidable candidate than the president's campaign staff had anticipated, while Anderson's candidacy inserted a discomfiting wild card in the race. Any adverse change in affairs at home or abroad could be fatal to Carter's reelection drive.

Three weeks after the Wisconsin primary, Kennedy narrowly defeated Carter in Pennsylvania and in the Michigan caucuses. In Pennsylvania, the senator won by only 10,000 votes out of 1.6 million votes cast, acquiring 93 delegates to the president's 92. In Michigan, Kennedy again captured only 1 more delegate than Carter, gaining 71 delegates to the president's 70. In contrast, the president collected 60 delegates in Missouri to the senator's 10. As the primary campaign entered its final month, the president was reported to have 1,175 of the 1,666 first-ballot votes needed for nomination; Kennedy had only 664. The president's own figures indicated that he had 1,507 votes to the Massachusetts senator's 707.

Nevertheless, Kennedy's victories in Pennsylvania and Michigan, combined with his earlier wins in New York and Connecticut, meant that he had enough staying power to carry his uphill campaign into the 3 June primaries. His assaults on the president were also becoming increasingly effective, thereby whittling away at Carter's prospects in November. At the very least, Carter's strategists anticipated a loud and divisive brawl with Kennedy forces over the party platform.

The major news story during the week of 25 April, however, was not the campaign but the failed attempt to rescue the Iranian hostages. Preparation for some form of military action against Iran had been under way at the White House since 6 November 1979, the day after the hostages were first taken, and Zbigniew Brzezinski had also asked the Joint Chiefs of Staff (JCS) to draft a plan for a rescue mission. For five months, Carter resisted proposals for military measures. "The problem with all the military options," he said, "is that we could use them and feel good for a few hours—until we found that they had killed our people. And once we start killing people in Iran, where does it end?"[7]

But by the second week of April, the president had changed his mind, since all efforts to win the freedom of the hostages (or even their transfer to the Tehran government) had foundered. In February, a political moderate, Abolhassen Bani-Sadr, had been elected as Iran's first president, leading the White House to hope for an early resolution of the crisis. In an interview with ABC news, Bani-Sadr had expressed his own expectation that the situation would soon be sorted out. Secret negotiations between Hamilton Jordan and two men with close ties to Iran's Revolutionary Council—one a French lawyer and the other an Argentine businessman living in Paris—fed these hopes. Through the two intermediaries, Bani-Sadr agreed to a plan by which a UN fact-finding mission would go to Iran to hear Tehran's grievances and then obtain the release of the hostages. But Khomeini subverted the plan by instructing the militants holding the hostages not to hand them over to the new government.

As the possibility of a quick release faded, interest shifted at the White House from unofficial negotiations to some type of military rescue action. The fact that a small plane had successfully penetrated Iranian airspace and had examined a potential rescue staging site without being detected convinced Carter that such a mission was feasible. On 7 April, therefore, the president informed the NSC that he was breaking diplomatic relations with Tehran and imposing new sanctions, including an embargo on all U.S. goods except for food and medicine. An inventory of frozen Iranian assets would be compiled for possible distribution to American citizens and businesses with claims against Iran. Four days later, at another meeting of the NSC, he announced his decision to go forward with the rescue mission. In his opinion, nothing less than the nation's honor was at stake in freeing the hostages from their illegal and immoral bondage.[8]

Of the NSC members, only Secretary of State Vance, who had been vacationing in Florida and was not even present at the hastily called 11 April meeting, was opposed to the president's decision. Vance had previously advised against cutting off relations with Iran, arguing that it was much easier to sever ties with a country than to restore them. Moreover, by isolating Iran, the United States would be handing the Soviets a target of opportunity in the Middle East. Believing that a rescue mission could not succeed without many hostages being killed or wounded, he asked that another attempt be made at diplomacy. Here, too, the secretary of state failed to budge Carter.

According to the intricate JCS scheme for rescuing the hostages, eight helicopters would fly from the aircraft carrier *Nimitz* in the Gulf of Oman to a site south of Tehran designated Desert One. There they would be joined by six C-130s carrying ninety members of a rescue team plus fuel and supplies. Having delivered their cargo, the transport planes would leave Iran. The helicopters would then take the rescue team to cover in mountains one hundred miles outside of Tehran. The next night, trucks purchased in Tehran by American agents would carry the rescue team into the city. The highly trained force would attack both the foreign ministry building (where American chargé Bruce Laingen and two of his colleagues were being held) and the American embassy compound, overpowering the guards and freeing the hostages. The team and the hostages would then be retrieved by the helicopters (still hidden outside Tehran) and flown to an abandoned airstrip near the city. There two C-141s would be waiting to take them across the desert to safety in Saudi Arabia.

Military experts continue to debate the feasibility of the rescue mission. Some argue that more helicopters should have been used, others that the plan was too complex and dependent on too many variables to succeed. But three points are clear. First, the president did not issue the order to begin the operation until he was confident it would work. Second, the ill-fated mission was the victim of circumstances that doomed it almost from the outset. Third, its failure was a devastating political and personal blow to Carter, from which he and his administration never fully recovered.

Although the president was assured by his military advisers and by the rescue team itself that the chances for the mission's success were good, the carefully constructed plan began to fall apart within hours after the raid commenced on 24 April. The setup provided for two spare aircraft in addition to the six helicopters required for the mission. Soon after entering Iranian airspace, one of the choppers developed mechanical problems and had to be abandoned. A second helicopter got lost in a sandstorm and had to return to the *Nimitz*, taking with it the margin of safety built into the plan. The remaining aircraft proceeded to Desert One, only to encounter a busload of Iranians crossing the normally desolate area; shortly thereafter, a fuel truck and a pickup truck were also spotted. Although the bus was immobilized and the fuel truck blown up, the driver of the truck escaped in the pickup that had been following him.

Concluding that the escapees were probably smugglers who would not report what they had seen to Iranian officials, the leader of the rescue force, Army Col. Charles Beckwith, a Green Beret veteran of the Vietnam War, decided to carry on. But then a third helicopter developed a hydraulic problem after refueling and could not take off. Because the plan called for six operating helicopters, the mission was aborted.

As the force was boarding the C-130s and preparing to evacuate, one of the five operational helicopters rose fifteen to twenty feet in the air and then banked sharply to the left, slashing the fuselage of one of the transports. Eight servicemen were killed and four others badly burned. The survivors abandoned the scene, leaving the four remaining helicopters and the dead behind in the flaming wreckage. A few hours later, in the early morning, a visibly shaken Carter went on national television to report to the American people on the disaster that had taken place.

Although initial reaction to the hapless mission was supportive of the president, the failure of the rescue attempt probably did more to undercut the Carter presidency than any other single event. Even before this incident, the hostage crisis had become a political liability for the president. A *Newsweek*/Gallup poll taken on 9 and 10 April showed that approval for the president's handling of the crisis had fallen to just 40 percent of the people surveyed. As details of the botched plan were revealed, it became another entry in a long list of failures that many Americans attributed to the president. On Capitol Hill, some lawmakers expressed indignation that Congress had not been consulted before the venture. American allies were also distressed that they had not been briefed in advance. Indeed, they were disturbed by the president's entire approach to the situation, including the imposition of new sanctions on Iran, which they believed would be ineffective, and a trade embargo, which they feared might be the first step on the road to war with Iran.[9]

As the primary season entered its final month, the president's whole foreign policy seemed in disarray, and this perception was further strengthened by the resignation of Secretary of State Vance. Although the immediate cause for Vance's decision was his objection to the Iranian rescue mission, he had watched his influence with the president wane steadily since the Soviet invasion of Afghanistan. As Carter turned more and more to Brzezinski for counsel, the secretary appeared increasingly tired, drained, and withdrawn.

The news media seized on Vance's resignation as evidence that the president's foreign policy was in a quagmire. "As things now stand," *Newsweek* reported, "the President's uncertain diplomatic strategy has left allies perplexed, enemies unimpressed and the nation as vulnerable as ever in an increasingly dangerous world." Because of his high profile and combative Cold War views, Brzezinski came under particular attack, prompting Jody Powell to urge Carter to curb the NSC adviser's public appearances. "To put it bluntly," Powell stated, "Zbig needs to almost drop from public view for the next few months at least."[10]

In response to his mounting political problems, Carter decided to abandon his Rose Garden campaign in favor of a more public candidacy. His staff had been urging him to change course since at least the New York primary, on the grounds that his standing with the American people and his fundraising were being hurt by his stay-at-home strategy. His argument that he needed to remain at the White House to deal with fast-breaking developments in the hostage crisis was being met with increasing skepticism. Critics charged instead that he was hiding behind the hostages to avoid debating Kennedy. The debacle of the rescue mission provided a convenient moment to break out from his six-month hermitage in the White House. As Carter returned to the campaign trail, his ascendancy over Kennedy seemed assured. In the Indiana primary on 6 May, he beat the senator by a two-to-one margin. In Tennessee and North Carolina he overwhelmed him by four to one. Only in the predominantly black District of Columbia did he lose to Kennedy. Of the 1,666 convention votes needed for nomination, the president now had at least 1,500.

Carter became an active candidate again just as he received some encouraging economic news. After growing at a rate of 18 percent per annum during the first quarter of 1980, the annual increase in the CPI slowed in May to only 10.9 percent—the slowest rise in nearly a year and a half. Some economists even predicted that the annual rate might dip as low as 5 percent or 6 percent before the end of the year. Interest rates also began to tumble almost as fast as they had escalated at the beginning of the year. Major banks dropped their prime interest rate to 13 percent, well below the peak of 20 percent reached in April.

On Capitol Hill, moreover, the president scored two political victories when Congress passed a $227-billion windfall profits tax and the Energy Security Act, which established a Synthetic Fuels Corporation with authority to spend up to $88 billion over the next ten years developing alternative energy sources. Both laws were key parts of the energy program Carter had sent to Congress almost a year before. These measures, along with earlier legislation deregulating natural gas prices and gradually decontrolling domestic oil, represented the most sweeping energy legislation in the nation's history and a great personal achievement for the president.

Yet Carter's struggle for reelection was far from over. The Democratic party remained divided and clearly unenthusiastic about either the president or Kennedy. Governor Hugh Carey of New York urged both candidates to throw the convention totally open by releasing their delegates. The *Des Moines Register* called on Carter to stand down in favor of Vice-President Walter Mondale. Meanwhile, the Republican party was uniting behind Ronald Reagan, who took a commanding 9-percent lead over Carter in the latest Harris poll.

Compounding Carter's political troubles was a still-mutinous Congress. Except for energy legislation, in fact, the president's scorecard on Capitol Hill was nearly blank during the first half of 1980. For example, lawmakers never acted on his only new domestic initiative—a youth employment program aimed primarily at minority teenagers. They also neglected other measures the White House supported, such as the president's three-year-old plan to upgrade health benefits for poor children and his proposal to expand the Commerce Department's Economic Development Association in order to place more federal development programs under its jurisdiction.

However, these setbacks paled beside two crushing defeats for the White House: Congress's rejection of the president's proposal to establish an Energy Mobilization Board, which lawmakers feared would trample on states' rights and environmental laws; and the peremptory override of his veto of a joint resolution that would have prevented him from imposing a ten-cents-per-gallon surcharge on imported oil. The surcharge, which Carter had implemented as part of his 14 March anti-inflation program and which was supposed to take effect on 15 May, had run into trouble on Capitol Hill because lawmakers were concerned about imposing a new tax during an election year. Under provisions of the newly enacted windfall profits tax, Congress could block enactment of the surcharge by passage of a joint resolution subject to a presidential veto, which it could still override by a two-thirds vote in both houses. On 4 June, both the House and the Senate passed by overwhelming margins (73 to 16 in the Senate and 376 to 30 in the House) a resolution killing the duty.

Why the president insisted on challenging Congress on such an unpopular measure when relations with Capitol Hill were already so strained and his administration was in such deep water politically remains something of a mystery. Clearly Carter thought the tax was necessary to balance the budget, and he was angry with the Democratic leadership in both the House and Senate, which had actually encouraged him to impose the fee. "This is a new low in performance for the Congress since I've been in office," he recorded in his diary on 13 May. He also regarded the willingness of the House and Senate to uphold his right to impose the tax a test of his ability to work with the members of Congress. Nevertheless, the override of his veto represented a humiliation not inflicted by a House and Senate on a president of its own party since the Truman administration in the 1950s—an embarrassment Carter could easily have avoided.[11]

Relations with Congress, then, continued to undermine the administration's political viability—just as they had throughout most of Carter's presidency. Economic developments had a similar impact. Despite some favorable statistics on inflation and interest rates, the economy was still in trouble. Although inflation was down, most economists, including the administration's top analyst, Alfred Kahn, believed that the underlying rate of inflation would hold at a disturbing 8 percent. Interest rates, while falling, also were higher than at any period before 1979.

Although inflation and interest rates appeared to be dropping, the same could not be said for unemployment. As the recession spread from housing and automobiles to other industries, unemployment shot up to 7.8 percent in May. Meanwhile, sales of American-made cars and the number of new housing starts continued their descent. New orders received by U.S. factories in April also fell 5.6 percent from the month before, the sharpest drop in more than five years. As a result of these and other economic indicators, including a slump in industrial and commercial construction, Time's Board of Economists concluded that the 1980 recession would be longer, deeper, and more painful than it had forecast just a few weeks earlier.[12]

In order to stimulate the economy, Republican candidate Reagan called in May for an across-the-board 10-percent cut in personal income taxes, and Republican lawmakers on Capitol Hill seconded the idea. So popular was the proposal for a tax cut that Democratic leaders in the Senate offered a preemptive bill of their own despite Carter's plea for fiscal austerity and his opposition to a tax cut, which would forestall any chance of achieving the balanced budget he had promised for fiscal 1981.

Mindful of the coming election, however, the White House became less concerned with balancing the budget and more concerned with winning in November. Eizenstat told the president in May that his economic policy was widely "viewed solely as austerity, pain, and sacrifice" and that he knew "of no President who had been re-elected during a serious recession for which he could be blamed." For that reason, Eizenstat joined CEA Chairman Schultze, OMB Director McIntyre, Vice-President Mondale and the president's other economic advisers in urging a moderate spending program and a tax-cut pledge as a way to satisfy Kennedy, preempt the Republicans, and prod the economy.[13]

Carter rejected both increased spending and reduced taxes as fiscally imprudent. He also lobbied against a Senate budget resolution that would have offset an increase in defense spending by cuts in domestic programs; instead, the president endorsed a House budget resolution more in line with his own spending recommendations. Despite vigorous efforts by the White House, the joint budget agreement approved in conference committee was much closer to the Senate version and authorized $6.8 billion more for defense and $4.3 billion less for domestic programs than what the White House considered acceptable. After weeks of bedlam on Capitol Hill, during which Senate Democrats rebelled against the president for denouncing the budget compromise, Congress approved the plan with only minor modifications—another slap in the administration's face.

As the primary campaign neared its close in June, therefore, President Carter could look forward with confidence to his renomination. But in his bid for reelection, he was clearly at a disadvantage. His domestic and foreign policies were largely in ruin; the economy seemed incurable; the hostage crisis was dragging on with no end in sight; major differences had surfaced between the United States and its allies over Iran and Afghanistan; a Congress controlled by his own party had rebuked him; not even Democratic loyalists were enthusiastic about his candidacy; and he had the lowest approval rating of any president ever—lower even than Richard Nixon's during the height of the Watergate affair. Given these factors, what now seems surprising is not the outcome of the November election but how close the presidential race was up to the last days of the campaign.

13

★ ★ ★ ★ ★

GLOOM AND DOOM

In some respects, the period from June through early September 1980 was the worst for the Carter presidency. Not only did the president suffer major defeats on Capitol Hill concerning the oil import surcharge and the budget resolution, voters in five of eight states casting ballots on 3 June—"Super Tuesday," as the final day of the primaries was dubbed—rejected his administration by voting for Ted Kennedy. The economy shuffled along in recession, which contributed to a flare-up of racial unrest in the nation's urban ghettos. In Europe, U.S. allies openly impugned Carter's leadership of the Western alliance. In the Middle East, a deadline established at Camp David for settling the Palestinian question passed without any progress, and relations between Israel and Egypt sputtered to their lowest point since the Camp David accords. Ronald Reagan received the Republican nomination for president on 16 July and jumped into a 28-percent lead over Carter in public opinion polls. Potentially damaging congressional hearings began on Billy Carter's relations with the Libyan government. No headway was made toward freeing the Iranian hostages. In a convention whose most memorable moment was when Kennedy stepped up to the podium, Democrats nominated Carter for a second term without much excitement and with real doubts as to whether he could beat Reagan in November.

According to most delegate counts, including the president's, Carter was less than 25 votes shy of securing the Democratic nomination before Super Tuesday. The 321 delegates he won that day, therefore, were more than enough to fend off any challenge at the convention in August from Ted Kennedy. But the results of the final primaries represented another repudiation of the president by Democratic voters. Of the three biggest states holding elections that day, Kennedy took California and New Jersey, and the president carried Ohio. Kennedy also won in Rhode Island, South Dakota, and New Mexico, while Carter prevailed in Montana and West Virginia.

A month earlier, Carter, confident of his party's nod, had ordered his staff to stop attacking Kennedy. He also took other conciliatory steps to turn his political rival into an ally against Reagan. In a television interview on the eve of Super Tuesday, the president described his relationship with the Massachusetts senator as "one of respect, one of personal friendship, one of admiration." But the senator did not reciprocate. Buoyed by his victories over the president, Kennedy told a cheering throng on primary night that he was unwilling to concede the nomination to Carter. Later, when the president phoned to congratulate him and to invite him to the White House for a discussion on the campaign, an aide to the senator said he was resting and could not be disturbed. When he finally did return the president's call four hours later, Kennedy proposed they confer the next day.

The meeting in the Oval Office did not heal the breach between the two men. The president again tried to appease Kennedy. Instead of asking him to get out of the race now that the primaries were over, he stressed the importance of a unified party, offered to help Kennedy pay off his campaign debts, and pledged that the senator would be treated properly at the convention. But with his own nomination practically assured, Carter was not prepared to make any major concessions—for instance, allowing Kennedy to write the party platform so as to include comprehensive health insurance or wage and price controls. More than any other issue, NHI had contributed to the falling-out between Kennedy and Carter. Now Kennedy wanted the Democratic party on record as supporting a comprehensive insurance program; Carter was determined to prevent that from happening.

As the meeting proceeded, its tone became increasingly acerbic. "It took him about an hour to fumble around and say we had issues dividing us, and we needed to have a personal debate in front of the TV cameras in order to resolve those differences," the president wrote about Kennedy after the session. "However, he would not agree to support me and Fritz [Mondale] even if we had such a debate." For his part, the senator, looking grim, told reporters as he left the White House only that the meeting had been a step toward party unity.[1]

Following his talk with Carter, Kennedy pressed to have an "open convention." Current party rules required delegates to vote on the first ballot for the candidates whom they had pledged to support in the primaries and caucuses; the senator claimed that this made delegates little more than automatons. The Kennedy campaign assumed that if the rules were changed, many of the delegates obligated to Carter would switch to the senator because of the president's dismal showing in the opinion polls. The proposal enraged Carter. The senator's "overwhelming defeat in the primaries," he later wrote, "having disproved Kennedy's major premise for running—that he could win and I could not—there was no logical reason for him to persist in the debilitating campaign which so weakened his party's chances for success in November."[2]

With Carter's comfortable lead in the delegate count, it was highly unlikely Kennedy could persuade the Democratic convention to change the rules. But because the senator refused to bow out, the overarching political reality facing Carter after the primaries was a potentially explosive convention showdown with Kennedy and a badly splintered party, which seemed to be hoping for an alternative to both Democratic contenders.

More recession and continued high unemployment added to the sense of gloom at the White House and of doom among the Democratic faithful. Although inflation appeared to be under control and interest rates were dropping, the recession continued. Despite a 1.4-percent increase in retail sales and a significant pickup of housing starts in June, consumer demand remained anemic, resulting in a drastic decline in corporate profits. Although the automobile industry was the hardest hit, the bottom line for other basic industries, such as steel, rubber, and chemicals, withered. Between April and June, corporate profits plunged by more than 18 percent, the third biggest drop since World War II.

As the recession prolonged into July, unemployment replaced inflation as the nation's most serious economic trouble. The Department of Labor set the number of jobless in July at 8.2 million, up a startling 1.9 million since February. Even Carter's own economists predicted that the unemployment rate of 7.8 percent would reach 8.5 percent by the end of the year and stay there through most of 1981. Other analysts broached the idea of impending double-digit unemployment.

Economic hard times helped spark the worst summer of racial violence in more than a decade. There had been earlier incidents in Boston and Wichita, Kansas, but the most serious outbreak occurred at the end of May in the Liberty City section of Miami. After an all-white jury in Tampa acquitted four white policemen charged with the beating death of a black insurance salesman, three days of looting, shooting, overturning cars, and burning property ensued, leaving 16 dead, more than 400 injured, and an estimated $100 million in property damage. "Black folks ain't worth a damn in this country," Benjamin Hooks of the NAACP commented afterwards. Sporadic violence erupted in the Miami area throughout the summer. In Chattanooga, a demonstration turned into a riot when another all-white jury acquitted whites accused of murdering blacks.[3]

President Carter responded to the twin problems of recession and unemployment in several ways, although none offered any immediate relief for impoverished minorities. First, he ordered restrictions removed on consumer credit, which the Federal Reserve Board had imposed in March. Second, he encouraged the FRB to increase the money supply, which Chairman Paul Volcker had earlier tightened to fight inflation. To help the battered automobile industry, he also announced a $1-billion government assistance program that included a relaxation of some emission standards, up to $400 million in loans to car dealers, and $50 million in aid to local communities to rebuilt old auto plants. In addition, he promised a faster review of a UAW request for restrictions on imports of Japanese cars.

The president also reconsidered his position on taxes. Ronald Reagan had made a $36-billion tax cut—including a 10-percent blanket reduction in personal income taxes and faster tax write-offs for business investment—the centerpiece of his plan for overcoming the recession. Reagan's call for a tax cut put the White House on the defensive. Carter had long resisted the idea, identifying inflation as the nation's chief economic culprit and believing that a balanced budget was essential to winning the inflation battle. As inflation receded and the recession worsened, however, the president began to look more favorably on a tax cut. Firmly opposed to a reduction as large as the Republicans were suggesting, he was nonetheless persuaded by Eizenstat and some of his other economic advisers to present a more modest proposal—one that encouraged business investment through accelerated appreciation rather than reducing personal income taxes. Such a plan could be economically stimulating, help improve the nation's industrial productivity, which had been declining for a number of years and was a matter of considerable concern to the president, and be noninflationary at the same time.

In July Carter announced his third economic recovery program for the year at Detroit's Metro Airport—deliberate timing, since the Republicans were simultaneously holding their convention in that city and nominating Reagan as their candidate for president. Reaction to the president's plan was mixed. On Capitol Hill, the response mainly followed party lines—Democrats defending the program as "statesmanlike," Republicans charging it was "too little, too late, too political." Within the business and financial community, the reaction was described by Carter's own staff as "ho-hum." While business leaders generally approved of the thrust of the program, some commented that it had been put together too hastily and lacked a comprehensive economic strategy. Likewise, other commentators described the plan as an "economic smorgasbord," with some morsels for business, some for individual taxpayers, and some even for government (by increasing its involvement in the economy).

Considering the poor state of the economy and the uneven response to his newest economic proposals, Carter prepared for the political campaign ahead aware of his vulnerability on domestic issues. In contrast, Reagan was widely believed to be weakest on foreign policy because of his inexperience and often simplistic views and because of the president's own achievements in that area—most notably the Panama Canal treaties and the Camp David accords. It behooved the president, therefore, to stress his mastery of world politics as compared with his Republican opponent. But even here, Carter's credibility was tarnished by the presence of several serious problems concerning the Atlantic alliance, the unresolved Arab-Israeli dispute, U.S.–Soviet relations, and Iran's holding of the American hostages.

When Carter took office in 1977, Zbigniew Brzezinski had said that "wider cooperation" with the United States' key allies would be the very first priority of the new administration's foreign policy. However, by the spring of 1980, Washington's relations with its allies had slipped into alarming disorder. A former top aide to Henry Kissinger, Helmut Sonnefeldt, told an influential European audience that the Atlantic alliance was undergoing its "deepest tensions in thirty years." No one challenged that assessment.

Part of the friction was attributable to the barely concealed disdain that West German Chancellor Helmut Schmidt had for Carter as well as the president's view of Schmidt as unstable, unreliable, and egotistical. The latest problem between the two leaders arose over a message Carter sent to Schmidt regarding his stand on the placement of additional weapons in Europe. While campaigning for reelection, Schmidt was quoted by the press as calling for a three-year moratorium on the disposition of new missiles despite an allied decision in December 1979 to go forward with the deployment of the Pershing 2 and ground-launched cruise missiles. In a telephone call to the president, Schmidt said that he had been misquoted, although he did acknowledge supporting talks with the Soviets on arms limitation. But after a time new stories circulated in which the German chancellor was again reported as favoring a suspension of new missiles. Carter then sent Schmidt a communiqué expressing concern about the confusion his statements were creating. The message became public and Schmidt became furious, convinced the president was trying to undermine efforts at arms control.

French President Valéry Giscard d'Estaing also harbored a low opinion of Carter, whom he accused of being inconsistent, ineffective, and unnecessarily provocative in his dealings with the Soviet Union. He also criticized the American president for allegedly expecting Europe to follow every twist and turn of American foreign policy. Like other European leaders, d'Estaing sought a more balanced American approach to the Middle East, one that took into account Europe's heavy dependency on Persian Gulf oil. Similarly, he urged a more reasoned response to the Soviet invasion of Afghanistan, which reflected Western Europe's close proximity to the Soviet Union.

In May, the French president met privately in Warsaw with Soviet President Leonid Brezhnev; plans for the five-hour session had been kept secret from the United States. About the same time, rumors spread around Washington that the annual economic summit of the western industrial powers and Japan, scheduled for Venice on 12 and 13 July, would be the occasion of a European demand: that the Palestine Liberation Organization be allowed to participate in all future negotiations in the Middle East and that UN Resolution 242, the heart of most long-range peace formulas for the Middle East, be revised to remove its reference to the Palestinians as mere "refugees."

President Carter's new secretary of State, former Senator Edmund Muskie of Maine, turned livid when he learned of the Brezhnev-d'Estaing summit and the plans afoot to pressure the United States and Israel into accommodation on the Palestinian question. Strong-willed and known to have a fiery temper, Muskie was nevertheless highly respected in Washington, and his appointment as Cyrus Vance's replacement was generally well-received even though he had no particular expertise on foreign affairs. Although Muskie had initially been one of the president's most outspoken critics, he was also one of the few lawmakers on Capitol Hill with whom the president had cultivated a warm personal relationship. Carter had selected Vance for his management and negotiating talents, but he intended Muskie to serve as the administration's spokesman on foreign policy, leaving other matters to his able deputy secretary of state, Warren Christopher, whom many at the State Department had expected to succeed Vance.

While in Vienna to attend a foreign ministers meeting, Muskie had been scolded by French Foreign Minister Jean Francois-Poncet on the failure of the United States to consult with its allies. But the minister had neglected to mention d'Estaing's forthcoming meeting with Brezhnev. When he finally learned of the Soviet-French conference, therefore, the secretary of state did not mince words about French hypocrisy. "I'm concerned that when I was being given a lecture on consultation, the lecturer was not inclined to practice what he was preaching," he commented caustically to reporters. In a thinly veiled reference to the allies, he also attacked what he referred to as the meddling in the Mideast "from the sidelines."[4]

By the time Carter left for the Venice summit in June, so much distrust had emerged among the western powers and so much scorn heaped upon the president that many political observers feared the meeting would be a disaster. Although the allies agreed on most strategic issues, they remained sharply at odds on a peace prospectus for the Mideast, on the proper response to the crises in Iran and Afghanistan, and on a unified policy for dealing with the nuclear threat posed by the Soviet Union.

Instead of a diplomatic fiasco, however, the Venice summit proved to be a personal success for Carter. Before the start of the gathering, the president met with Schmidt to try to settle their conflicts. In a stormy session, Schmidt claimed that he had been insulted by Carter's last message to him and that Germany was not the United States' fifty-first state. But after Carter agreed to make a public statement expressing confidence in Schmidt and noting their concurrence on theater nuclear forces, matters quieted down, and the surface cordiality between the two men reappeared.

Once the summit began, Carter was determined to use it to restore his own standing as leader of the western alliance. Although the agenda was devoted to economic issues, he saw to it that the Soviet invasion of Afghanistan was placed high on the list. Believing that the allies underestimated the Soviet menace, he urged them to take a stronger position on Afghanistan. At the same time, he stressed the need to maintain allied unity. Through skillful negotiation and sheer doggedness, Carter was able to dominate the meeting. Brezhnev had tried to upstage the American president by announcing on the first day of the summit that he was pulling an unspecified number of Soviet troops out of Afghanistan. However, the seven leaders at Venice ended their conference with a final communiqué condemning the Soviet Union for endangering world peace. In return, Carter agreed to shelve his demand for further punitive measures against the Soviets and to consider the possibility of negotiations with Moscow at some later date. On the economic front, the president also achieved most of the goals he set for himself in Venice, including an agreement by the world leaders on oil import limits lower than the levels set at Tokyo the previous year and a commitment on their part to double the use of coal by the end of the decade.

Yet as most political observers recognized, the heads of state at Venice had papered over their differences rather than resolved them. The president cautioned the Japanese about the growth of protectionist sentiment in the United States because of Japanese imports and barriers to American exports. He also feared that Schmidt would make concessions to Moscow on arms control even though the German leader promised at Venice not to break ranks with the allies. For their part, Europe's leaders retained their suspicions of Carter and wondered whether an Atlantic alliance, predicated on American economic and military dominance after World War II and crafted for the recovery of Europe and the defense of the North Atlantic, was still sustainable or even desirable.

Disharmony also reigned between the United States and its Mideast friends, Israel and Egypt. Despite repeated affirmations by both countries of their solid commitment to the Camp David peace process, they made little progress in resolving the Arab-Israeli dispute. The immediate problem remained Palestinian autonomy in the West Bank and Gaza Strip. Although the 1979 Camp David accords called for an agreement on self-rule by 26 May 1980, Israeli Prime Minister Menachem Begin held steadfastly to a definition of Palestinian autonomy limited largely to municipal affairs. Under no circumstances would he permit Palestinian self-determination, which was what Sadat eventually intended for the Palestinians. President Carter tilted toward the Egyptian position, believing that the Palestinians were entitled to "full autonomy."

At the end of March, the president sent Sol Linowitz to the Mideast with instructions to develop a package of proposals on the Palestinian question acceptable to both Egypt and Israel. But Linowitz's mission was a failure. Although Israel agreed to view the May date as a "positive incentive" for deciding the autonomy issue rather than a fixed deadline, Begin refused the American envoy's request that he suspend the building of new settlements on the West Bank until after 26 May. Egyptian Foreign Minister Mustapha Khalil responded that Israel would have to declare a moratorium on new construction before Cairo would agree even to an extension of the deadline.

In addition to dispatching Linowitz to Egypt and Israel, Carter invited Sadat and Begin to Washington for separate talks on the full panoply of Middle East concerns. But those negotiations also proved largely unproductive. Sadat agreed to ignore the May cutoff and even said that if Israel assented to a formula for Palestinian autonomy, he would be willing to state publicly that there should be no separate Palestinian state. But Begin would not budge from his often-stated positions on either Palestinian independence or the building of Israeli settlements in the occupied territories. All that the president achieved was Begin's acquiescence to nonstop talks between Egypt and Israel during the forty days before 26 May.

The true significance of the Carter-Begin discussions, in fact, was the president's realization of the fundamental weakness of the Camp David accords. Perhaps for the first time, he understood that the terms contained in the documents—such as 'autonomy' 'security,' 'Palestinian rights,' and even 'West Bank'—had different connotations for each of the parties involved in the Arab-Israeli strife. At issue, moreover, was not semantics but the foundation of a final agreement. For Israel that meant security; for the Palestinians, their legitimate rights as a people; for Egypt, its credibility and influence within the Arab world. Under these circumstances, there was scant room for compromise. As a result, weeks of talks between Egyptian and Israeli negotiators bore no fruit.

Two weeks before the 26 May target date, Sadat broke off the sessions for two months after Begin stated that security in the West Bank and Gaza "must remain exclusively in Israel's hand." During this interval, Begin lost considerable public support even in Israel for his hard-line approach to the Palestinian problem and the occupied territories. There was also vocal criticism of Begin's policies from the American Jewish community. In July, 56 prominent American Jews signed a statement already endorsed by 250 influential Israelis censuring "extremists" within the Israeli government who "distort Zionism and threaten its realization."[5]

Nevertheless, the Israeli prime minister and his Likud coalition remained defiant. At the beginning of August, the Knesset passed a measure making an undivided Jerusalem the capital of Israel, even though U.S. Ambassador Samuel Lewis had already warned Begin that the United States might not be able to conduct face-to-face meetings with him if he moved his offices to East

Jerusalem. With Begin resistant to outside pressures, with little hope of further progress in the bilateral talks between Egypt and Israel, with Carter increasingly distracted by his campaign for relection, and with European leaders anxious to undertake their own Mideast initiative, the peace process begun at Camp David a year earlier had simply run out of time.

The Arab-Israeli controversy compounded Carter's political problems at home. Although American Jews were now more apt to criticize Begin, this did not translate into praise for the president. As Stu Eizenstat and Al Moses, the White House's liaison with the Jewish community, told the president in early October, American Jews simply did not trust the administration. They believed that if Carter was reelected, he would "recognize the PLO or put an untenable amount of pressure on the state of Israel to make concessions to the Arabs that would run counter to their national interest and security."[6]

Foreign policy spilled over into domestic politics even more dramatically during the summer of 1980. In July the press reported that President Carter's brother Billy was being investigated by the Senate and the Justice Department. At issue was whether he had violated federal law by accepting $220,000 as the first installment of what he called a "loan" from the Libyan government without registering as their agent. Even more serious were suggestions by the news media that the White House might have interceded improperly in Billy's affairs and in the probes into them.

Ever since Billy's highly publicized trip to Libya in 1978, his fortunes had declined drastically. His "good ol' boy" image no longer seemed charming or amusing, and he was shunned by the celebrity circuit. Loss of the considerable fees he received for his public appearances left him deeply in debt. He began to drink so heavily that he had to admit himself for seven weeks into an alcoholic treatment center in California. A recovering alcoholic with outstanding obligations, Billy turned to his Libyan friends for assistance— and they were pleased to oblige the brother of the American president. In January 1979, they advanced him $20,000, followed in April by $200,000, as the first installments of a $500,000 "loan" from the Libyan government. Although this business deal eventually fell through because of a cutback in Libyan oil production, Billy could have made as much as $5 million annually by helping to procure an additional 100,000 barrels per day of high-grade Libyan oil for a Florida business concern, the Charter Oil Company.

Because of Billy's close association with Libya, the Justice Department asked him clearly in 1979 to register as a foreign agent under a 1933 law requiring all persons who did political or public relations work for a foreign government to list with the department their activities and pay. Billy ignored the request on the grounds that he never acted as an agent for Libya. Lacking sufficient evidence to take action against him, the department began an investigation into his affairs. In May, it discovered his $220,000 "loan." Two weeks later, Billy agreed to be interviewed by Justice Department officials.

On 14 July, he registered as a foreign agent and filed a report showing the $220,000 he had received as compensation.

News that Billy Carter had accepted $220,000 from Libya and was listed as a foreign agent produced a political storm, which the White House clumsily turned into a hurricane. Legitimate questions were immediately raised as to what Billy had done to earn the Libyan largesse and why he had agreed to register as a foreign agent after insisting for nearly eighteen months that he was just a friend of the Libyans'. More specifically, reporters and lawmakers wanted to know what role the White House played in Billy Carter's Libyan activities and in the Justice Department inquiry into his affairs. Had Billy Carter hawked his influence with the White House for $220,000?

Aware that some Republicans were already drawing comparisons to Watergate by referring to Billy's money dealings with the Libyans as "Billygate," the White House issued a statement on 22 July disclosing what it knew about the matter and flatly asserting that at no time had there been any contact between the Justice Department and White House concerning the investigation into Billy's finances. On the same day, the president released a separate statement saying that he did not believe it was "appropriate for a close relative of the President to undertake any assignment on behalf of a foreign government."

Intended to lay to rest any hint of impropriety on the president's part, the official disclaimers made a bad situation worse. In the first place, the White House acknowledged in its release that at Zbigniew Brzezinski's request, Billy and a Libyan official had met with the NSC adviser in November to explore the possibility of Libyan help in recovering the Iranian hostages. In addition, the White House conceded that even though Carter had learned in March that Billy was attempting to obtain more Libyan oil for the Charter Oil Company, he had done nothing about it.

Taken at face value, the 22 July statement did exonerate the president: Carter had not intervened on his brother's behalf, and there was no evidence of illegal influence peddling at the White House, which would have destroyed Carter's presidency. But the episode raised questions about the president's judgment in allowing his brother to act as a diplomatic emissary to a hostile country and in permitting him to profit from that relationship.

Over the next several weeks, apparent errors and omissions were discovered in the White House's initial release. Although none was serious enough to suggest a Watergate-type cover-up, they kept the political caldron boiling. On 22 July, the president revealed that after checking his records, he found that Attorney General Benjamin Civiletti had in fact told him six weeks earlier that Billy needed to register as a foreign agent. Lawmakers then learned that in early 1980 Billy had traveled to Libya for a second time and that, before leaving the country, he had been given some confidential cables from the State Department.

As it turned out, the cables were routine ones that the State Department often made available to individuals and companies doing business abroad. But the fact that the White House had not mentioned the documents in its earlier statement caused many political observers to wonder about their content and whether they enhanced Billy's credibility with the Libyans. Many people were also dismayed to learn that First Lady Rosalynn Carter had raised the idea of using Billy's Libyan connection to help free the Iranian hostages and that Billy had arranged meetings between the president, Brzezinski, and Ali Houderi, the Libyan envoy to Washington. Was the president trying to conceal this evidence of amateur diplomacy?

In truth, the White House concealed nothing. To avoid even the semblance of wrongdoing, it adopted a policy as soon as news broke of Billy's "loan" of total openness and candor—of letting the chips fall where they may. On Capitol Hill, the Senate Judiciary and Foreign Relations committees appointed an ad hoc committee to conduct an investigation of Billy's activities. In response, the president announced that he would waive executive privilege and furnish whatever documents the committee requested. He also made clear that he and his staff would be available for interviews. But as the White House had to keep amending its 22 July account, there was doubt cast on Carter's forthrightness with the American people.

It was again Carter's presidential timber rather than his integrity, however, that hung in the balance for the American public. Few Americans believed the president was guilty of some misconduct that he was now attempting to hide, just as few Americans ever contested his moral character. But on the eve of the Democratic convention, the Billy Carter affair added new misgivings about Carter's competence to serve a second term. "The damn Billy Carter stuff is killing us," Hamilton Jordan told Pat Caddell.[7]

The release of the hostages would almost certainly have improved Carter's drive for reelection. Although the death of the shah on 27 July led to some speculation that the Iranians might free the captives in return for some face-saving concession—such as a UN inquiry into Iran's grievances, as had been proposed earlier in the year—absolutely no progress was made toward their release.

Washington's relations with Moscow also remained stalemated, primarily because of the Soviet occupation of Afghanistan. Another great concern for Moscow was the decision by the NATO powers in December 1979 to place intermediate-range nuclear weapons in Europe to counter Soviet SS-20 rockets aimed at the West. And Washington was equally anxious about a Soviet military buildup that seemed to exceed what was necessary for defense purposes. In May 1980, Secretary of State Muskie met in Vienna with his Soviet counterpart, Andrei Gromyko, in the first high-level contact between the two countries since the beginning of the Afghan crisis last December. But the talks were unproductive. Moscow had dangled the possibility of a military pullout from Afghanistan in exchange for recognition of the Soviet-installed government in Kabul, but Muskie dismissed the proposal as cosmetic. Afterwards, the secretary flew from Vienna to Brussels for a NATO meeting, where he told European allies that they would have to assume a heavier defense burden in Europe so that American military resources could be redirected to the Persian Gulf and Indian Ocean.

In July, President Carter signed Presidential Directive 59 (PD-59) authorizing the largest arms procurement program in thirty years. Conceived by Brzezinski and Defense Secretary Harold Brown, PD-59 was intended to break away from the doctrine of mutual assured destruction (MAD), which provided the rationale for much of the nation's strategic planning. MAD presumed that the ability of the Soviet Union and the United States to devastate each other's civilian population centers would deter both superpowers from beginning a nuclear war. Brzezinski and Brown contended, however, that the buildup of Soviet strategic forces and the improved accuracy of its nuclear warheads gave the Soviets the means to engage in more limited nuclear war against military targets. Therefore, a nuclear strategy based on the existence of a countervailing force left Washington in the untenable position of either responding with a massive strike against civilian population centers, resulting in the full-scale Soviet retaliation projected in the MAD scenario, or giving in to nuclear blackmail. PD-59 proposed to address this strategic deficiency by requiring defense planners to target military installations as well as population centers. If it could respond in kind to a Soviet attack, the United States would achieve a credible nuclear deterrent.

In reality, PD-59 was not so much a new doctrine as a modification of existing doctrine. Defense planners had been moving toward a more flexible nuclear strategy since at least 1962, when Defense Secretary Robert McNamara considered the idea of a counterforce but rejected it because of its cost. Nevertheless, the disclosure that President Carter had signed PD-59 led to a new round of complaints against the administration. Critics accused Brzezinksi of purposely leaking the story in order to embarrass Secretary Muskie—who did not even know the details of PD-59 until he read them in the newspaper. Other commentators suspected its political motive—perhaps to blunt the charge in the Republican party platform that the administration's nuclear and strategic policy provided "a Hobson's choice between mass mutual suicide and surrender."[8]

Advocates of arms reduction asserted that PD-59 actually increased the chances of a nuclear conflict because the president would be more tempted to resort to war during a crisis. Others maintained that the Soviets might decide on a preemptive first strike of their own. Former CIA Deputy Director Herbert Scoville, Jr., observed that anything that made it easier to fight a nuclear war was "a step in the wrong direction." Lawrence Korb of the American Enterprise Institute, a conservative think tank, added that the "irony" of this doctrine was that "it could make war either more or less probable. . . . It is stoppable, but because it is, it is also more startable."[9]

Moscow also blasted the White House's revised strategy. *Tass* referred to it as "madness"; *Pravda* called it "nuclear blackmail" and warned of an accelerated arms race. Considering PD-59 in the same context as the planned deployment of Pershing missiles in Europe, the White House's decision to construct the MX missile system, and the indefinite shelving of the SALT II treaty, Soviet analysts became convinced the United States was seeking a strategic advantage over the Soviet Union. Despite administration claims to the contrary, they also concluded that Washington's long-standing acceptance of strategic parity with Moscow—the very basis of détente—was now a thing of the past and that the United States and the Soviet Union were entering a new period of confrontation.[10]

As Democrats prepared to hold their nominating convention in New York, the president, therefore, was being battered by domestic and foreign problems. Inflation, recession, and unemployment; racial unrest; Billygate and the Libyan connection; the Mideast crisis; the Iranian hostage crisis; and the Afghan crisis—all these were working against Carter. A Gallup poll in early August showed the president with a 21-percent approval rating, three points lower than that of Richard Nixon during the depths of Watergate and the worst rating of any American president in the history of polling. A survey in California placed Carter third in the state, behind Reagan and John Anderson. An ABC/Harris poll also revealed major shifts throughout the country in favor of Republicans in races for Congress, governorships, and state legislatures.

The convention itself did little to instill confidence about the president's chances for reelection in November. On the first day, Carter's forces were able to defeat Senator Kennedy's motion to eliminate the rule binding delegates to the candidates they had supported in the primaries and caucuses. Although Kennedy subsequently announced that he was withdrawing his candidacy, he fully intended to have his views reflected in the party platform. At issue were four economic planks favored by Kennedy but opposed by Carter. The first called for wage and price controls. The second urged a $12-billion program to create 800,000 new jobs. The third put the Democratic party on record as against any action "whose effect will be a significant increase in unemployment." The fourth barred the party from fighting inflation with high interest rates and unemployment. The president's position on wage and price controls was well established, and he believed that passage of these planks would leave him vulnerable to Republican charges that he favored big government and was unwilling to take the steps needed to revive the economy.

Speaking for his platform proposals the next night, Kennedy delivered a powerful address in which he excoriated Republican candidate Reagan for such idiocies as attributing 80 percent of air pollution to trees and calling unemployment insurance "a prepaid vacation plan for freeloaders." But the heart of his message was an emotional appeal to the convention not to abandon traditional Democratic values. Do not let "the great purposes of the Democratic party become the bygone passages of history," he told the delegates. "For all those whose cares have been our concern the work goes on, the cause endures, the hope still lives, and the dream shall never die."

Kennedy's speech moved even Carter delegates in the convention hall, who joined the Kennedy people in a demonstration lasting almost forty minutes. Meanwhile, a deal was being struck below the podium between the Carter and Kennedy forces. Kennedy consented to withdraw the plank on wage and price controls; in return, Carter agreed not to contest the other economic proposals. After a voice vote from the floor, Tip O'Neill ruled the three planks approved. Rather than endorse the articles outright, the president simply promised to "accept and support the intent" of the jobs plank and "pursue policies that will implement [its] spirit and aims."

The main business of the convention, nominating the Carter-Mondale ticket for a second term, took place on 13 August, but it was really anticlimactic. The major battles were over, and all that remained was for Mondale and Carter to give their acceptance speeches. Mondale's remarks consisted mainly of humorous barbs directed against Reagan. Calling out a list of Democratic programs, he asked in each case who had supported them and then responded by shouting, "Not Ronald Reagan!" The delegates soon joined in the refrain.

In contrast, there was little humor in the president's speech, but it was carefully crafted and well presented. Carter gave clear notice that he intended to make Reagan rather than his own presidential record the key issue of the campaign. The election, he said, was a "choice between two futures." His was one of "security, justice, and peace," his opponent's one of "despair" and "surrender." Carter's future would strive toward world peace, Reagan's would court "risk—the risk of international confrontation, the risk of an uncontrollable, unaffordable, and unwinnable nuclear war."

Of more immediate interest to most of the delegates in the convention hall was whether or not Kennedy would join the president after his speech in a final show of party unity. Almost deferentially Carter reached out for the senator's support and spoke directly to him through the medium of television. "Ted, your party needs—and I need—you," he said. "And I need your idealism and your dedication working for us." Kennedy's response was a keen disappointment to Carter and to other Democratic leaders. The senator arrived late to the convention hall, found himself in the midst of a milling crowd that had also been called to the podium, and was clearly uncomfortable even in his brief appearance next to Carter. As soon as possible, he left the hall and returned to his hotel. "If that's the best they can do in unity," observed Reagan, who was watching the convention on television, "they have a long way to go."[11]

As the convention adjourned, Carter clearly faced a herculean task in the coming campaign. In the weeks following his nomination, the president's fortunes actually improved, so that the two major candidates ran virtually neck and neck in all of the polls. But Carter's turnaround was not enough to stave off defeat. For the next twelve weeks, Reagan asked the American people if they wanted four more years of Carter. In November they answered no.

14

★ ★ ★ ★ ★

DEFEAT

Despite his instability in the polls, the president returned to the White House from the Democratic convention in August confident of victory in November. His campaign staff was in place, the Democratic party had survived intact, and the news media could be expected to turn its attention from his intraparty battle with Kennedy to his presidential contest with Reagan. That, the president was convinced, would work in his favor. Other circumstances gave additional cause for optimism. "Billygate," which had dogged him for months, proved to be a puff of wind without much political impact. The threat to his campaign posed by independent candidate John Anderson diminished, and signs also pointed to an economic improvement in the fourth quarter of 1980, which could have a substantial impact on the election.

However, these developments did not add up to victory. Had he not tried to make Reagan the central issue of the campaign, or had economic recovery occurred faster, or had he secured the release of the Iranian hostages, perhaps Carter would have succeeded in his drive for a second term. As it was, he made a remarkable comeback in the polls and, until the last week of the campaign, seemed close to winning. But Reagan was a more adept campaigner than the president had anticipated; indeed, the president's competency, not Reagan's, became the recurring theme of the campaign. In the end, Carter became the first elected president since Herbert Hoover in 1932 to fail in his bid for reelection.

Well before the Democratic convention, Hamilton Jordan had decided to focus the campaign on Reagan. In June, Pat Caddell and Jerry Rafshoon had persuaded him to give up his position as White House chief of staff and to join the campaign full-time. Jordan was delighted to escape the straitjacket of his

White House duties. By agreement with the chairman of the campaign, Robert Strauss, Jordan would be responsible for overall strategy while Strauss would handle the nuts and bolts.

On 25 June, Jordan prepared a memorandum for Carter laying out the obstacles the president would have to overcome in order to win in November and proposing a blueprint for victory. It was a sobering report. Two weeks before, he had met with a group of prominent California Democrats to learn more about Carter's likely opponent in the fall. California State Treasurer Jesse Unruh warned Jordan not to "make the mistake that every person in this room has made at one time or another and underestimate Ronald Reagan." Jordan took this advice seriously, but his main concern was the damaging impact of Kennedy's challenge to Carter. "The most costly consequence is that support for you based on your being a likable, well-intentioned, compassionate and at times atypical politician has eroded badly," he told Carter.

A growing number of Americans had come to believe that it did not really matter who was elected president—that there was not a great deal of difference between Carter and Reagan. To win the election, therefore, Carter had to turn the campaign away from the controversial issues that alienated voters (particularly liberal Democrats). At the same time, he had to convince the American people that this was indeed a critical election with two very distinct candidates. Jordan's idea, then, was that Carter should hammer away at Reagan's fitness to be president. "I was troubled by the insinuation of my own analysis that we couldn't just run on our record," he later acknowledged.[1]

Carter had anticipated as early as October 1979 that he would be running against Reagan, and he agreed that Reagan's qualifications, rather than his own position on the major issues, should dominate Democratic campaign strategy in 1980. By no means were current affairs ignored entirely, since that would have been politically impossible. However, both Jordan and pollster Pat Caddell believed the president could not win reelection without offering the American public his conception of the country's future. "You must tell us what your vision, your plans and hopes are for our people and nation," Jordan told the president. "I know that you have such a vision, but it must be communicated to us."[2]

Repeating a mistake of his presidency, however, Carter did not offer his campaign staff, much less the American voter, a clear sense of where he intended to lead the country over the next four years. As a result, he was unable to define himself in a way that might have affected the election's outcome. By attacking Reagan's presidential fitness, moreover, he opened himself to counterattacks about his own competency as president.

For most of the campaign, though, it appeared that the president's strategy might work. Carter kicked off his bid for reelection on 1 September with a huge rally at Tuscumbia, Alabama. At the event were about twenty robed members of the Ku Klux Klan, whom the president denounced as cowards who "counsel[ed] fear and hatred." Nevertheless, Reagan insinuated the next day that Carter was seeking the support of racists. Reagan realized immediately that the comment was a mistake: "I shouldn't have said it because the minute after I said it, I knew that this was what would be remembered."

The Republican candidate's remark was only the latest of a series of gaffes on his part. Earlier he had called the Vietnam War a "noble cause," expressed personal doubts about the theory of evolution, remarked that the New Deal was patterned after Benito Mussolini's state socialism, proposed making social security voluntary, and voiced pro-Taiwan views that threatened relations with the Beijing government. "If Reagan keeps putting his foot in his mouth for another week or so we can close down campaign headquarters," Pat Caddell gloated after one of Reagan's blunders.[3]

Other political developments also seemed to break in Carter's favor. First, Billygate was successfully defused as a campaign issue. A week before the Democratic convention, Carter prudently held a televised news conference devoted mostly to answering questions about his role in his brother's dealings with Libya. The president admitted that Billy's case gave the appearance of favoritism, but he denied any effort at a cover-up. Carter informed reporters that his legal counsel, Lloyd Cutler, was drafting an order prohibiting any executive branch employee from associating with a member of the president's family under circumstances that might suggest improper influence. He also stressed that Billy had had no say in U.S. foreign policy.

The president's earnest, nothing-to-hide manner, buttressed by a lengthy White House report and thousands of official documents and excerpts from his personal diary, sapped the sensationalism of Billygate. But it was Billy Carter's own nine hours of testimony on 21 and 22 August before the Senate committee looking into his activities that finally put the controversy to rest. Denying that he was "a buffoon, a boob, or a wacko," he described himself as "a common citizen with uncommon financial and family problems." He also disputed charges that he had been an influence-peddler for Libya. "I have not asked anything of Jimmy Carter or of any U.S. Government representative on behalf of the Libyan government," he said. Rather than profiting from being the brother of the president, Billy also maintained that he had suffered financially from the connection. Ten separate investigations into his affairs, including several by the Internal Revenue Service, had meant enormous legal fees, while negative publicity about his ties with Libya had cost him as much as $500,000 a year in public appearances.

Instead of the beer-guzzling clown often depicted by the news media, Billy proved to be an articulate, courteous, even sympathetic witness. His testimony, moreover, supported the president's claims that he knew nothing about his brother's $220,000 loan and that the White House had extended no special treatment to Billy. On 2 October, the Senate investigation concluded with a report criticizing the president for trying to involve his brother in attempts to free the Iranian hostages but acquitting him of any other charge.[4]

Even the economy seemed to be smiling on the president's endeavors. The economic signals had been mixed and indicated at best a slow recovery, but by the beginning of October, there were a number of signs that the recession was bottoming out. Housing starts were up, businesses were borrowing more to expand production and increase inventories, and the Department of Commerce was estimating that the GNP, which had been falling since the first quarter, would rise in the fourth quarter and continue to grow slowly through the second quarter of 1981.

As a result of these occurrences, the president managed to close the gap separating him from his Republican opponent. A *Newsweek* poll taken at the end of September showed Reagan leading Carter by a margin of only 4 percent with 12 percent of the voters surveyed still undecided. According to the president's own polls, in states like Connecticut, where Carter had been trailing Reagan by more than a two-to-one margin in the middle of July, or in Iowa, where he had been behind by almost a three-to-one margin, he had by the middle of September pulled even or close to even. In other states like Maryland or North Carolina, where he was already ahead, he had enlarged his lead. A potential political blowout thus seemed to be turning into a cliffhanger.[5]

The fall brought a tactical dilemma for the Carter campaign over whether or not to participate in a three-way debate sponsored by the League of Women Voters. The president's advisers were anxious to have Carter face Reagan alone, and they were opposed to a debate that included independent candidate John Anderson. Conducting a National Unity campaign with the former Democratic governor of Wisconsin, Patrick J. Lucey, as his running mate, Anderson had issued a lengthy and detailed platform in September that called for gun control, passage of an Equal Rights Amendment, overhaul of the nation's mass transportation system, and a fifty-cents-a-gallon tax on gasoline. Not only would Anderson's appearance with Carter and Reagan add to the legitimacy of his campaign, it would provide an opportunity for Reagan and him to gang up on the president. Since the polls showed support for the inclusion of Anderson in any presidential matchup, the president's staff did agree to a three-way exchange on the condition that Carter would first debate Reagan alone. But the League of Women Voters took the position that Anderson should participate in all the sessions if he received at least 15 percent in the national public opinion polls. When the polls showed that Anderson had that level of support, the league sent out invitations to all three candidates for the first debate in Baltimore on 21 September.

Carter was in a political bind. Either he would strengthen Anderson's campaign by appearing with him or he would be accused of refusing to debate the issues before the American public. Regardless, Reagan would come out ahead. In this no-win situation, the president's staff concluded that Carter had more to lose than gain by joining Reagan and Anderson on stage. Afterwards, Hamilton Jordan, who had watched the debate on television, acknowledged that Carter had been hurt by not participating. "When it was over," he remarked, "I didn't feel very good. Reagan had not made any big mistakes and Anderson had handled himself well." Yet the damage was not lasting. Polls taken a few days after Anderson's dialogue with Reagan showed him still running a distant third behind his Republican and Democratic opponents. Reagan also seems to have profited little from the debate. Thirty-three percent of survey respondents said they were now more likely to vote for him, while 30 percent said they were less likely.[6]

Another source of consternation for the Carter campaign was the so-called meanness issue. After Reagan had accused him of seeking the votes of racist elements in the South, the president retaliated by suggesting strongly that Reagan was himself a racist. Carter also delivered a series of hard-hitting speeches in which he portrayed the choice between the Republican candidate and himself as one between war and peace. His attacks on Reagan culminated in an address in Chicago on 6 October in which he said that Reagan's election would divide the nation, "black and white, Jew from Christian, North from South, rural from urban" and could well "lead our country toward war."

Jordan, Rafshoon, Caddell, and other campaign advisers had urged the president to tone down his denunciations of Reagan. "Mr. President, you've just got to be careful what you say," Jordan had entreated him after a talk in Atlanta. Whatever most Americans thought of Carter's conduct of the presidency, his advisers realized that he was still largely perceived as a decent and honorable person. By attacking Reagan in this way, the president could damage one of his most valuable campaign assets—especially since his mudslinging was directed against an opponent who, like himself, was widely regarded as a good and fair-minded individual. Reagan played on his own "nice guy" image by responding to Carter's remarks with expressions of "sorrow" and "regret" rather than by lunging for the jugular as the president seemed to be doing.

Other Republicans were less restrained. Carter's "intemperate and totally misleading statements demean the office of the Presidency," former President Gerald Ford retorted. "I'm appalled at the ugly, mean little remark Jimmy Carter made," added Republican vice-presidential candidate George Bush. The news media also seized on the temper of Carter's speeches and peppered him with questions. "We have a major problem on our hands, and we are going to have to eat a little crow to put this 'meanness' thing behind us," Jordan finally told the president on 7 October, the day after his Chicago speech. The president got the message. In a televised interview, he admitted that the campaign had "departed from the way it ought to be between two candidates for the highest office in this land" and that he had gotten "carried away" in some of his comments. In the future, he said, he would lay aside personalities and stick to the issues.[7]

In reality, the president merely repackaged his attacks on Reagan, making them less strident and more statesmanlike. He no longer claimed that Reagan would divide America, only that Carter would unite it. With increased effectiveness, he also put Reagan on the defensive by pounding on the theme that a Reagan presidency would be more likely to lead the nation into war than his own. Almost overnight, "war and peace" replaced "meanness" in campaign priorities, as Carter tore into Reagan's proposals to scrap the SALT II agreement and to use the threat of a new arms race to force Moscow back to the bargaining table.

The Carter campaign also had a field day with Reagan's statements on the environment. After his early bloopers, Reagan's staff assigned a top-level political adviser to travel with him in order to make certain his speeches did not contain any embarrassing bombshells. He was also urged to refrain from making any impromptu remarks. As a result, Reagan's blunders decreased—but they did not disappear entirely. Reagan commented on one occasion that while he was not a scientist, he suspected that the recent Mount St. Helen's volcano in Washington state had "probably released more sulfur dioxide into the atmosphere of the world than has been released in the last ten years of auto driving or things of that kind." The next day the Environmental Protection Agency (EPA) reported its estimate that man-made sulfur dioxide emissions amounted to 81,000 tons a day while total emissions from the Mount St. Helen's explosion were between 500 and 2,000 tons. Another time, Reagan said that air pollution in Los Angeles had been "substantially controlled," only to have his plane diverted from Los Angeles shortly thereafter because the city was enveloped in some of the worst smog in its history.[8]

In contrast to Reagan, Carter was generally considered to be strong on environmental issues. Unlike his opponent—who claimed that "environmental extremists in Washington wouldn't let you build a house unless it looked like a bird's nest"—the president insisted on strict enforcement of EPA regulations, spoke out against sacrificing air or water quality for the sake of economic development, and favored new legislation to clean up chemical dumps. On Capitol Hill, his administration was working hard for passage of legislation that would protect much of the federal wilderness in Alaska.[9] Worried about the world's rapidly growing population, its shrinking resources, and what he believed to be its worsening environment, the president even had the Council on Environmental Quality and the Department of State undertake a comprehensive study of trends in global resources and the environment outside of the United States.

By the middle of October, the momentum of the campaign had shifted in Carter's favor. Reagan's own pollsters reported that, for the first time in the race, the president had moved ahead of Reagan (by two percentage points) and that in several key states, like Illinois and Texas, the Republican lead was narrowing. The Reagan camp became concerned that the president might pull an "October surprise" by obtaining the release of the Iranian hostages. As they were aware, economic sanctions, dwindling financial reserves as a result of cutbacks in oil production, the freezing of Iranian assets in the United States, and Iran's inability to resupply its military were taking their toll on the country. Border skirmishes between Iraq and Iran were also escalating into a major war. Faced with an economic and military crisis, the Tehran government might seek to cast off its image as an international pariah by freeing the hostages.

There was ample reason for Republican apprehension. On 9 September, Iran let the United States know through the German ambassador in Tehran that it was ready to discuss a resolution of the hostage issue. Having already been disappointed several times by Iran, the White House was extremely leery about these new overtures. Confirming the sincerity of Iran's offer, however, the Ayatollah Khomeini announced later in September new conditions for a settlement: a pledge by the United States not to intervene in Iran's internal affairs, release of all of Iran's frozen assets, cancellation of all claims by Americans against Iran, and return of the shah's wealth to Iran. Notably absent was an earlier demand that the United States make an apology for its past policies toward Iran. Although considerable negotiation was still required on all these points, their presentation offered the best hope yet that an end to the crisis was possible, even imminent.

On 13 September, a five-person delegation, headed by Deputy Secretary of State Warren Christopher, left Washington for Bonn, West Germany, to hold exploratory talks with Sadegh Tabatabai, a distant relative of Khomeini's. Tabatabai took back to Iran the United States' detailed but generally positive response to the Ayatollah's recent demands. The outbreak of the Iran-Iraq war stalled negotiations for several weeks. But when Tabatabai was finally able to return to Bonn in October, he brought encouraging news: The American reply to Khomeini's conditions had "fallen on fertile ground."

In mid-October, Iranian Prime Minister Mohammed Ali Rajai came to the United States to present Iran's case against Iraq to the United Nations. Although he declined a White House invitation to meet with the president, he told a New York press conference that Washington now seemed "ready to cooperate" in resolving the hostage situation. Carter also received word that the hostages, who had been separated into groups following the ill-fated rescue mission in April, had been returned to the American embassy in Tehran and that there seemed to be a consensus among Iranian leaders that it was time to free the American captives.

These developments led to widespread public speculation that the hostages might be released before the election. Carter fed the conjectures by promising during an Ohio campaign speech to thaw Tehran's assets and lift the American trade embargo after the hostages were freed. For Republican candidate Reagan, who had earlier assured NSC Adviser Brzezinski that he would not criticize the administration's Iranian policy, the release of the Americans just before the election would be a political disaster. In private, Republican leaders even accused the president of playing politics with the hostages.[10]

Sensing that the campaign was slipping out of their grasp, Reagan and his advisers reconsidered their refusal to debate the president without John Anderson. All of the surveys of public opinion indicated that voters were turning to Carter mainly because of the cogency of the war-and-peace argument and concerns that the Republican nominee was not very smart. There was, however, no ground swell of enthusiasm for the president; rather, many voters supported him simply as the lesser of two evils. If Reagan could dispel his image as a war-mongering zealot lacking the intellect to be president, he stood a good chance of breaking Carter's toehold. The best way to achieve this was to debate Carter one-on-one.

For these very reasons, some of the president's advisers opposed a Carter-Reagan meeting. In particular, Caddell was concerned about Reagan's well-deserved reputation as the "great communicator," a skill that he displayed once more by upstaging the president when they both appeared on 15 October at the annual Alfred E. Smith dinner in New York. "Isn't there any way we can avoid debating him?" Caddell asked Jordan when he learned two days later that Reagan was ready to proceed without Anderson, whose own ranking in the polls had fallen below the 15-percent mark required by the League of Women Voters for participation. But Jordan believed that there was no way to dodge the confrontation without irreparable harm to Carter's candidacy. The president had been committed to a debate with Reagan alone too long to reject it now. Besides, Jordan and most of the president's other advisers were confident that, in a forum pitting the president's superior intellect and mastery of the issues against Reagan's superior showmanship, Carter would prevail.[11]

They were wrong. Strategically, Reagan's decision to debate Carter was the crucial move of the campaign and probably won him the election. The debate was held in Cleveland on 28 October, just one week before election day. During his ninety-minute session with Reagan, Carter handled himself well. Having spent long hours in preparation, Carter projected himself as a deliberate and thoughtful policymaker with a firm grasp of complex issues. Much of the time he was on the attack, emphasizing the substantial differences between himself and his opponent, especially on foreign policy. His one major mistake was to relay a conversation he had had that day with his daughter Amy; asking Amy what she regarded as today's most important issue, she had responded, "nuclear weaponry and the control of nuclear arms." By seeming to trivialize a serious problem, the president opened himself to ridicule. Some reporters quipped later that if Carter was re-elected, the country would be run by a teenager. But most political pundits agreed that in terms of debating points, the president had bested his opponent.

In terms of style and image, however, Reagan was the clear winner. Appearing relaxed, reasonable, and informed and avoiding any obvious mistakes, he effectively undermined the single concern that had propelled Carter into a virtual tie with him in the polls—that he was not up to the job of chief executive. He also came across as warmer than the president and more intimate with the voters, often fending off Carter's jabs with a sorrowful shake of the head followed by "aw, shucks" or "there you go again."

But the masterful stroke of the debate came at the end when Reagan returned to the two issues—the economy and America's position in the world—that had surfaced in the polls more than any others save Reagan's own fitness to be president. "Are you better off than you were four years ago?" he asked. "Is it easier for you to go and buy things in the stores than it was four years ago? Is there more or less employment in the country . . . ? Is America as respected throughout the world as it was? Do you feel that our security is safe, that we're as strong as we were four years ago?" If the voters answered no, he concluded, "Why then I think your choice is very obvious as to whom you'll vote for."

In all the polls taken after the debate, Reagan was the victor. A *Newsweek* survey of people who had watched the debate showed the Republican beating the president by a margin of 34 percent to 26 percent, with 31 percent calling the event a draw. An ABC news/Harris poll favored Reagan over Carter by an even wider margin, 44 percent to 26 percent. Even Pat Caddell acknowledged that the debate had produced "a pause" in the president's momentum: "It seems basically a wash with maybe a slight edge for Reagan."[12] Reagan's senior adviser, James Baker, had predicted that all the Republican candidate had to do to win the debate was to stay even with the president. But he had done more than that. With seven days remaining in the campaign, he had returned the attention of the American voters back to the issues on which Carter was most vulnerable. Once more the election had become a referendum on the Carter presidency.

During the final days of the race, the Republicans also benefited from a new twist in the hostage crisis. Always anxious about an "October surprise," they had strongly implied that voters should be on guard against political manipulation of the hostage situation. The president seemed to be guilty of precisely that type of gamesmanship when, on the Sunday before election day, he broke off campaigning to return to Washington and announced to the

American people that the Iranian parliament had set terms for the release of the hostages in what he called a "significant development." In effect, the Iranian legislature informed the United States through intermediaries that they were now prepared to free the American captives if the United States met the four conditions stated by Khomeini in September.

Carter and his advisers were of two minds in learning of the latest Iranian communication. They understood that the hostages would not be released before the election because provisions such as canceling Iranian debts could take months of negotiations and adjudication. They were also aware that the Republicans had primed the American people so well about a last-minute ploy that publication of the latest dispatch could cause a backlash against the president.

Nevertheless, Carter was optimistic that a breakthrough had been made in the hostage crisis, which could ultimately bring about the liberation of the Americans. Jordan also felt that a "statesmanlike response" to the Iranians would still constitute "a political plus." On Jordan's advice, the president decided to follow this course. "We are within two days of an important national election," he told the American people. "Let me assure you that my decision on this crucial matter will not be affected by the calendar."[13] Yet the president's eleventh-hour announcement turned many undecided voters against him. Not only were they suspicious of his motives, but his televised message highlighted his inability to secure the hostages' release before this. The realization that the long Iranian hostage crisis was still not over also left many Americans with a sense of futility and impotence for which they blamed Carter.

On 4 November, a majority of voters expressed their displeasure by rejecting the president's bid for reelection. Reagan received 51 percent of the vote to Carter's 41 percent and John Anderson's 7 percent. In terms of electoral votes, Reagan's victory was even more clear-cut: He lost in the District of Columbia but carried every state except Rhode Island, West Virginia, Georgia, Minnesota, and Maryland, for a total of 489 electoral votes to Carter's 49. Reagan's performance in his debate with Carter and the president's final report on the hostage crisis seem to have been decisive. According to an ABC postelection analysis, more than one out of every four voters settled on a candidate during the last week of the campaign. Of this group, 44 percent voted for Reagan and 38 percent for Carter.

Another reason for Carter's loss was that the voter turnout among several traditional Democratic groups—Catholics, Jews, blacks, union members, and urban dwellers—was significantly lower than four years earlier. Among blacks, Carter captured an estimated 80 percent to 90 percent of the vote, about the same as in 1976, but about 5 percent fewer blacks voted in 1980 than in 1976. Indeed, the voter turnout in 1980 was just over 52 percent of eligible voters—2 percent lower than the turnout in 1976 and the lowest since

1948. Many people expressed their disinterest in or dislike of all three candidates by not voting at all.

In thirteen states, John Anderson received a vote greater than Reagan's margin of victory over Carter, but he appears to have been a spoiler for Carter in only a few states—most notably New York and Florida. Had Anderson not run, exit polls nationwide indicated that Carter would have picked up barely half (49 percent) of his votes while 37 percent would have switched to Reagan. This would not have been enough to change the election's outcome.[14]

Vice-President Mondale and a few other members of the Carter entourage had sensed the swing in voter sentiment just before the campaign ended. "What I heard," said Mondale after the election, "was a series of negative, cynical questions suggesting a different public mood. I do not know, something sour happened. The last two days you could cut it with a knife." But only as Carter was returning to Plains from his final day of campaigning did he fully realize that he was going to lose. While on Air Force One, he took a message from Pat Caddell that his last poll showed Reagan beating the president by ten percentage points. "We're losing the undecided voters overwhelmingly," Caddell told him, "and a lot of working Democrats are going to wake up tomorrow and for the first time in their lives vote Republican."[15]

Results of the election stunned political analysts, few of whom had predicted such an unequivocal outcome. The final Gallup poll before the election placed Reagan ahead of Carter by only 3 points, and the final ABC news/ Harris poll had him leading by 5 points. A *Newsweek* poll actually gave the president an edge over the former California governor, 41 percent to 40 percent. As late as the end of October, the president's advisers thought he had a good chance to win even in California, Reagan's home state. What the pollsters did not foresee was the shift of the undecided vote to Reagan in the closing days of the campaign and the decision of so many loyal Democrats to stay home on election day.[16]

The American electorate's repudiation of Carter and the Democratic party was overwhelming. Not only did the Republicans take possession of the White House, but Republicans gained control of the Senate for the first time in twenty-eight years as seven liberal Democrats, including the party's 1972 standard-bearer, George McGovern, went down to defeat. Republicans also picked up thirty-three seats in the House and, on the state level, finished with a net gain of four governorships.

Carter had conceded defeat an hour before the polls even closed on the West Coast, although his own staff had warned that his announcement might cause late voters to skip the polls. The president's decision to yield so early in the evening angered Democratic leaders throughout the country, who accused Carter of sabotaging the reelection of several Democratic congressmen.

In many ways, this one episode was illustrative of the entire Carter presidency. Throughout his nearly four years in office, Jimmy Carter had remained a political outsider in Washington who acted according to his own instincts of propriety, often irrespective of the counsel of his own advisers and frequently when it defied accepted political practices and placed him at odds with those whose political support he needed and should have nurtured.

After his defeat, Carter demonstrated that he was still president for the next ten weeks and that he had an agenda to pursue regardless of the election results. His most pressing priority, of course, was the release of the hostages. The news from Iran continued to be encouraging, as the Ayatollah Khomeini gave permission to the militants holding the Americans to turn them over to the Tehran government. Prime Minister Mohammed Ali Rajai appointed a commission to work out the terms for the release of the hostages, using Algeria as Iran's intermediary with Washington.

The negotiations themselves were long and complex. Although the Tehran government wanted Washington to confiscate and return the shah's wealth in the United States, the president did not have the legal power to do this. Nor could the White House simply sweep away all legal claims against Iran or unfreeze its assets in the United States. As the historian Gaddis Smith pointed out, "The problem of unfreezing the assets was an almost indescribable labyrinth of disagreement over how many dollars were involved, fluctuations in the value of currencies, the status of loans, the payment of interest on frozen accounts, the banking laws of other countries where some of the funds were located, and hundreds of interlocking claims."[17]

Diplomats, financial experts, bankers, and lawyers worked around the clock in a desperate effort to overcome these obstacles. By 18 January, two days before Carter would leave office, they had settled on $9 billion in frozen assets as the amount to be transferred to Iran upon the return of the Americans. Having spent most of his last year as president preoccupied with the hostage crisis, Carter was anxious to see their liberation during his term. But he was denied this consolation prize. The Iranians completed their deal only a few minutes after Reagan had taken the oath of office on 20 January.

A week after the election, Congress met in an unusual postelection session to wrap up a number of unfinished matters. In addition to bargaining for the hostages' freedom, Carter busied himself in the remaining weeks of his presidency by lobbying on Capitol Hill for several of his high priority measures—a youth jobs bill, a superfund to clean up toxic wastes, and an Alaskan lands bill. Determined to keep Democrats in the lame-duck Congress from enacting any last-minute legislation before Reagan assumed office, Republicans in the Senate managed to keep the jobs bill tied up in committee even though it passed the House overwhelmingly and had strong bipartisan support in the upper chamber.

The president had better luck in persuading Congress to approve his two pieces of environmental legislation. The first of these established a $1.6-billion toxic waste superfund. A proposal for a superfund had been in the drafting stages since 1977; that year, residents of the Love Canal near Niagara Falls had been forced to abandon their homes after it was learned they had been built on a former chemical dump and that emissions from the dump were poisoning the area. The measure that lawmakers passed was substantially weaker than what the president and environmentalists wanted. In particular, the superfund could not be used to clean up oil spills, only chemical contamination. A number of lawmakers in the House preferred to hold out for a tougher bill that would cover such spills. But the president believed that the Senate would not agree to a stricter and more comprehensive measure and that the version approved by the upper chamber was better than no legislation at all. Consequently, Carter made several last-ditch telephone calls to guarantee final House approval.

Passage on 12 November of the Alaskan lands bill represented a more significant victory for the president. The most sweeping proposal of its kind ever approved by Congress, the legislation more than doubled the size of the country's national parks and wildlife refuge system and almost tripled the amount of land designated wilderness. For more than two years, Carter had labored to get an Alaskan lands bill through Congress, telling Frank Moore in 1978 to push the measure. But opposition from oil, gas, mineral, and timber interests, from the state government, and from Alaska's two senators, who sought to open the land for development, was strong enough to prevent land legislation from making it onto the Senate floor.[18]

In 1980, however, Carter decided to make the bill his "highest environmental priority." Working closely with Congressman Morris Udall of Arizona and other lawmakers seeking to protect the wilderness, he brought environmentalists from all over the country to the White House in July to kick off the campaign promoting the legislation. In order to ensure action on the measure and give its backers some leverage against prodevelopment forces, who hoped to force concessions through delaying tactics, the president's interior secretary, Cecil Andrus, also withdrew 40 million acres of Alaskan land from development, under authority given to the Interior Department in 1976. Andrus said he would rescind this withdrawal, which provided even stricter protection of this acreage than the legislation before Congress, when an Alaskan lands bill was approved. He explained his action as an "insurance policy [against] deliberate obstructionism."[19]

The legislation that the House and Senate finally passed after a long and acrimonious struggle on Capitol Hill did not entirely satisfy environmentalists or the president. Environmental groups were unhappy with the protection afforded calving grounds for caribou and habitats for migratory birds. They disliked a provision allowing seismic exploration of certain parts of Alaska's North Slope believed to hold millions of barrels of oil, and another permitting mining and logging operations in previously forbidden areas until such time as environmentalists and prodevelopment forces agreed over how much to preserve. But considering the legislation's sweep and what it did exclude from development—104 million acres, or about one-third of Alaskan lands—it is understandable why Carter termed the legislation "among the most gratifying achievements" of his administration.[20]

Resolving the Iranian hostage crisis and lobbying for his environmental legislation consumed most of Carter's last two months in office. There were also other presidential duties, such as a farewell meeting with Israeli Prime Minister Begin, which the president had earlier hoped would be a prelude to another Begin-Sadat summit, and the preparation of a budget for fiscal 1982, which Reagan was almost certain to amend once he took office. Another, more serious matter arose in early December when the Soviets deployed fifteen or twenty divisions along the Polish border, possibly to squelch the growing Solidarity movement there. Carter promptly dispatched a warning to Soviet leader Brezhnev not to send forces into Poland, and the divisions were soon moved back.

During his last days in the White House, Carter found time to reflect on his four years in the White House. Although acknowledging he had made mistakes as president, he attributed his defeat not to these errors but to his willingness to tackle difficult and politically risky issues, ranging from the Mideast crisis to the energy crisis. When asked by a group of reporters how he thought history would judge him, he answered, "I don't know yet," and then went on to list some of his achievements as president—interestingly, all in the international realm. "I think, in general," he told them, "that the opening of access into Africa, the normalization of relations with China, the Middle East peace effort, the maintaining of our nation's peace—in international affairs [history] will look on us well."

There can be no gainsaying the truth of what the president said about the problems he confronted and his accomplishments while in office. At the same time, it is hard to avoid the conclusion that his was a mediocre presidency and that much of the reason for this was his own doing. What the American people had witnessed in his four years in office was a political figure long on good intentions but short on know-how; a novice in the Oval Office who never reached an accommodation with the institutions and interests in Washington he had run against but whose support he needed; a chief executive who was smart, caring, honest, and informed but who self-righteously believed that what he thought was right should prevail; an administrator who micromanaged but not always well; a leader who worked diligently in support of his policies and programs but failed to educate or influence public opinion; and, most important, a president who never adequately defined a mission for his government, a purpose for the country, and a way to get there. This was not a formula for a successful presidency.

15

$\star\ \star\ \star\ \star\ \star$

EPILOGUE

Immediately after the inauguration of Ronald Reagan as the nation's new chief executive on 20 January 1981, Carter, Rosalynn, and Amy returned to Plains. The next day, at President Reagan's invitation, Carter flew to Wiesbaden, West Germany, to welcome back to freedom the Iranian hostages. It was an exhilarating moment for Carter, but it was followed by a difficult period of transition from president to private citizen. Carter had not recovered fully from the shock of his defeat, particularly the dimension of Reagan's victory. He was also faced with personal financial problems. Before taking office in 1977, he had put his financial assets into a blind trust only to discover as he was about to leave office that his principal asset, the Carter peanut warehouse business, was broke and that he was deeply in debt. For Rosalynn, the return to Plains was even more traumatic. "There was no way I could understand our defeat," she later wrote. "It didn't seem fair that everything we had hoped for, all our plans and dreams for the country could have been gone when the votes were counted on election day."[1]

After a few months, however, the Carters settled into a new routine. They fixed up their home, which had not been occupied in ten years, sold the warehouse business, and signed lucrative book contracts, thereby assuring their financial security. They sent Amy, who had grown up in Atlanta and Washington, D.C., and had never really adjusted to living in Plains, to a private boarding school in Atlanta.

During the first half of the 1980s, the former president all but vanished from the national political scene. He took no part in the 1984 presidential election even though his former vice-president, Walter Mondale, was running against Reagan. He also made few public appearances and only occasionally pondered his own administration. In a 1984 interview with Tom Wicker of the *New York Times*, he defended what he considered his apolitical approach to the presidency, that is, making tough decisions regardless of their political consequences. "No way could I do it differently," he told Wicker. But President Reagan's success in getting his budget, tax cuts, and military spending increases through Congress seemed to highlight Carter's own ineptitude as the nation's chief executive and to prove what Carter's critics had said while he was in office—that the nation was governable if the right leader was at the helm.[2]

In forced retirement, the former president spent most of his time writing his memoirs, teaching at Emory University, and raising funds for the Jimmy Carter Library, Museum, and Presidential Center in Atlanta. Determined that the Carter complex be more than a monument to his presidency, Carter envisioned the center as an institution performing vital public service—a place where disputes between nations could be mediated in a nongovernmental and academic setting and where experts from various walks of life could come together to discuss, and even take action, on such important world issues as nuclear arms control, human rights, the environment, world hunger, and especially health care. "[Preventive health care] had been a very long-standing concern for me, dating back to my early childhood experiences," he later remarked.[3] Since opening in 1986, the Carter Presidential Center has become a locus of research and social and political activism for all these problems and more. The former president has been intimately involved with these endeavors, spending about five days a month at the center where he and Rosalynn maintain a small apartment. He has also traveled throughout the world, promoting improved agricultural methods and better health care in the world's most poverty-stricken countries, especially in Africa.

Although the programs at the Carter Presidential Center remain a major part of Carter's life, they have not been his only commitment. Beginning with a bus trip in 1984 to the Lower East Side of New York in order to help renovate a dilapidated building, he and Rosalynn have been very active in Habitat for Humanity, a charitable organization started in 1973 to provide housing for the poor. The former president has often been seen swinging a hammer at construction sites in New York, Philadelphia, and Chicago, and he has raised large sums of money in support of Habitat's work.

Since the mid-1980s, Carter has become publicly more vocal and politically more visible. Around 1985, he began to speak out frequently on national issues and to criticize the Reagan administration's policies and programs. In an interview in March 1986, for example, he attacked the president for his policy of "constructive engagement" with South Africa, by which the administration kept close ties with that nation despite its adherence to apartheid. This stance was "a disaster," Carter said, "because of the general presumption of the world that [it] in effect means approval [of apartheid]." He also objected to Reagan's Strategic Defense Initiative (the so-called Star Wars program intended to protect the United States from incoming missiles through a shield of orbiting satellites), arguing that it would cost $1 trillion to build and "could be easily and cheaply counteracted."[4]

The former president has also played an increasingly important role as an elder statesman, attempting to mediate the long-running war in Ethiopia between its Marxist government and Eritrean rebels (1989), and monitoring elections in Panama (1989) and Nicaragua (1990). But the Middle East has remained the region of most concern to him, as he has watched the promise of the Camp David agreements of 1978 go largely unfulfilled. He has written a short study of the Middle East, has been openly critical of Israel for its refusal to stop building settlements on the West Bank and its unwillingness to grant Palestinians greater autonomy, and has proposed an international peace conference to mediate the Arab-Israeli dispute. Carter also spoke out strongly against military intervention in the Persian Gulf following Iraq's invasion of Kuwait in 1990. Once the United Nations sanctioned the war, he urged President George Bush to insist on less than the complete destruction of Iraqi forces; any other course, he argued, would only contribute to greater instability in the region.[5]

As Carter has reentered the public arena, the news media has given more attention to his activities as a private citizen, and he has gained a degree of popularity and stature with the American people that would have been hard to imagine when he left office in 1981. In April 1990, *Newsweek* referred to Carter as "the modern model of a successful ex-president of the United States." The next month he was awarded the Liberty Medal and a $100,000 prize for his involvement in "issues of liberty around the world." An ABC/ *Wall Street Journal* poll at the beginning of 1990 showed Carter's public approval rating nearly equaling Reagan's, and only 29 percent of Americans surveyed gave Carter an unfavorable rating while 36 percent disapproved of Reagan.[6]

Ironically, one issue that has contributed to Carter's rising reputation has been his management of the 1979/80 hostage crisis. Even though this was a crucial factor in his defeat, political commentators have favorably compared the way he handled this situation with Ronald Reagan's handling of a similar crisis in 1984 involving Americans kidnapped in Lebanon. In nationally televised congressional hearings in 1987, Americans learned how the Reagan administration tried to barter arms for Iran in return for the release of these hostages. Its back-room approach appeared in sharp contrast to the former president's refusal to make such deals during the 1979/80 hostage crisis. Carter himself has condemned the Reagan arms deal. "To me, the bribery of kidnappers is unconscionable," he remarked in an interview in April 1987. "What we did in Iran, in the most recent scandal, has not only encouraged additional taking of hostages but it rewarded those who did kidnap Americans."[7]

There has been a recent twist to the Iran hostage crisis of 1979/80, with implications for the public's perception of Carter's presidency. On 15 April 1991, Gary Sick, who as a member of Carter's National Security Council had been intimately involved in the hostage episode, made a startling assertion in the *New York Times*: In the 1980 presidential election, Reagan's campaign managers, fearing that the early release of the American captives would assure Carter's victory, arranged a deal with the Tehran government to keep the hostages until after the election. According to Sick, the Iranians were promised large quantities of arms once the new Reagan administration took office. Sick based his allegations of an arms-for-hostages deal on a computerized data base on the crisis, which he claimed revealed "a curious pattern" of events suggesting that such a bargain had been struck. Sick later elaborated on these charges in his book *October Surprise.*[8]

Sick has admitted that he has "no 'smoking gun'" and that he cannot "prove exactly what happened at each stage" of the arms-for-hostages deal. President George Bush, who Sick asserts was a participant in at least one of the meetings that supposedly took place between members of the Reagan campaign and Iranian officials, has emphatically denied these allegations, calling them "rumor mongering." The director of the Ronald Reagan Library, Ralph Bledsoe, has said that he can find no evidence in Reagan's 1980 campaign files to support Sick's theories. Certainly no member of the Carter campaign in 1980 appears to have suspected that the Republicans were maneuvering to delay the release of the hostages until after the November elections. As earlier noted, in fact, Hamilton Jordan was worried that the preelection return of the hostages might actually work against Carter, being construed as political manipulation of the most repugnant kind.[9]

Nevertheless, the former president has since stated his belief that there might be substance to Sick's charges, and a number of Democratic lawmakers on Capitol Hill have called for a congressional investigation into the matter—as have eight former hostages. In October 1991, the Senate voted to conduct an inquiry, but the next month, Senate Republicans were able to block funding for it. Short of new evidence to substantiate Sick's allegations, it is highly unlikely that Congress will act.

NOTES

This study follows the practice of other volumes in the American Presidency Series of limiting citations mainly to quotations. Undocumented remarks by President Jimmy Carter come from *Public Papers of the Presidents of the United States: Jimmy Carter,* 9 vols. (Washington, D.C.: Government Printing Office, 1977–1982); polls and surveys are from the news media, mainly *Time, Newsweek, U.S. News and World Report,* and the *New York Times.* The primary and secondary literature on which this work is based can be found in the Bibliographic Essay.

CHAPTER 1
INTRODUCTION

1. Haynes Johnson, *In the Absence of Power* (New York: Viking Press, 1980).

2. See, for example, Michael J. Krukones, "The Campaign Promises of Jimmy Carter: Accomplishments and Failures," *Presidential Studies Quarterly* 15 (Winter 1985): 136–44; David Lee, "The Politics of Less: The Trials of Herbert Hoover and Jimmy Carter," *Presidential Studies Quarterly* 14 (Spring 1984): 265–84; and William F. Mullen, "Perceptions of Carter's Legislative Successes and Failures: Views from the Hill and the Liaison Staff," *Presidential Studies Quarterly* 12 (Fall 1982): 522–24.

3. Charles O. Jones, *The Trusteeship Presidency: Jimmy Carter and the United States Congress* (Baton Rouge: Louisiana State University Press, 1988); Erwin C. Hargrove, *Jimmy Carter As President: Leadership and the Politics of the Public Good* (Baton Rouge: Louisiana State University Press, 1988); Richard V. Pierard and Robert D. Linder, *Civil Religion and the Presidency* (Grand Rapids, Mich.: Academie Books, 1988), p. 255; Aaron Wildavsky, *The Beleaguered Presidency* (New Brunswick, N.J.: Transaction Publishers, 1991), p. xiv. For an earlier defense of the Carter administration, see Reo M. Christenson, "Carter and Truman: A Reappraisal of Both," *Presidential Studies Quarterly* 12 (Spring 1983): 313–21. For a discussion of the Carter revisionism that is

under way, see especially Gary W. Reichard, "Early Returns: Assessing Jimmy Carter," *Presidential Studies Quarterly* 19 (Summer 1990): 603–20, but see also *Wall Street Journal*, 24 June 1988, pp. 1 and 6.

4. See, for example, Paul Charles Light, *The President's Agenda: Domestic Policy Choice from Kennedy to Carter (with Notes on Ronald Reagan)* (Baltimore: Johns Hopkins University Press, 1982), pp. 1–12.

5. Charles O. Jones, "Carter and Congress: From the Outside In," *British Journal of Political Science* 15 (July 1985): 271–98; Jones, "The Separated Presidency—Making It Work in Contemporary Politics," in Anthony King, ed., *The New American Political System: Second Version* (Washington, D.C.: AEI Press, 1990), pp. 26–27; Mark J. Rozell, *The Press and the Carter Presidency* (Boulder, Colo.: Westview Press, 1989), p. 226. See also Light, *The President's Agenda*, p. 80, and Reichard, "Early Returns," pp. 610–11.

6. Mark A. Peterson, *Legislating Together: The White House and Capitol Hill from Eisenhower to Reagen* (Cambridge, Mass.: Harvard University Press, 1990), pp. 17–19. See also Nelson W. Polsby, *Consequences of Party Reform* (New York: Oxford University Press, 1983), pp. 105–14.

CHAPTER 2
WHAT MAKES JIMMY RUN?

1. Jimmy Carter, *Why Not the Best?* (Nashville, Tenn.: Broadman Press, 1975), p. 8.

2. Ibid., p. 60.

3. Ibid.

4. Ibid., p. 80.

5. *Time*, 31 May 1971, pp. 14–20.

6. Hugh Carter, *Cousin Beedie and Cousin Hot: My Life with the Carter Family of Plains, Georgia* (Englewood Cliffs, N.J.: Prentice-Hall, 1978), p. 112.

7. Cited in Kandy Stroud, *How Jimmy Won: The Victory Campaign from Plains to the White House* (New York: William Morrow, 1977), pp. 185–87.

8. Carter, *Why Not the Best?* p. 141.

9. *Time*, 22 March 1976, pp. 8–10.

10. Ibid., 19 April 1976, pp. 14 and 16.

11. Cited in Stroud, *How Jimmy Won*, pp. 277–81; *Time*, 26 April 1976, p. 16.

12. "Campaign Plan—Final Copy," n.d., Box 13, Michael Raoul Duval Papers, Gerald Ford Library, Ann Arbor, Michigan.

13. Cited in David F. Hahn, "The Rhetoric of Jimmy Carter," *Presidential Studies Quarterly* 14 (Spring 1984): 273.

14. Memorandum for Bailey to Cheney and Teeter, 30 September 1976, Box 1, Special Files, Gerald Ford Papers, Gerald Ford Library.

15. "The Foreign Policy Debate," 3 October 1976, Box 2, Gerald Ford Papers.

16. Ibid.

17. "The Public's Response to Gerald Ford's Statement on Eastern Europe during the Second Debate," May 1977, Box 62, Robert Teeter Papers, Gerald Ford Library.

18. Cited in Betty Glad, *Jimmy Carter: In Search of the Great White House* (New York: W. W. Norton, 1980), p. 398.

CHAPTER 3
TRANSITION AND HONEYMOON

1. Ernest S. Griffith, *The American Presidency: The Dilemmas of Shared Power and Divided Government* (New York: New York University Press, 1976), pp. v–vii, 1–15, and 221–25.

2. Thomas E. Cronin, *The State of the Presidency* (Boston: Little, Brown, 1975), esp. pp. 6–10.

3. *New Republic*, 27 January 1979, pp. 16–18.

4. Cronin, *State of the Presidency*, p. 25. For a similar verdict, see also Griffith, *American Presidency*, p. 208.

5. Nelson W. Polsby, *Consequences of Party Reform* (New York: Oxford University Press, 1983), p. 113.

6. Patrick Caddell, "Initial Paper on Political Strategy," November 1976, Box 4, Jody Powell Papers, Jimmy Carter Library, Atlanta, Georgia.

7. Memorandum from Schultze to Economic Policy Group, 18 January 1977, Box 192, Stuart Eizenstat Papers, Jimmy Carter Library.

8. "Attorney General," n.d., Box 8, Hamilton Jordan Papers, Jimmy Carter Library.

9. Jimmy Carter, *Keeping Faith: Memoirs of a President* (New York: Bantam Books, 1982), p. 65.

10. Ibid., pp. 73–74.

11. *Time*, 24 January 1977, p. 45.

12. *Newsweek*, 18 April 1977, pp. 85–86.

13. Carter's handwritten comments are in the margin of Memorandum for the President from Eizenstat, 18 June 1977, Box 42, Powell Papers.

14. Thomas P. O'Neill with William Novak, *Man of the House: The Life and Political Memoirs of Speaker Tip O'Neill* (New York: Random House, 1987), p. 302.

15. Rich Hutcheson to the President, 23 January 1977, Box 51, Jordan Papers; *Time*, 31 January 1977, pp. 20–21.

16. *Time*, 7 February 1977, p. 19.

17. Carter to Eizenstat, 15 April 1977, Box 315, Eizenstat Papers.

18. *Congressional Quarterly Almanac* 33 (1977): 95–96.

19. Memorandum for the President-elect from Fritz Mondale, n.d., Box 6, Powell Papers.

20. *Time*, 24 January 1977, pp. 8–13.

21. *Newsweek*, 2 May 1977, pp. 16–18.

22. Memorandum for the President from Hamilton Jordan, 29 March 1977, Box 55, Jordan Papers (Jordan's italics).

23. *Newsweek*, 2 May 1977, p. 39.

CHAPTER 4
MORALITY AND FOREIGN POLICY

1. Memorandum for President Carter from Hamilton Jordan, n.d., Box 59, Hamilton Jordan Papers, Jimmy Carter Library, Atlanta, Georgia.

2. Jimmy Carter, *Keeping Faith: Memoirs of a President* (New York: Bantam Books, 1982), p. 53.

3. *The Presidential Campaign 1976*, 3 vols. (Washington, D.C.: Government Printing Office, 1978), 1:110, 245–46; 3:97.

4. Ibid., 1:83–84, 712–14, and 1043–44.

5. Ibid., pp. 39–42.

6. Ibid., p. 953; 3:93.

7. Carter, *Keeping Faith*, pp. 212–17.

8. J. C. to Zbig, 14 February 1977, Box 58, Jordan Papers; J. C. to Zbig, Jack, Rick, 21 February 1977, Box FG-25, Presidential Papers of Jimmy Carter, White House Central Files, Jimmy Carter Library (hereafter cited as WHCF).

9. Memorandum for the President from Jody Powell, 21 February 1977, Box 208, Stuart Eizenstat Papers, Jimmy Carter Library.

10. *Time*, 7 February 1977, p. 38.

11. *New Republic*, 16 April 1977, p. 55; *Time*, 14 March 1977, p. 22.

12. *Presidential Campaign 1976*, 3:113.

13. Ibid., 1:56–57, 81–82, 202, 215–21, 709–14; 3:104.

14. Cyrus Vance, *Hard Choices: Critical Years in America's Foreign Policy* (New York: Simon and Schuster, 1983), p. 170.

15. "Work Plan: Middle East," n.d., Box 34, Jordan Papers (Jordan's italics); Benjamin Rosenthal to Jimmy Carter, 28 April 1977, and Carter to Rosenthal, 19 May 1977, Box CO-34, WHCF.

16. *Time*, 30 May 1977, p. 22.

17. Carter, *Keeping Faith*, p. 288.

18. Vance, *Hard Choices*, pp. 128–30.

19. "Letter from Washington," *New Yorker*, 22 July 1977, p. 58.

20. *Time*, 8 August 1977, pp. 8–23.

CHAPTER 5
THE DOG DAYS OF SUMMER AND FALL

1. Memorandum for the President from Stu Eizenstat, 20 June 1977, Box 315, Stuart Eizenstat Papers, Jimmy Carter Library, Atlanta, Georgia.

2. Memorandum for the President from Charles Schultze, 23 June 1977, Box 194, Eizenstat Papers.

3. Joseph A. Califano, Jr., *Governing America: An Insider's Report from the White House and the Cabinet* (New York: Simon and Schuster, 1981), pp. 329–30.

4. Memorandum for the President from Joe Califano, 11 April 1977, attached to Memorandum for the President from Jack Watson, 15 April 1977, Box 60, Hamilton Jordan Papers, Jimmy Carter Library.

5. Califano, *Governing America*, pp. 336–37.

6. Memorandum for the President from Hamilton Jordan, n.d., Box 37, Jordan Papers.

7. Memorandum to Jimmy Carter from Hamilton Jordan, n.d., Box 34, Jordan Papers (Jordan's italics).

8. Thomas P. O'Neill with William Novak, *Man of the House: The Life and Political Memoirs of Speaker Tip O'Neill* (New York: Random House, 1987), pp. 320–23.

9. Memorandum for the President from Stu Eizenstat and Bob Ginsburg, 16 May 1977 (Eizenstat's italics); Memorandum for the President from Jim Fallows, 6 June 1977, Box 287, Eizenstat Papers.

10. Memorandum for the President from Charles Schultze, 15 October 1977, Box BE-4, WHCF.

11. Bert Lance with Bill Gilbert, *The Truth of the Matter: My Life In and Out of Politics* (New York: Summit Books, 1991), pp. 130–36; Jimmy Carter, *Keeping Faith: Memoirs of a President* (New York: Bantam Books, 1982), p. 130.

12. *New Yorker*, 12 September 1977, pp. 130–36.

13. Ribicoff to the President, 3 September 1977, and enclosure attached to Memorandum for President Carter from Frank Moore, 3 September 1977, Box 31, Staff Offices, Robert J. Lipshutz, Presidential Papers of Jimmy Carter, Jimmy Carter Library (hereafter cited as Lipshutz Papers).

14. Memorandum for the President from Robert Lipshutz, 6 September 1977, Lipshutz Papers.

15. Carter, *Keeping Faith*, p. 132.

16. Lance, *The Truth of the Matter*, pp. 139–41; *Newsweek*, 26 September 1977, pp. 20–31.

17. Carter, *Keeping Faith*, pp. 133–34.

18. Ibid., pp. 134–36; Lance, *The Truth of the Matter*, pp. 148–51.

19. Bob Haldeman to the President, 21 September 1977, Box FG-85, WHCF.

20. "Summary of Issue Concerns of the American People," 12 September 1977, Box 33, Jordan Papers, *Time*, 22 August 1977, p. 28; *National Review*, 2 September 1977, p. 978.

CHAPTER 6
CAN CARTER COPE?

1. Memorandum to Robert Lipshutz and Stuart Eizenstat from Joyce R. Starr, Box 208, Stuart Eizenstat Papers, Jimmy Carter Library, Atlanta, Georgia; Douglas J. Bennett, Jr., to Honorable E. de la Garza, 15 March 1978, and attachment, Box "Andrew Young," Name File, WHCF.

2. Memorandum for the President, Secretary Schlesinger, and Frank Moore, 23 December 1977, Box 198, Eizenstat Papers.

3. Memorandum for Bob Lipshutz and Stu Eizenstat from Doug Huron, 2 September 1977, Box 120, Staff Offices, Counsel Margaret McKenna, Presidential Papers of Jimmy Carter, Jimmy Carter Library. See also Memorandum for the President from Stu Eizenstat and Bob Lipshutz, 6 September 1977, Box 33, Hamilton Jordan Papers, Jimmy Carter Library.

4. Memorandum for the President from Stu Eizenstat and Bob Lipshutz, 6 Sep-

tember 1977, Box 33, Jordan Papers; Griffin B. Bell with Ronald J. Ostrow, *Taking Care of the Law* (New York: William Morrow, 1982), pp. 29–30.

5. Joseph A. Califano, Jr., *Governing America: An Insider's Report from the White House and the Cabinet* (New York: Simon and Schuster, 1981), pp. 235–38.

6. Memorandum for the President and Vice-President from Bob Lipshutz and Stu Eizenstat, 16 September 1977, Box 33, Jordan Papers.

7. Califano, *Governing America*, p. 243; Bell, *Taking Care of the Law*, p. 24.

8. Memorandum to President Carter from Hamilton Jordan, [September 1977], Box 33, Jordan Papers.

9. Minutes of the Cabinet Meeting, 16 January 1978, Box 159, Eizenstat Papers.

10. Jimmy Carter to Pat Harris et al., 7 October 1977, Box 301, Eizenstat Papers.

11. Memorandum for the President from Stu Eizenstat, 20 January 1978, Box 309, Eizenstat Papers.

12. *New York Times*, 18 December 1977, p. 47; Memorandum for the President from James T. McIntyre, Jr., 20 December 1977, Box 152, Eizenstat Papers.

13. *Time*, 12 December 1977, pp. 12–16.

14. *Business Week*, 16 January 1978, pp. 28–29.

15. Memorandum to the President from Hamilton Jordan, 14 December 1977, Box 34, Jordan Papers.

16. To the Baron Report from Peter D. Hart, n.d., attached to Memorandum for the President from the Vice-President, 20 March 1978, Box 44, ibid.

17. Memorandum to the President from Hamilton Jordan and Jack Watson, 14 February 1978, Box 9, Lipshutz Papers.

18. *New York Times*, 7 March 1978, p. 35; *Time*, 3 April 1977, p. 26.

19. *Business Week*, 23 January 1978, pp. 90–91, and 6 February 1978, p. 39; *Newsweek*, 30 January 1978, pp. 23–25.

20. Memorandum for the President from W. Michael Blumenthal and Charlie Schultze, 15 March 1978, Box 144, Eizenstat Papers.

21. Memorandum to President Carter from Hamilton Jordan, 22 March 1978, Box 56, Jordan Papers.

CHAPTER 7
THE YEAR OF NEGOTIATIONS

1. Jimmy Carter, *Keeping Faith: Memoirs of a President* (New York: Bantam Books, 1982), p. 293.

2. *Time*, 28 November 1977, pp. 28–47.

3. Carter, *Keeping Faith*, p. 300.

4. *Newsweek*, 16 January 1978, p. 23.

5. Ibid., pp. 40–47.

6. Zbigniew Brzezinski, *Power and Principle: Memoirs of the National Security Adviser, 1977–1981* (New York: Farrar, Straus, Giroux, 1985), pp. 235–36.

7. Moshe Dayan, *Breakthrough: A Personal Account of the Egypt-Israel Negotiations* (New York: Alfred A. Knopf, 1981), pp. 117–18.

8. Brzezinski, *Power and Principle*, p. 246; Dayan, *Breakthrough*, p. 123.

9. Edward Tivnan, *The Lobby: Jewish Political Power and American Foreign Policy* (New York: Simon and Schuster, 1987), pp. 124–25.

10. Memorandum to President Carter from Hamilton Jordan, [January 1978], Box 37, Hamilton Jordan Papers, Jimmy Carter Library, Atlanta, Georgia.

11. Barry Goldwater to the President, 12 September 1977, attached to Kathy Baker to the President, 15 September 1977, Box FO-16, WHCF.

12. See, for example, *Time,* 15 May 1978, pp. 18–20; *Newsweek,* 15 May 1978, pp. 28–30; *U.S. News and World Report,* 22 May 1978, pp. 19–24.

13. Gaddis Smith, *Morality, Reason, and Power: American Diplomacy in the Carter Years* (New York: Hill and Wang, 1986), p. 115.

14. See miscellaneous correspondence in Box "Andrew Young," Name File, WHCF; *Time,* 8 August 1977, p. 23.

15. Brzezinski, *Power and Principle,* pp. 140–41.

16. Memorandum for the President from Jody Powell, 7 July 1978, Box 40, Jody Powell Papers, Jimmy Carter Library.

17. *Newsweek,* 17 April 1978, pp. 34–37; *Time,* 17 April 1978, pp. 10–14.

CHAPTER 8
WAR ON INFLATION

1. *Newsweek,* 21 August 1978, pp. 56–59.

2. Memorandum for Jody Powell and Jerry Rafshoon from Stu Eizenstat and Bob Ginsburg, 21 June 1978, Box 289, Stuart Eizenstat Papers, Jimmy Carter Library, Atlanta, Georgia.

3. Joseph A. Califano, Jr., *Governing America: An Insider's Report from the White House and the Cabinet* (New York: Simon and Schuster, 1981), p. 89.

4. Memorandum to President Carter from Hamilton Jordan, 23 May 1977, Box 34, Hamilton Jordan Papers, Jimmy Carter Library, Memorandum for Peter Bourne from Hamilton Jordan, and attachment, 8 July 1977, Box 240, Eizenstat Papers.

5. Califano, *Governing America,* pp. 104–6.

6. Memorandum for the President from Stu Eizenstat, 14 June 1978, Box 242, Eizenstat Papers.

7. Memorandum for the President from W. Michael Blumenthal, n.d., attached to Mike to President, 13 September 1978, Box 145, Eizenstat Papers.

8. Memorandum for the President from Jerry Rafshoon, 18 July 1978, Box 28, Staff Offices, Gerald Rafshoon, Presidential Papers of Jimmy Carter, Jimmy Carter Library (hereafter cited as Rafshoon Papers).

9. See pp. 111–12.

10. *U.S. News and World Report,* 18 September 1978, pp. 20–21.

11. See pp. 117–21.

12. *Congressional Quarterly Alamanac* 34 (1978): 660–62.

13. Carter to Donald Riegle, 31 August 1978, Box 44, Jordan Papers.

14. M. Glenn Abernathy, "The Carter Administration and Domestic Civil Rights," in M. Glenn Abernathy, Dilys Hill, and Phil Williams, eds., *The Carter Years: The President and Policy Making* (New York: St. Martin's Press, 1984), pp. 106–22;

Steven F. Lawson, *In Pursuit of Power: Southern Blacks and Electoral Politics, 1965–1982* (New York: Columbia University Press, 1985), pp. 256–62.

15. Review of the Carter Administration, 29 September 1978, and Meeting with Congressional Black Caucus, 25 September 1978, Box 22, Staff Offices, Louis Martin, Presidential Papers of Jimmy Carter, Jimmy Carter Library (hereafter cited as Martin Papers).

16. Memorandum to President Carter from Hamilton Jordan, 6 October 1978, Box 42, Jordan Papers.

17. Jimmy Carter, *Keeping Faith: Memoirs of a President* (New York: Bantam Books, 1982), p. 32.

18. Memorandum for the President from Stu Eizenstat, Charles Schultze, and Alfred Kahn, 6 December 1978, Box 148, Eizenstat Papers.

19. *Time*, 20 November 1978, pp. 16–19.

20. Memoranda for Stu Eizenstat and Bert Carp from Bill Spring and Kitty Higgins, 9 and 20 November 1978, Box 152, Eizenstat Papers: Memorandum for the President from Jack Watson, 20 November 1978, Box 155, ibid.; Memorandum for Stu Eizenstat from Beth Abramowitz, 17 November 1978, Box 152, ibid.

CHAPTER 9
CRESCENT OF CRISIS

1. Cyrus Vance, *Hard Choices: Critical Years in America's Foreign Policy* (New York: Simon and Schuster, 1983), p. 216.

2. Jimmy Carter, *Keeping Faith: Memoirs of a President* (New York: Bantam Books, 1982), pp. 322–23.

3. Zbigniew Brzezinski, *Power and Principle: Memoirs of the National Security Adviser, 1977–1981* (New York: Farrar, Straus, Giroux, 1983), pp. 255–56.

4. William B. Quandt, *Camp David: Peacemaking and Politics* (Washington, D.C.: Brookings Institution, 1986), pp. 376–87.

5. Memorandum to President Carter from Hamilton Jordan, 30 November 1978, Box 49, Hamilton Jordan Papers, Jimmy Carter Library, Atlanta, Georgia.

6. *Time*, 12 March 1979, pp. 13–16; *Newsweek*, 12 March 1979), pp. 24–27.

7. Vance, *Hard Choices*, pp. 244–45.

8. Ibid.

9. Ibid., p. 314; Brzezinski, *Power and Principle*, p. 354; Carter, *Keeping Faith*, p. 435.

10. William Sullivan, *Mission to Iran* (New York: W. W. Norton, 1981), p. 168. See also Barry Rubin, *Paved with Good Intentions: The American Experience in Iran* (New York: Oxford University Press, 1980), p. 216.

11. Sullivan, *Mission to Iran*, pp. 182, 220, and 236.

12. Gary Sick, *All Fall Down: America's Tragic Encounter with Iran* (New York: Random House, 1985), pp. 3–4, 41–48, 62–66, 69, 81–88, 119, and 124.

13. "Talking Points on Iran," attached to Memorandum for David Aaron from Tom Thornton, 17 February 1979, Box CO-5, WHCF.

14. Memorandum for the President from Hamilton Jordan, 6 February 1979, Box 37, Jordan Papers.

15. *Time*, 15 January 1979, pp. 18–25; *Newsweek*, 8 January 1979, p. 14.

16. *Time*, 1 January 1979, pp. 39–40.

17. *Newsweek*, 26 February 1979, pp. 26–32.

18. Vance, *Hard Choices*, p. 112.

19. *Time*, 8 January 1979, p. 16.

20. Ibid., pp. 16–21.

21. *Time*, 5 February 1979, p. 34.

22. *Time*, 19 February 1979, pp. 12–14.

CHAPTER 10
A GROWING SENSE OF CRISIS

1. Joseph A. Califano, Jr., *Governing America: An Insider's Report from the White House and Cabinet* (New York: Simon and Schuster, 1981), p. 124; *Newsweek*, 18 December 1978, pp. 28–29.

2. *U.S. News and World Report*, 22 January 1979, pp. 16–18.

3. *Newsweek*, 18 December 1978, pp. 28–29.

4. Memorandum to the President from Alfred Kahn, 12 April 1979, Box BE-15, WHCF.

5. Memorandum for the President from Louis Martin, 12 March 1979, Box 80, Martin Papers.

6. *Newsweek*, 22 January 1979, pp. 24–25.

7. Memorandum for Hamilton Jordan and Jerry Rafshoon from Ed Sanders, 15 January 1979, Box 1, Staff Offices, Edward Sanders, Presidential Papers of Jimmy Carter, Jimmy Carter Library, Atlanta, Georgia (hereafter cited as Sanders Papers); *U.S. News and World Report*, 22 January 1979, p. 6.

8. *Time*, 16 April 1979, pp. 66–68.

9. *Atlantic Monthly*, May 1979, 33–48; Bert Lance with Bill Gilbert, *The Truth of the Matter: My Life In and Out of Politics* (New York: Summit Books, 1991), pp. 159–70.

10. Memorandum for President Carter from Patrick Caddell, 23 April 1979, Box 40, Jody Powell Papers, Jimmy Carter Library. See also James L. Sundquist, "The Crisis of Competence in Our National Government," *Political Science Quarterly* 95 (Summer 1980): 183–208.

11. Memorandum for the President from Stu Eizenstat and Joe Onek, 20 March 1979, Box 241, Stuart Eizenstat Papers, Jimmy Carter Library.

12. *Time*, 25 June 1979, pp. 20–21.

13. Jimmy to Jim Hanley, 23 May 1979, Box BE-3, WHCF.

14. James McGregor Burns, "Jimmy Carter's Strategy for 1980," *Atlantic Monthly*, May 1979, pp. 41–46.

15. Memorandum for the President from Stu Eizenstat, 4 May 1979, Box BE-3, WHCF.

16. "Economic Decision Making," 14 March 1979, attached to President Carter from Hamilton Jordan, 16 March 1979, Box 34, Hamilton Jordan Papers, Jimmy Carter Library.

17. See pp. 145–46.

18. *Time*, 26 November 1979, p. 60.

19. *Time*, 23 July 1979, p. 20.

20. "Camp David Domestic Summits," n.d., Box 162, Eizenstat Papers; "Notes/ Agenda Energy Meeting," ibid.; Memorandum for the President from Patrick Caddell, 12 July 1979, Box 40, Powell Papers; Memorandum to the President from Frank Moore, 8 July 1978, Box MC-16, Subject File, WHCF.

21. Memorandum to the President from Gerald Rafshoon, Copy to Hamilton Jordan, July 1979, and Powell to the President from Frank Moore, July 1979, Box 33, Jordan Papers; Califano, *Governing America*, pp. 429–31.

22. Jimmy Carter, *Keeping Faith: Memoirs of a President* (New York: Bantam Books, 1982), p. 121.

23. Memorandum for Members of the White House Staff from Hamilton Jordan, 18 July 1979, Box FG-48, Subject File; WHCF; Memorandum to President Carter from Hamilton Jordan, 26 July 1979, Box 37, Jordan Papers.

24. Jordan to the Speaker of the House, 2 August 1979, Box 43, Jordan Papers.

25. See pp. 436–37.

26. Memorandum for the President from Stu Eizenstat, 14 November 1979, Box BE-4, WHCF.

27. Memorandum for the President from Patrick H. Caddell, 6 November 1979, Box 33, Jordan Papers (Caddell's italics).

CHAPTER 11
FOREIGN POLICY, PATRIOTISM, AND POLITICS

1. Memorandum to the Democratic National Committee from Cambridge Survey Research, 24 May 1979, Box 33, Hamilton Jordan Papers, Jimmy Carter Library, Atlanta, Georgia; Memorandum on Current Public Attitudes on SALT from Patrick H. Caddell, [May 1979], Box 37, ibid.

2. Lloyd Bentsen et al. to the President, 14 June 1979, Box FO-46, WHCF.

3. Jimmy Carter, *Keeping Faith: Memoirs of a President* (New York: Bantam Books, 1982), pp. 111–13. On Schmidt, see also *Time*, 11 June 1979, pp. 26–35.

4. Memorandum for Hamilton Jordan from Edward Sanders, 8 February 1979, Box 1, Sanders Papers.

5. Carter, *Keeping Faith*, pp. 240–41.

6. Sam Nunn, John Tower, and Henry Jackson to the President, 2 August 1979, Boxes FO-40 and FO-42, WHCF.

7. *Newsweek*, 17 September 1979, pp. 28–30; *Congressional Quarterly Almanac* 35 (1979): 422–23.

8. On this point, see particularly Richard E. Neustadt and Ernest R. May, *Thinking in Time: The Uses of History for Decision-Makers* (New York: Free Press, 1983), pp. 92–96.

9. Memorandum to Dr. Brzezinski and Mr. Cutler from Hedley Donovan, 27 September 1979, Box 3, Staff Offices, Hedley Donovan, Presidential Papers of Jimmy Carter, Jimmy Carter Library.

10. Memorandum for Hamilton Jordan from Al McDonald, 8 November 1979, Box CO-32, WHCF.

11. On 18 July 1969, Mary Jo Kopechne drowned when the car Kennedy was driving went off the bridge at Chappaquiddick Island. He fled the scene under circumstances that even he admitted were "incomprehensible and completely inexcusable." Cited in Richard Harwood, ed., *The Pursuit of the Presidency 1980* (New York: Berkley Publishing Company, 1980), p. 68.

12. Hamilton Jordan, *Crisis: The Last Year of the Carter Presidency* (New York: Berkley Publishing Company, 1982), pp. 11–12.

13. Carter, *Keeping Faith*, pp. 471–72.

14. Memorandum for the President from Stu Eizenstat, 3 January 1980, Box 76, Staff Offices, Lloyd Cutler, Presidential Papers of Jimmy Carter, Jimmy Carter Library.

15. Carter, *Keeping Faith*, p. 476.

CHAPTER 12
ECONOMIC PAIN AND POLITICS

1. Memorandum for the President from Stu Eizenstat, 26 March 1980, Box BE-13, WHCF.

2. Ibid.

3. Memorandum for the President from Patrick H. Caddell, 11 February 1980, Box 10, Jody Powell Papers, Jimmy Carter Library, Atlanta, Georgia.

4. *New York Times*, 27 March 1980, p. 17.

5. *Time*, 14 April 1980, p. 28.

6. Jimmy Carter, *Keeping Faith: Memoirs of a President* (New York: Bantam Books, 1982), pp. 530–31.

7. Cited in Gaddis Smith, *Morality, Reason, and Power: American Diplomacy in the Carter Years* (New York: Hill and Wang, 1986), p. 201.

8. Paul B. Ryan, *The Iranian Rescue Mission: Why It Failed* (Annapolis, Md.: Naval Institute Press, 1986), pp. 45–50.

9. *Time*, 5 May 1980, pp. 26–31.

10. Memorandum for the President from Jody Powell, 1 May 1980, Box 40, Powell Papers; *Newsweek*, 12 May 1980, pp. 42–53.

11. Carter, *Keeping Faith*, p. 529.

12. *Time*, 16 June 1980, pp. 64–70.

13. Memorandum for the President from Stu Eizenstat, 24 May 1980, Box BE-13, WHCF.

CHAPTER 13
GLOOM AND DOOM

1. Jimmy Carter, *Keeping Faith: Memoirs of a President* (New York: Bantam Books, 1982), p. 532.

2. Ibid.

3. *Newsweek*, 2 June 1980, pp. 32–39.

4. Carter, *Keeping Faith*, pp. 535–36; Zbigniew Brzezinski, *Power and Principle:*

Memoirs of the National Security Adviser, 1977–1981 (New York: Farrar, Straus, Giroux, 1985), pp. 461–63.

5. *Time*, 4 August 1980, pp. 34–35.

6. Memorandum for the President from Stu Eizenstat and Al Moses, 30 September and 3 October 1980, Box 18, Staff Offices, Al Moses, Presidential Papers of Jimmy Carter, Jimmy Carter Library, Atlanta, Georgia.

7. Hamilton Jordan, *Crisis: The Last Year of the Carter Presidency* (New York: Berkley Publishing Company, 1982), p. 295.

8. *New Republic*, 30 August 1980, pp. 7–9.

9. *Time*, 25 August 1980, pp. 30–31.

10. Ibid.; Raymond Garthoff, *Détente and Confrontation: American-Soviet Relations from Nixon to Reagan* (Washington, D.C.: Brookings Institution, 1985), pp. 796–99.

11. Jack W. Germond and Jules Witcover, *Blue Smoke and Mirrors: How Reagan Won and Why Carter Lost the Election of 1980* (New York: Viking, 1981), pp. 190–93 and 207.

CHAPTER 14
DEFEAT

1. Hamilton Jordan, *Crisis: The Last Year of the Carter Presidency* (New York: Berkley Publishing Company, 1982), pp. 282–92.

2. Ibid., pp. 290–91.

3. Memorandum for the President from Stu Eizenstat, Box 12, Jody Powell Papers, Jimmy Carter Library, Atlanta, Georgia; Jack W. Germond and Jules Witcover, *Blue Smoke and Mirrors: How Reagan Won and Why Carter Lost the Election of 1980* (New York: Viking, 1981), pp. 209–21.

4. *U.S. News and World Report*, 1 September 1980, p. 21; *Time*, 1 September 1980, pp. 12–13.

5. Cambridge Survey Research, 23 September and 1 and 8 October 1980, Box 10, Powell Papers.

6. Jordan, *Crisis*, pp. 326–27.

7. Ibid., pp. 323–24 and 330–31.

8. Germond and Witcover, *Blue Smoke and Mirrors*, pp. 222–23.

9. See pp. 436–37.

10. Memorandum of Telephone Call between Brzezinski and Reagan, 24 September 1980, Box 13, Powell Papers; Jimmy Carter, *Keeping Faith: Memoirs of a President* (New York: Bantam Books, 1982), pp. 557–58 and 562; Warren Christopher et al., *American Hostages in Iran: The Conduct of a Crisis* (New Haven, Conn.: Yale University Press, 1985), pp. 289–90 and 297.

11. Jordan, *Crisis*, pp. 331–34.

12. Memorandum for the President from Zbigniew Brzezinski, 21 October 1980, Box 8, Powell Papers; Memorandum for Jody Powell, Pat Caddell, and Jerry Rafshoon from Al McDonald, 22 October 1980, ibid.; Memorandum for Al McDonald and Dave Rubenstein from Jody Powell, 22 October 1980, ibid.

13. Jordan, *Crisis*, pp. 342–43.

14. *Newsweek*, 17 November 1980, pp. 31–32; *U.S. News and World Report*, 17 November 1980, pp. 26–30.

15. Germond and Witcover, *Blue Smoke and Mirrors*, pp. 288–89; Jordan, *Crisis*, pp. 348–49.

16. Memorandum for Hamilton Jordan and Bob Strauss from Al McDonald, 28 October 1980, Box 10, Powell Papers.

17. Gaddis Smith, *Morality, Reason, and Power: American Diplomacy in the Carter Years* (New York: Hill and Wang, 1986), pp. 206–7; *Newsweek*, 17 November 1980, pp. 44–46.

18. Carter's marginal notation on Memorandum for the President from Frank Moore, 30 April 1978, Box 48, Hamilton Jordan Papers, Jimmy Carter Library.

19. *Congressional Quarterly Almanac* 36 (1980): 580.

20. Memorandum for the President from Gus Speth, Jane Yarn, and Bob Harris, 18 July 1980, Box FO-58, WHCF; Carter, *Keeping Faith*, pp. 582–83.

CHAPTER 15
EPILOGUE

1. Jimmy and Rosalynn Carter, *Everything to Gain: Making the Most of the Rest of Your Life* (New York: Random House, 1987), p. 9.

2. Tom Wicker, "Whatever Became of Jimmy Carter?" *Esquire*, July 1984, pp. 78–84.

3. Carter, *Everything to Gain*, p. 35.

4. *Christianity Today*, 21 March 1986, pp. 42–43.

5. Jimmy Carter, *The Blood of Abraham: Insights into the Middle East* (Boston: Houghton Mifflin, 1985); *Time*, 20 April 1987, pp. 38–39.

6. *Newsweek*, 2 April 1990, pp. 36–37; *New York Times*, 8 May 1990, p. B10.

7. *U.S. News and World Report*, 7 December 1987, pp. 19–20.

8. *New York Times*, 15 April 1990, p. A17; Gary Sick, *October Surprise: America's Hostages in Iran and the Election of Ronald Reagan* (New York: Random House, 1991).

9. *New York Times*, 4 May 1991, p. I3.

BIBLIOGRAPHICAL ESSAY

The place to begin any study of the Carter presidency is, of course, the vast holdings of the Jimmy Carter Library in Atlanta, Georgia, as it houses the 26 million documents shipped from the White House after Carter left office in 1981. The bulk of Carter's presidential papers held there are in the White House Central File (WHCF), but another important part is the 150,000-page Handwriting File. Carter made handwritten comments on just about every document he read, so this file provides a window to his thinking on major (and not so major) policy issues. Included in the presidential papers are records of members of the White House staff, most notably Lloyd Cutler, Hedley Donovan, Robert J. Lipshutz, Margaret McKenna, Louis Martin, Al Moses, and Edward Sanders.

There are separate collections for the papers of Carter's principal aides, Stuart Eizenstat, Hamilton Jordan, Jody Powell, and Gerald Rafshoon. The Eizenstat Papers are a treasure trove on just about every domestic issue confronting the administration, and the Jordan and Powell papers are rich with respect to political matters and underscore the close relationship of these men with the president; no other members of Carter's staff spoke to him with the same temerity and frankness. The Rafshoon Papers reveal the importance the White House attached to the presidential image. For matters having to do with foreign economic policy, one should consult the papers of Anthony Solomon, a highly respected authority on international monetary matters and an assistant secretary of the Treasury during the Carter presidency. Also at the Carter Library are a series of exit interviews with administration officials; most useful for this book were the interviews with Jody Powell, Stuart Eizenstat, and Robert Lipshutz. If one is studying the 1976 campaign, there are several important collections at the Gerald Ford Library in Ann Arbor, Michigan, including the Special Files, Presidential Papers of Gerald Ford; the Michael Raoul Duval Papers; and the Robert Teeter Papers.

A number of former officials in the Carter administration have written books and memoirs. Two review essays that discuss some of these works are Edward R.

Kantowicz, "Reminiscences of a Fated Presidency: Themes from the Carter Memoirs," *Presidential Studies Quarterly* 16 (Fall 1986): 655–65, and Walter LaFeber, "From Confusion to Cold War: The Memoirs of the Carter Administration," *Diplomatic History* 8 (Winter 1984): 1–12. Also important as a general introduction to the literature on the Carter presidency is Gary W. Reichard, "Early Returns: Assessing Jimmy Carter," *Presidential Studies Quarterly* 19 (Summer 1990): 603–20.

President Carter's own memoirs, *Keeping Faith: Memoirs of a President* (New York: Bantam Books, 1982), is highly selective in content, but the book does provide an especially full account of the Camp David summit of 1978 as well as the events leading to Carter's recognition of the People's Republic of China and his efforts on behalf of a national energy program. This book also contains important excerpts from Carter's diary, a document that is not yet open to the researcher.

Zbigniew Brzezinski's *Power and Principle: Memoirs of the National Security Adviser, 1977–1981*, (New York: Farrar, Straus, Giroux, 1983) is frank and extremely rich concerning foreign policy. Also valuable is Cyrus Vance's *Hard Choices: Critical Years in America's Foreign Policy* (New York: Simon and Schuster, 1983). Together the Brzezinski and Vance volumes cover the full range of Carter's foreign policy and illuminate the friction that developed between the White House and Department of State. Other memoirs by former members of the Carter administration include Joseph A. Califano, Jr., *Governing America: An Insider's Report from the White House and the Cabinet* (New York: Simon and Schuster, 1981), which provides much detail on such policy matters as welfare, social security, tax reform, national health insurance, and Califano's firing as HEW secretary in 1979; Hedley Donovan, *Roosevelt to Reagan: A Reporter's Encounter with Nine Presidents* (New York: Harper and Row, 1985), containing this senior adviser's brief comments on Carter's concern with energy legislation, black-Jewish tensions, and the firing of Andrew Young; Hamilton Jordan, *Crisis: The Last Year of the Carter Presidency* (New York: Berkley Publishing Company, 1982), almost a day-by-day diary of Jordan's involvement in 1980 in the negotiations for the release of the Iranian hostages and the Carter presidential campaign; Bert Lance with Bill Gilbert, *The Truth of the Matter: My Life In and Out of Politics* (New York: Summit Books, 1991), a spirited defense of Lance's banking practices, which makes clear Lance's continued admiration for Carter; Jody Powell, *The Other Side of the Story* (New York: William Morrow, 1984), an attack on the press's treatment of the Carter administration; Griffin B. Bell with Ronald J. Ostrow, *Taking Care of the Law* (New York: William Morrow, 1982), useful only for Bell's involvement in the Bakke case and as an indication of the tension that arose between Bell and the White House; Robert Pastor, *Condemned to Repetition: The United States and Nicaragua* (Princeton, N.J.: Princeton University Press, 1987), a defense of the administration's response to the Nicaraguan revolution by a former member of the NSC who was one of the architects of that policy; William B. Quandt, *Camp David: Peacemaking and Politics* (Washington, D.C.: Brookings Institution, 1986), an excellent history of the Camp David accords by another member of the NSC during the Carter administration who was responsible for handling the Arab-Israeli dispute; Gary Sick, *All Fall Down: America's Tragic Encounter with Iran* (New York: Random House, 1985), an account by yet a third NSC member that describes the American response to the Iranian Revolution and is highly critical of Ambassador William Sullivan's role in the fall of the shah; William Sullivan, *Mission to Iran* (New York: W. W. Norton,

1981), Sullivan's own defense of his actions; Stansfield Turner, *Secrecy and Democracy: The CIA in Transition* (Boston: Houghton Mifflin, 1985), an account of Turner's efforts as director of the CIA to balance the need for secrecy in intelligence gathering with the public's right to know; Jerry J. Jasinowski, "The First Two Years of the Carter Administration: An Appraisal," *Presidential Studies Quarterly* 9 (Winter 1979): 11–15, a defense of Carter's foreign policy by a former assistant secretary of commerce under Carter; and Harrison Wellford, "Staffing the Presidency: An Insider's Comments," *Political Science Quarterly* 93 (Spring 1978): 10–12, a brief discussion by a lower-level member of the White House staff of Carter's intention as president to have the executive office reflect his views on major policy matters.

In addition to these works by former members of the Carter administration, the reader should also consult Thomas P. O'Neill with William Novak, *Man of the House: The Life and Political Memoirs of Speaker Tip O'Neill* (New York: Random House, 1987), a description by the former Speaker of the House of the strained relations that existed between Congress and the White House during the Carter administration; Kenneth W. Thompson, ed., *The Carter Presidency: Fourteen Intimate Perspectives of Jimmy Carter* (Lanham, Md.: University Press of America, 1990), a series of oral interviews with President Carter, Rosalynn Carter, Vice-President Walter Mondale, and members of Carter's cabinet and White House staff; and Moshe Dayan, *Breakthrough: A Personal Account of the Egypt-Israel Peace Negotiations* (New York: Alfred A. Knopf, 1981).

Although not technically employed as a member of the administration, Rosalynn Carter served as one of her husband's closest advisers and was more involved in affairs of state than any presidential wife since Eleanor Roosevelt. Her memoirs, *First Lady from Plains* (Boston: Houghton Mifflin, 1984), therefore, give an insider's perspective on administration policy as well as personal information about the presidential family. Two Democratic elder statesmen who, at various times, were consulted by the president are Clark Clifford and George W. Ball. Clifford was also Bert Lance's lawyer during the so-called Lance Affair. For their memoirs, both critical of the president, see Clifford with Richard Holbrooke, *Counsel to the President: A Memoir* (New York: Random House, 1991), and Ball, *The Past Has Another Pattern: Memoirs* (New York: W. W. Norton, 1984). *Public Papers of the Presidents of the United States: Jimmy Carter*, 9 vols. (Washington, D.C.: Government Printing Office, 1977–1982), contain all of Carter's public speeches and papers as president.

For autobiographical material by the former president, see *Keeping Faith; Why Not the Best?* (Nashville, Tenn.: Broadman Press, 1975), Carter's campaign biography; *An Outdoor Journal: Adventures and Reflections* (New York: Bantam Books, 1988), musings on his love for the outdoors; and, with Rosalynn Carter, *Everything to Gain: Making the Most of the Rest of Your Life* (New York: Random House, 1987), in which the Carters discuss their adjustment to private life after Jimmy Carter's defeat in 1980 and also offer advice on preventive health care. On the former president's continued interest in the Middle East, consult his *Blood of Abraham: Insights into the Middle East* (Boston: Houghton Mifflin, 1985), a country-by-country historical synopsis and analysis of Middle East problems. For Carter's collection of his statements and speeches before becoming president, see *A Government As Good As Its People* (New York: Pocket Books, 1977). For a humorous but often biting account of the Carter family by the former president's cousin, see Hugh Carter, *Cousin Beedie and*

Cousin Hot: My Life with the Carter Family of Plains, Georgia (Englewood Cliffs, N.J.: Prentice-Hall, 1978).

There is no first-rate biography of Carter. The best to date is Betty Glad, *Jimmy Carter: In Search of the Great White House* (New York: W. W. Norton, 1980), long, detailed, and comprehensive but concluding with Carter's successful quest for the White House. A psycho-biography that has all the faults of that genre is Bruce Mazlish and Edwin Diamond, *Jimmy Carter: A Character Portrait* (New York: Simon and Schuster, 1979). Mazlish and Diamond stress three themes of Carter's development: 1) belonging and being apart; 2) the need to measure up and win; and 3) the power of thinking and acting positively. Even less satisfactory is Peter Meyer, *James Earl Carter: The Man and the Myth* (Kansas City, Mo.: Sheed Andrews and McMeel, 1978), written while Carter was still in office by a person who had voted for the president and then became disillusioned with his performance after he took office. An incisive character analysis of Carter, also written while he was in office, is William Lee Miller, *Yankee from Georgia: The Emergence of Jimmy Carter* (New York: Quadrangle/New York Times Books, 1978). Miller argues that Carter was a southerner with the mind of a Yankee Puritan—logical, methodical, and punctual rather than creative and innovative.

Four books dealing with Carter's deeply held religious views are David Kucharsky, *The Man from Plains: The Mind and Spirit of Jimmy Carter* (New York: Harper and Row, 1976); Niels C. Nielsen, *The Religion of President Carter* (Nashville, Tenn.: Thomas Nelson, 1977); Wesley G. Pippert, *The Spiritual Journal of Jimmy Carter: In His Own Words* (New York: Macmillan, 1978); and Howard Norton and Bob Slosser, *The Miracle of Jimmy Carter* (Plainfield, N.J.: Logos International, 1976). Kucharsky emphasizes Carter's quest for a revival of old values. Nielsen maintains that Carter's faith was a mixture of southern evangelicalism, eighteenth-century religious pluralism, and more recent and sophisticated Christian political realism. Pippert argues that the central theme of both Carter's faith and political philosophy is his belief that individuals and nations are fallible and sinful and require forgiveness. Also useful on Carter's civil religion is Richard V. Pierard and Robert D. Linder, *Civil Religion and the Presidency* (Grand Rapids, Mich.: Academie Books, 1988). Pierard and Linder attribute Carter's drive for excellence to his Christian mindset and his experience working for Adm. Hyman Rickover.

A number of books also have chapters that furnish important insights into Carter's character and beliefs. Among these are William R. Leuchtenburg, *In the Shadow of FDR: From Harry Truman to Ronald Reagan* (Ithaca, N.Y.: Cornell University Press, 1983); Alonzo Hamby, *Liberalism and Its Challengers: FDR to Reagan* (New York: Oxford University Press, 1985); Barbara Kellerman, *The Political Presidency: Practice of Leadership from Kennedy through Reagan* (New York: Oxford University Press, 1984); and Richard E. Neustadt, *Presidential Power: The Politics of Leadership from FDR to Carter* (New York: John Wiley and Sons, 1980). Leuchtenburg argues that part of Carter's problem as president was his effort to distance himself from the New Deal tradition of Franklin Roosevelt, while Hamby maintains that New Deal liberalism was exhausted by the time Carter took office. On the basis of her analysis of Carter's energy program, Kellerman concludes that the president was a failed politician because he refused to play politics. Finally, Neustadt attributes many of Carter's problems as president to his operational style.

For Carter's political career before running for the presidency, the reader should consult the works by Glad, *Jimmy Carter*, and Norton and Slosser, *Miracle of Carter*. Also useful is James Wooten, *Dasher: The Roots and the Rising of Jimmy Carter* (New York: Summit Books, 1978). An important work on Carter's term as governor of Georgia is Gary Fink, *Prelude to the Presidency: The Political Character and Legislative Leadership Style of Governor Jimmy Carter* (Westport, Conn.: Greenwood Press, 1980), which contends that much of Carter's later difficulties with Congress were foreshadowed by his struggle as governor with the Georgia legislature over reorganization of state government.

There are several books on the 1976 presidential campaign. The most thorough is Jules Witcover, *Marathon: The Pursuit of the Presidency, 1972–1976* (New York: Viking Press, 1977). Hamilton Jordan's plan for winning the Democratic nomination can be found in Kandy Stroud, *How Jimmy Won: The Victory Campaign from Plains to the White House* (New York: William Morrow, 1977). Elizabeth Drew—*American Journal: The Events of 1976* (New York: Random House, 1977)—is one of the nation's most astute political observers. Drew is critical of candidate Carter, whom she describes as a pragmatic liberal, for being too thin-skinned and not offering voters any vision of the future. In *Running for President, 1976: The Carter Campaign* (New York: Stein and Day, 1977), Martin Schram makes the point that Carter failed to reestablish the FDR Democratic coalition. In *Dasher*, Wooten remarks that Carter was purposefully enigmatic during the campaign and did whatever was necessary to win the election. A good analysis of the Catholic vote in the election can be found in George Gallup, Jr., and Jim Castelli, *The American Catholic People: Their Beliefs, Practices, and Values* (Garden City, N.J.: Doubleday, 1987). A discussion of how Carter was able to stop, momentarily at least, the flight of white voters from the Democratic party is in William J. Keefe, *Parties, Politics, and Public Policy in America* (Washington, D.C.: CQ Press, 1988). For campaign speeches by Carter and Ford, consult *The Presidential Campaign 1976*, 3 vols. (Washington, D.C.: Government Printing Office, 1978).

On the 1980 election, see Jack W. Germond and Jules Witcover, *Blue Smoke and Mirrors: How Reagan Won and Why Carter Lost the Election of 1980* (New York: Viking, 1981), a journalistic interpretation by two political commentators. Also useful is Richard Harwood, ed., *The Pursuit of the Presidency 1980* (New York: Berkley Publishing Company, 1980), which is an account of the campaign by reporters from the *Washington Post*. A group of essays on the election generally critical of the rightward swing of the electorate is Thomas Ferguson and Joel Rogers, *The Hidden Election: Politics and Economics in the 1980 Presidential Campaign* (New York: Pantheon Books, 1981). Ferguson and Rogers develop this theme further in *Right Turn: The Decline of the Democrats and the Future of American Politics* (New York: Hill and Wang, 1986). For an analysis of voting patterns in both the 1976 and 1980 elections, see also Euel W. Elliott, *Issues and Elections: Presidential Voting in Contemporary America—A Revisionist View* (Boulder, Colo.: Westview Press, 1989). Always insightful are the comments of the dean of presidential campaign historians, Theodore White. See his *America in Search of Itself: The Making of the President, 1956–1980* (New York: Harper and Row, 1982). Useful for anecdotal information is Paul F. Boller, Jr., *Presidential Campaigns* (New York: Oxford University Press, 1984).

Although there are no comprehensive histories of the Carter administration, there are a number of general studies. Two of the most important are Erwin C.

Hargrove, *Jimmy Carter As President: Leadership and the Politics of the Public Good* (Baton Rouge: Louisiana State University Press, 1988), and Charles O. Jones, *The Trusteeship Presidency: Jimmy Carter and the United States Congress* (Baton Rouge: Louisiana State University Press, 1988). Both these books are based on extensive interviews with Carter administration officials under the auspices of the White Burkett Miller Center of Public Affairs at the University of Virginia. A useful collection of essays, several of which will be noted individually in the course of this essay, is M. Glenn Abernathy, Dilys Hill, and Phil Williams, eds., *The Carter Years: The President and Policy Making* (New York: St. Martin's Press, 1984). Three harsh indictments of the Carter presidency are Haynes Johnson, *In the Absence of Power: Governing America* (New York: Viking Press, 1980); Clark Mollenhoff, *The President Who Failed: Carter Out of Control* (New York: Macmillan, 1980); and Laurence H. Shoup, *The Carter Presidency and Beyond: Power and Politics in the 1980s* (Palo Alto, Calif.: Ramparts Press, 1980). Johnson criticizes Carter for his weak leadership, although he also comments that the president did not receive credit for the things he did right. Mollenhoff accuses Carter of hypocrisy and of being too willing to compromise on policy matters—something most other writers have criticized him for *not* doing. Shoup maintains that a small group of the corporate upper class shaped the 1976 presidential campaign and dominated the administration. Both the Mollenhoff and Shoup volumes are unconvincing. For an enjoyable general history of the 1970s, see Peter N. Carroll, *It Seemed Like Nothing Happened: The Tragedy and Promise of the 1970s* (New York: Holt, Rinehart, and Winston, 1982).

Several books and articles deal with Carter's efforts to assemble his administration and with his first few months in office. The most comprehensive treatment is Bruce Adams and Kathryn Kavanagh-Brown, *Promises and Performance: Carter Builds a New Administration* (Lexington, Mass.: D. C. Heath, 1979). For a good discussion of the struggle between Hamilton Jordan and Jack Watson over staffing the White House, see Carl M. Brauer, *Presidential Transitions: Eisenhower through Reagan* (New York: Oxford University Press, 1986). Also useful are James L. Sundquist, "Jimmy Carter As Public Administrator: An Appraisal at Mid-Term," *Public Administration Review* 39 (January–February 1979): 3–8; Richard E. Neustadt, "Staffing the Presidency: Premature Notes on the New Administration," *Political Science Quarterly* 93 (Spring 1978): 1–9 and 12–14; Richard E. Neustadt and Ernest R. May, *Thinking in Time: The Uses of History for Decision-Makers* (New York: Free Press, 1983); Nelson W. Polsby, "Presidential Cabinet Making: Lessons for the Political System," *Political Science Quarterly* 93 (Spring 1978): 15–25; Leslie Gelb, "Reflections on the Carter Transition," in Kenneth W. Thompson, ed., *History and Current Issues* (Lanham, Md.: University Press of America, 1986), pp. 69–86; and Robert Shogan, *Promises to Keep: Carter's First Hundred Days* (New York: Crowell, 1977). Sundquist maintains that at the beginning of his administration, Carter did not recognize the need for overall management of his administration. Neustadt criticizes Carter for not appointing a chief of staff early in his administration and for making peremptory decisions. Neustadt and May also believe that Carter could have been more effective in gaining public and congressional support for his policies if he had emphasized a few familiar themes after taking office. Polsby contrasts Richard Nixon's effort to control the entire executive apparatus through "political commissars" with Carter's effort to have in his cabinet "subject-matter" experts. Gelb thinks that Carter should have appointed Paul Nitze rather than Harold Brown as secretary of defense. Shogan maintains that Carter got off to a vigorous but erratic start during his first hundred days in office.

There are numerous books and articles on various aspects of Carter's domestic policies. In addition to Jones, *The Trusteeship Presidency,* and Hargrove, *Jimmy Carter As President,* see Dilys Hill, "Domestic Policy," and Stephen Woolcock, "The Economic Policies of the Carter Administration," in Abernathy, Hill, and Williams, eds., *The Carter Years,* pp. 13–34 and 35–53 respectively. Hill argues that Carter's program was overly ambitious and took too much time to legislate. Woolcock considers Carter's economic program as a compromise between his conservative preferences and the views of more liberal Democrats in Congress.

On the constraints on Carter's influence over domestic policy, see Paul Charles Light, *The President's Agenda: Domestic Policy Choice from Kennedy to Carter (with Notes on Ronald Reagan)* (Baltimore: Johns Hopkins University Press, 1982); Ernest S. Griffith, *The American Presidency: The Dilemmas of Shared Power and Divided Government* (New York: New York University Press, 1976); and Michael Nelson, ed., *The Presidency and the Political System,* 2d ed. (Washington, D.C.: CQ Press, 1988).

On the management of the Carter administration, consult Larry Berman, *The Office of Management and Budget and the Presidency, 1921–1979* (Princeton, N.J.: Princeton University Press, 1979); Colin Campbell, *Managing the Presidency: Carter, Reagan, and the Search for Executive Order* (Pittsburgh, Pa.: University of Pittsburgh Press, 1986); A. Whitfield Ayres, "The Carter White House Staff," and Donald A. Marchand, "Carter and the Bureaucracy," both in Abernathy, Dilys, and Williams, eds., *The Carter Years,* pp. 144–64 and 192–207 respectively; and Richard Polenberg, "Roosevelt, Carter, and Executive Reorganization: Lessons of the 1930s," *Presidential Studies Quarterly* 9 (Winter 1979): 35–46. According to Berman, one of the obstacles Carter confronted was the fact that the executive office of the president had not historically managed or executed policy directly. Campbell maintains that Carter's much-vaunted cabinet consultation amounted to little more than a ritual. Ayres argues that Carter's staff was inexperienced and ill suited for its tasks. Marchand states that of all the recent presidents, Carter took the keenest interest in presidential management but that the results of his initiatives were limited. Polenberg observes that efforts at executive reorganization, such as Carter's attempts, have historically been a minefield for the incumbent because of the resistance they encounter.

Carter's rocky relations with Congress have been the subject of considerable scholarship. Mark A. Peterson, *Legislating Together: The White House and Capitol Hill from Eisenhower to Reagan* (Cambridge, Mass.: Harvard University Press, 1990), claims that most chief executives have been able to work with Congress. Peterson believes that presidents should be agenda-focused; Carter was not, and this was the root of his problems. Nelson W. Polsby, *Consequences of Party Reform* (New York: Oxford University Press, 1983), regards Carter's troubled relations with Congress as one by-product of party reform. In "The Campaign Promises of Jimmy Carter: Accomplishments and Failures," *Presidential Studies Quarterly* 15 (Winter 1985): 136–44, Michael J. Krukones concludes that while Carter fulfilled about 60 percent of his campaign promies, he neglected many of his major ones, such as tax reform and price supports for farmers. Similarly, William F. Mullen, in "Perceptions of Carter's Legislative Successes and Failures: Views from the Hill and the Liaison Staff," *Pres-*

idential Studies Quarterly 12 (Fall 1982): 522–44, states that Carter's failures on Capitol Hill were his own doing, since Congress was willing to work with him. For a somewhat different view, see Charles O. Jones, "Carter and Congress: From the Outside In," *British Journal of Political Science* 15 (July 1985): 271–98, and "The Separated Presidency—Making It Work in Contemporary Politics," in Anthony King, ed., *The New American Political System: Second Version* (Washington, D.C.: AEI Press, 1990), pp. 1–28. In these articles, Jones emphasizes the difficulties every modern president encounters in working with Congress.

One reason given for this legislative stonewall is the power of special interest groups and political action committees (PACs) on Capitol Hill. Although the huge and growing literature on special interest groups and PACs is beyond the scope of this review, the reader should consult the essays in Allan J. Cigler and Burdett A. Loomis, eds., *Interest Group Politics* (Washington, D.C.: CQ Press, 1983), which collectively present a balanced view of both the benefits and the dangers inherent in interest group politics. Also useful are Robert H. Salisbury, "The Paradox of Interest Groups in Washington—More Groups Less Clout," in King, ed., *New American Political System*, pp. 203–29, and Benjamin Ginsberg and Martin Shefter, "The Presidency and the Organization of Interests," in Nelson, ed., *The Presidency and the Political System*, pp. 311–49. For an excellent study of one interest group active on Capitol Hill during the Carter administration, see Edward Tivnan, *The Lobby: Jewish Political Power and American Foreign Policy* (New York: Simon and Schuster, 1987).

An early but still excellent study of Carter's endeavors on behalf of welfare reform is Laurence E. Lynn, Jr., and D. F. Whitman, *The President as Policymaker: Jimmy Carter and Welfare Reform* (Philadelphia: Temple University Press, 1982). On Carter's battle with Congress over the water projects, consult Paul Scheele, "President Carter and the Water Projects: A Case Study in Presidential and Congressional Decision-Making," *Presidential Studies Quarterly* 8 (Fall 1978): 348–64, in which Scheele argues that the eventual compromise was a limited victory for Carter that showed he could be educated politically. On Carter's urban policy, see Harold L. Wolman and Astrid E. Merget, "The Presidency and Policy Formulation: President Carter and the Urban Policy," *Presidential Studies Quarterly* 10 (Summer 1980): 402–15. On Carter and civil rights, see M. Glenn Abernathy, "The Carter Administration and Domestic Civil Rights," in Abernathy, Hill, and Williams, eds., *The Carter Years* pp. 106–22, and Steven F. Lawson, *In Pursuit of Power: Southern Blacks and Electoral Politics, 1965–1982* (New York: Columbia University Press, 1985). On Carter's energy program, consult Kellerman, *The Political Presidency*, and J. William Holland, "The Great Gamble: Jimmy Carter and the 1979 Energy Crisis," *Prologue* 22 (Spring 1990): 63–69. Holland discusses the crisis of confidence surrounding Carter's decision to postpone his 1979 speech on energy. Another study of the 1979 malaise and Camp David domestic summit is Robert Strong, "Recapturing Leadership: The Carter Administration and the Crisis of Confidence," *Presidential Studies Quarterly* 16 (Fall 1986): 636–50.

During his four years as president, Carter faced an increasingly critical press. One study of the news media's treatment of the Carter administration argues that the press evaluated Carter on the basis of what it thought a successful president should do rather than on what Carter sought to achieve—see Mark J. Rozell, *The Press and the Carter Presidency* (Boulder, Colo.: Westview Press, 1989). A somewhat different approach is taken by John William Tebbel and Sarah Miles Watts in *The Press and the Presidency: From George Washington to Ronald Reagan* (New York: Oxford University Press, 1985). Tebbell and Watts argue that Carter and his press secretary Jody Powell overestimated the power of the press.

The Carter administration's foreign policy has also received substantial scholarly attention. The place to begin is Gaddis Smith, *Morality, Reason, and Power: American Diplomacy in the Carter Years* (New York: Hill and Wang, 1986). The book's title indicates what Smith believes were the three themes of Carter's foreign policy. Smith's volume should be supplemented with David S. McLellan's *Cyrus Vance* (New York: Cooper Square, 1985) and Raymond Garthoff's monumental *Détente and Confrontation: American-Soviet Relations from Nixon to Reagan* (Washington, D.C.: Brookings Institution, 1985), which is arguably the single best book on the Cold War. About a third of the book's eleven hundred pages are on Soviet-American relations during Carter's term. For a brief account of Carter's foreign policy, which describes it as amateurish, see Vincent Davis, "Carter Tries on the World for Size," in Vincent Davis, ed., *The Post Imperial Presidency* (New York: Praeger, 1980). Also critical of Carter's conduct of diplomacy, which he calls erratic, is Raymond Moore, "The Carter Presidency and Foreign Policy," in Abernathy, Hill, and Williams, eds., *The Carter Presidency,* pp. 54–83. In a test of decision making known as multiple advocacy, Alexander Moens concludes in *Foreign Policy under Carter: Testing Multiple Advocacy Decision Making* (Boulder, Colo.: Westview Press, 1990) that Carter's advisers on foreign policy failed to give the president enough policy options.

Probably no aspect of Carter's foreign policy has elicited more appraisal than the president's commitment to human rights. The literature on human rights and foreign policy is daunting, but the most complete study of Carter's human rights policy, although highly critical, is Joshua Muravchik, *The Uncertain Crusade: Jimmy Carter and the Dilemmas of Human Rights* (New York: Hamilton Press, 1986). This should be supplemented with Sandy Vogelgesang, *American Dream, Global Nightmare: The Dilemma of U.S. Human Rights Policy* (New York: W. W. Norton, 1980). For Carter's human rights policy as applied to Latin America, see Lars Schoultz, *Human Rights and U.S. Policy towards Latin America* (Princeton, N.J.: Princeton University Press, 1981). Schoultz focuses on the bureaucracy that has thwarted human rights policy. For more general treatments of the human rights issue, see also A. H. Robertson and J. G. Merrils, *Human Rights in the World: An Introduction to the Study of the International Protection of Human Rights,* 3d ed. (New York: St. Martin's Press, 1989); Kenneth W. Thompson, *Morality and Foreign Policy* (Baton Rouge: Louisiana State University Press, 1980); Kenneth W. Thompson, ed., *Moral Dimensions of American Foreign Policy* (New Brunswick, N.J.: Transaction Books, 1984); and Peter G. Brown and Douglas MacLean, eds., *Human Rights and U.S. Foreign Policy* (Lexington, Mass.: D. C. Heath, 1979).

The writings on the Mideast and the Arab-Israeli dispute are also so large as to be beyond the scope of this essay. But three good overviews of U.S. Middle East policy are Seth P. Tillman, *The United States in the Middle East: Interests and Obstacles* (Bloomington: Indiana University Press, 1982); T. G. Fraser, *The USA and the Middle East since World War II* (New York: St. Martin's Press, 1989); and Steven L. Spiegel, *The Other Arab-Israeli Conflict: Making America's Middle East Policy, from Truman to Reagan* (Chicago: University of Chicago Press, 1985). Spiegel has a chapter on Carter, whose Mideast policy he concludes was based on a creative global philosophy that was overtaken by world events.

A widely cited account of the United States' response to the Iranian Revolution, which, however, contains a number of inaccuracies, is Michael Ledeen and William Lewis, *Debacle: American Failure in Iran* (New York: Knopf, 1981). More reliable are Barry Rubin, *Paved with Good Intentions: The American Experience in Iran* (New York: Oxford University Press, 1980), and especially James A. Bill, *The Eagle and the Lion: The Tragedy of American-Iranian Relations* (New Haven, Conn.: Yale University Press, 1988). On Carter's decision to let the shah into the United States for medical treatment, see Edward B. McMahon et al., *Medical Cover-Ups in the White House* (Washington, D.C.: Farragut Publishing Company, 1987). On the Huyser mission to Iran, consult Robert E. Huyser, *Mission to Iran* (New York: Harper and Row, 1986). On the failed hostage rescue, see Paul B. Ryan, *The Iranian Rescue Mission and Why It Failed* (Annapolis, Md.: Naval Institute Press, 1986), and Charlie Beckwith and Donald Knox, *Delta Force* (New York: Harcourt Brace and Jovanovich, 1983). The excruciating diplomacy leading to the final release of the hostages is covered in Warren Christopher et al., *American Hostages in Iran: The Conduct of a Crisis* (New Haven, Conn.: Yale University Press, 1985).

On the Panama Canal treaties, see Walter LaFeber, *The Panama Canal: The Crisis in Historical Perspective* (New York: Oxford University Press, 1978); J. Michael Hogan, *The Panama Canal in American Politics* (Carbondale: Southern Illinois University Press, 1986); and Robert Strong, "Jimmy Carter and the Panama Canal Treaties," *Presidential Studies Quarterly* 21 (Spring 1991): 269–84. On Carter's policy with respect to Central America, again see Walter LaFeber, *Inevitable Revolutions: The United States in Central America* (New York: W. W. Norton, 1984). On the Soviet brigade issue, see David Newsom, *The Soviet Brigade in Cuba: A Study of Political Diplomacy* (Bloomington: Indiana University Press, 1987). Two books that deal with Carter's African policy are Gerald J. Bender et al., eds., *African Crisis Areas and U.S. Foreign Policy* (Berkeley and Los Angeles: University of California Press, 1985), and Thomas J. Noer, *Cold War and Black Liberation* (Columbia: University of Missouri Press, 1985).

There is relatively little scholarship on Carter's defense policy. One early study is S. Sarkesian, ed., *Defense Policy and the Presidency: Carter's First Years* (Boulder, Colo.: Westview Press, 1979). For a general overview, see also Phil Williams, "Carter's Defense Policy," in Abernathy, Hill, and Williams, eds., *The Carter Years*, pp. 84–105. Hill argues that during his first two years in office, Carter and the liberal Democrats basically agreed on defense policy, producing a conservative backlash that damaged him for the remainder of his administration. A brilliant study of the politics and diplomacy of the SALT II treaty is Strobe Talbott, *Endgame: The Inside Story of SALT II* (New York: Harper and Row, 1979). For a discussion of organizational change in the NSC and Defense Department, see R. Gordon Hoxie, *Command Decision and the Presidency: A Study of National Security Policy and Organization* (New York: Readers Digest Press, 1977). On PD-59, see Jeffrey Richelson, "PD-59, NSDD-1, and the Reagan Strategic Modernization Program," *Journal of Strategic Studies* 6 (June 1983): 125–26. An excellent study of the B-1 bomber controversy by a Pulitzer-prize-winning journalist is Nick Kotz, *Wild Blue Yonder: Money, Politics, and the B-1 Bomber* (New York: Pantheon Books, 1988).

INDEX

and Habitat for Humanity, 2, 212
and health insurance, 102–5, 135, 140, 149, 182
and hospital cost containment, 100–101, 103, 135, 142–43
and housing, 110
and human rights, 38–41, 49, 95
and Iran, 86, 125–29, 153, 158–61, 162, 165, 173–75, 179, 181, 190, 191, 193, 203–4, 205–6, 208, 211, 213–14
and Japan, 47, 96, 187
and labor, 19, 20, 29–30, 53, 55, 73, 80, 81–82, 101, 102–5, 110–11, 115, 134, 206
and legislative priorities, 28, 52
and Memphis midterm conference, 133–35
and Mexico, 131–32
and Middle East, 44–47, 83–89, 117–28, 137, 151, 163, 171, 181, 187–89, 210, 213
and NATO, 93–95, 191–92
and neutron bomb, 95–96
and Nicaragua, 130, 152, 157–58, 213
oil and energy policy of, 32–34, 55, 57–58, 66–68, 81, 107–9, 137–39, 140, 141, 142, 143–45, 147–48, 151–53, 169–70, 176–77, 181, 187
and Panama Canal treaties, 42–43, 83, 89–90, 153
and People's Republic of China, 93–94, 129–30, 131, 151, 164–65
and Persian Gulf War, 213
and post-presidential career, 211–14
on the presidency, 2, 212
and the press, 2, 5
and preventive health care, 212
public perceptions of, 1–2, 22, 23, 28, 31, 50, 51, 65, 71, 73, 76, 77, 78, 81–82, 83, 90, 105, 106–7, 109–10, 133, 139, 140, 141, 143, 145, 147–49, 151–52, 160–61, 168, 170, 171, 172, 175, 190–91, 193, 213
religious faith of, 8, 16
and sale of jet fighters to Saudi Arabia, 88–90
and social security reform, 72, 73, 81
and Soviet Union, 38–42, 49, 83–84, 92–94, 128–29, 130–31, 152, 153–54, 156, 155–57, 162–66, 179, 187, 191–93, 210
and staffing of administration, 25–28, 34, 71–72, 107, 141
as state senator, 8
and Taiwan, 129
and tax policy, 52, 55, 58–59, 72–73, 76, 81, 100, 101–2, 103, 106, 109, 177–78, 184
as trustee president, 1, 2, 3, 28, 34–35
and urban issues, 29, 32, 74–76, 77, 81, 110, 149

and welfare reform, 12, 52–55, 102, 149
and withdrawal of U.S. troops from South Korea, 48
and women's issues, 25–26, 111–12
and youth employment program, 177
Carter, John William ("Jack"), 6
Carter, Lillian Gordon, 5, 15, 161
Carter, Rosalynn, 6, 9, 14, 112, 161, 191, 211, 212
Carter, Ruth, 5
Carter Doctrine, 164
Carter Presidential Center, 2, 212
CETA, 52
Charter Oil Company, 189–90
Cheney, Richard, 17, 27
Chicago, Council on Foreign Relations, 38
China, People's Republic of, 199. *See also under* Carter, Jimmy; Brzezinski, Zbigniew
Christopher, Warren, 186, 203
Chrysler Corporation, 149
Church, Frank, 14, 155–56
Civiletti, Benjamin, 147, 190
Civil service reform, 2, 101
Clark, Dick, 115
Clark, Ramsey, 160
Clifford, Clark, 63, 144, 156
Clinch River breeder reactor, 108–9
Coal strike (1978), 78–79
Cochran, Thad, 115
Committee for Economic Development, 21
Comprehensive Employment and Training Act (CETA), 52
Congressional Black Caucus, 69, 110–11, 134
Congressional Budget Office, 52
Connally, John, 149
Consumer Protection Agency, 32
Conyers, John, 111
Costanza, Midge, 107
Council on Environmental Quality, 202
Council on Wage and Price Stability (COWPS), 100–101, 112, 114–15, 171. *See also* Carter, Jimmy: and economic issues; Economy
Crane, Philip M., 106
Cronin, Thomas E., 21–22, 23
Cutler, Lloyd, 156, 199

Dayan, Moshe, 83, 87, 122
Dellums, Ron, 111
Democratic National Committee (DNC), 24
Demographic trends, 22–23
Deng, Xiaoping, 129–30, 131
Derian, Patricia, 124
Derrick, Butler, 141

D'Estaing, Valéry Giscard, 49, 185–86
Dobrynin, Anatoli, 40, 153
Domestic Policy Staff (DPS), 26, 116
Dole, Robert, 15
Dubs, Adolph, 128
Duncan, Charles, 147

Economic Policy Group (EPG), 58, 71
Economy, 22, 25, 52, 59, 71, 73, 76, 80, 99–
    100, 103, 105–6, 112–14, 135–36, 139,
    142–43, 167–69, 176, 178, 183–84, 200
Egypt. *See* Carter, Jimmy: and Middle East
Egyptian-Israeli Peace Treaty. *See* Carter,
    Jimmy: and Middle East
Eilberg, Joshua, 79–80
Eisenhower, Dwight, 51
Eizenstat, Stuart, 9, 26, 30, 31, 51, 52, 66, 71,
    72, 104, 134, 141, 145, 148, 163, 170, 189
    and *Bakke* case, 69–71
    and Domestic Policy Staff, 26, 116
    and oil and energy policy, 67–68
    and relationship with Blumenthal, 58–59,
        113, 141–42, 146
    and tax policy, 58–59, 72, 102, 178–79, 184
    and urban issues, 74
Election of 1976. *See under* Carter, Jimmy
Election of 1978. *See under* Carter, Jimmy
Election of 1980. *See under* Carter, Jimmy
Election of 1984. *See under* Carter, Jimmy
Emergency Natural Gas Act (1977), 33. *See
    also* Carter, Jimmy: oil and energy
    policy of
Energy, Department of, 57. *See also* Carter,
    Jimmy: oil and energy policy of
Energy Mobilization Board, 145, 147, 177.
    See also Carter, Jimmy: oil and energy
    policy of
Energy Policy and Conservation Act, 137–
    38. *See also* Carter, Jimmy: oil and
    energy policy of
Energy Security Act, 176–77. *See also* Carter,
    Jimmy: oil and energy policy of
Energy Security Corporation, 145, 148. *See
    also* Carter, Jimmy: oil and energy
    policy of
Enriched Radiation Weapon (ERW), 95–96
Environment, 22–23. *See also* Carter, Jimmy:
    and the environment
Environmental Protection Agency (EPA),
    202
Equal Employment Opportunity Commis-
    sion (EEO), 70, 110
Equal Rights Amendment (ERA), 25–26,
    107, 111–12, 200
Ethiopia. *See* Carter, Jimmy: and Africa
Evans, Rowland, 16

Fahd, ibn Abd al-Aziz, Al Saud, 45
Fallows, Jim, 59, 139
Federal Energy Administration, 32
Federal Reserve Board (FRB), 76, 77, 100,
    142, 183–84
Foley, Thomas, 56
Ford, Gerald, 2, 39, 40, 46, 65, 76, 79
    and election of 1976, 14, 15–20, 43, 55, 81,
        110, 201
Francois-Poncet, Jean, 186
Fraser, Douglas, 103–4, 110, 136

Garn, Jake, 154
Garner, John, 144
Geneva Conference. *See* Carter, Jimmy: and
    Middle East
Ginsburg, Alexander, 40, 93
Glenn, John, 48
Goldschmidt, Neil, 147
Goldwater, Barry, 30, 89, 129
Griffith, Ernest S., 21
Gromyko, Andrei, 42, 94, 130, 191

Habitat for Humanity, 2, 212
Haldeman, H. R., 27, 63
Hanley, James, 140
Hansen, Clifford, 108
Harriman, W. Averell, 156
Harris, Fred, 12
Harris, Patricia, 26, 74–75, 112, 116, 134, 147
Hart, Peter D., 77, 78
Haskell, Floyd, 115
Hatcher, Richard, 14
Hathaway, William, 115
Hee, Park Chung, 47
Heimann, John, 61–62
Helms, Jesse, 91, 115
Helsinki accords, 38, 40. *See also* Carter,
    Jimmy: and human rights
Hooks, Benjamin, 183
Horst, Jerald ter, 18
Hostage crisis. *See* Carter, Jimmy: and Iran
Houderi, Ali, 191
Humphrey, Gordon, 115
Humphrey, Hubert, 9, 14, 48
Humphrey-Hawkins bill, 110–11
Hunt, James, 143
Hunt, Nelson Bunker, 168
Hussein (king of Jordan), 45, 86–87, 120,
    123
Huyser, Robert, 126–27

Interagency Task Force on Women. *See*
    Carter, Jimmy: and women's issues

National Association for the Advancement
   of Colored People (NAACP), 21
National Education Act, 149
National Health Insurance. *See* Carter,
   Jimmy: and health insurance; Kennedy,
   Edward: and national health insurance
National Security Council (NSC), 38
National Unity Campaign. *See* Anderson,
   John
National Women's Conference. *See* Carter,
   Jimmy: and women's issues
NATO, 93–95, 191–92
Neustadt, Richard, 21
Neutron bomb. *See under* Carter, Jimmy
New York City, loan guarantee for, 101
Nixon, Richard, 3, 11, 12, 21, 39, 56, 93, 110,
   125, 142, 179, 193
Nkomo, Joshua, 91
Norton, Eleanor Holmes, 70
Novak, Robert, 16
Nunn, Sam, 48, 97, 155

Oil and Energy Policy. *See under* Carter,
   Jimmy
Okun, Arthur, 80
O'Neill, Thomas ("Tip"), 30, 48, 66, 102,
   134–35, 147, 194
   and energy legislation, 57, 68, 108
Organization of American States (OAS),
   157
Organization of Petroleum Exporting
   Countries (OPEC), 125, 137, 138, 143–
   44, 145, 152
Orlov, Yuri, 40, 93

PACs, 1, 23
Pahlavi, Muhammad Reza Shah, 123–27,
   159–60, 162, 191
Palestinians. *See* Carter, Jimmy: and Middle
   East
Palestinian Liberation Organization (PLO),
   44, 84, 186, 189
Panama Canal Treaties, 2, 83, 117, 185
PD-59 (Presidential Directive 59), 192–93
Percy, Charles, 61–62
Peres, Shimon, 118
Peterson, Esther, 32
Pierard, Richard V., 1
PLO, 44, 84, 186, 189
Political Action Committees (PACs), 1, 23
Pol Pot, 129
Polsby, Nelson, 24
Portillo, Jose Lopez, 131–32
Powell, Jody, 9, 26, 34, 39, 62, 80–81, 94,
   143, 147
Precht, Henry, 128

Proposition 13, 106
Proxmire, William, 60, 154–55

Rabin, Yitzhak, 45
Rafshoon, Gerald, 10, 106–7, 141, 144–45,
   197, 201
Rajai, Mohammed Ali, 203, 208
Reagan, Ronald, 15, 43, 149, 211, 213
   and election of 1980, 161, 172, 178, 181,
   184, 193–95, 197–208
Rhodesia. *See* Carter, Jimmy: and Africa
Ribicoff, Abraham, 60, 61–62
Rickover, Hyman, 6
Rockefeller, David, 12, 159
Rosenthal, Benjamin, 46
Rozell, Mark, 2
Rumsfeld, Donald, 26
Rusk, Dean, 156

Sadat, Anwar, 44, 45, 84–88, 107, 117–23,
   187–88
Safire, William, 60, 171
Sakharov, Andrei, 40
SALT I Agreement, 39, 40, 130
SALT II Agreement, 42, 130–31, 151, 153–
   57, 165, 202. *See also* Carter, Jimmy:
   and arms control; Carter, Jimmy: and
   Soviet Union
Sanders, Carl, 9
Sandinistas, 131, 157–58
SAVAK. *See* Iranian revolution; Carter,
   Jimmy: and Iran
Schlesinger, James, 26, 33, 68, 143, 144
   resignation of, 145–46
Schmidt, Helmut, 49–50, 95–97, 152, 165,
   185, 187
Schultze, Charles, 25, 26, 34, 52, 57, 59, 71,
   72, 73, 80–81, 103, 113, 115, 141–42,
   146, 178–79
Schweiker, Richard, 79
Scoville, Herbert, Jr., 192
Shah of Iran. *See* Pahlavi, Muhammad Reza
   Shah
Shcharansky, Anatoly, 93, 105
Sick, Gary, 126, 214
Sidey, Hugh, 31
Siegel, Mark, 88
Singlaub, John K., 47–48
Smith, Gaddis, 90, 208
Smith, Ian, 91
Social security system, 72
Solidarity movement, 210
Somalia. *See* Carter, Jimmy: and Africa
Somoza, Anastasio, 131, 152, 157–58
Sonnefeldt, Helmut, 185